WILEY COMPUTER PUBLISHING

John Wiley & Sons, Inc.

New York ♦ Chichester ♦ Weinheim ♦ Brisbane ♦ Singapore ♦ Toronto

Publisher: Robert Ipsen
Editor: Robert M. Elliott
Managing Editor: Angela Murphy
Text Design and Composition: North Market Street Graphics

Designations used by companies to distinguish their products are often claimed as trademarks. In all instances where John Wiley & Sons, Inc., is aware of a claim, the product names appear in initial capital or ALL CAPITAL LETTERS. Readers, however, should contact the appropriate companies for more complete information regarding trademarks and registration.

This book is printed on acid-free paper.⊗

This publication is designed to provide accurate and authoritative information in regard to the subject matter covered. It is sold with the understanding that the publisher is not engaged in professional services. If professional advice or other expert assistance is required, the services of a competent professional person should be sought.

Internet World, Web Week, Web Developer, Internet Shopper, and Mecklermedia are the exclusive trademarks of Mecklermedia Corporation and are used with permission.

Case study of the Time Warner Full Service Network excerpted from "Interactive News: State of the Art," by Peter M. Zollman, copyright © 1997 by Radio and Television News Directors Foundation; published by the News In The Next Century Project, supported by the Robert R. McCormick Tribune Foundation.

Library of Congress Cataloging-in-Publication Data
Miles, Peggy.
    Internet world guide to webcasting / Peggy Miles.
       p.   cm.
    "Wiley Computer Publishing."
    Includes index.
    ISBN 0-471-24217-9 (pbk. / Online : alk. paper)
    1. Webcasting. I. Title.
  TK5105.887.M55   1998
  070.5'797—dc21   97-52093

Printed in the United States of America.

10 9 8 7 6 5 4 3 2 1

CONTENTS

Foreword vii
Introduction xv

Chapter 1 What Is Webcasting? 1

How Is Webcasting Likely to Affect Our Lives? 6
Benefits of Webcasting 7
It's All Happening Now! 13
Types of Webcasts 20
Who Is Webcasting? 37
State of the Webcast Market 46

Chapter 2 Business Opportunities for Webcasting 57

Websites Literally Don't Deliver, or Do They? 57
Determining if Webcasting Is Feasible 69
Choice of Media 77
Cost Justifying Webcasting 89
A Caution Signal 90

Chapter 3 Webcasting Technologies 93

Technology Standards and Protocols 94
IETF Standards 96

ISO (International Standards Organization)   101
ITU Standards   103
World Wide Web Consortium (W3C) Standards   105
Proprietary Protocols and De Facto Standards   106
Webcasting Transmission and Content   108
Implementing a Webcasting System   118
Receiving a Webcast   123

Chapter 4 Developing a Webcasting Website   129

Who Can Webcast?   130
Selection Criteria: Choosing the Right Vendors and Components   136
What's It Going to Cost to Establish a Website and Begin Webcasting?   160
Maintaining the Website   176

Chapter 5 Developing Content   181

Developing a Content Strategy   181
Selecting the Content   183
Scheduling Your Content   192
Content Design Considerations   197
Producing the Content for Webcasting   209
Summary   220

Chapter 6 Marketing and Promotion   223

Generating the Marketing Plan   224
Promoting the Webcast   243
Measuring Success   260

Chapter 7 Managing Your Website   263

MANAGEMENT ISSUES AND GOALS   263
PERSONNEL/STAFFING ISSUES   275
BUDGETING FOR THE WEBCASTING DEPARTMENT   284
SITE MANAGEMENT ISSUES   288

Chapter 8 Legal and Regulatory Issues in Webcasting   291

PROTECTING YOUR WEBCAST CONTENT   292
USING CONTENT OWNED BY OTHERS   298
OTHER CONTENT ISSUES   309
SOME CURRENT WEB CONTENT DISPUTES   315
VISITOR AGREEMENTS AND STATEMENTS   320
SECURITY   325
AGREEMENT CHECKLISTS   333

Appendix A Webcasting Industry Associations   335

Appendix B Marketing and Promotion   359

Appendix C Recommended Reading   385

Glossary   387

Index   411

FOREWORD

Convergence isn't a business today. It's a word that gets bandied around far too often with far too little to show for it.

Yes, the previously disparate worlds of television and the computer are merging, but the economic models online haven't fully jelled and all the technological issues and debates are not yet resolved. Yet I find myself today at the helm of one of the first ships navigating the convergence surf, CNBC/Dow Jones Business Video (born as MSNBC Business Video). Indeed, my parent companies, NBC, Microsoft and Dow Jones, are not in this business for the stakes as they exist today, but for those of the not-too-distant future.

The end game is all about getting convergence to mean something to consumers weaned on 50 years of watching television in a linear format on sets that actually behave the way they're supposed to. And we're not at this point yet. Most of today's new interactive technology not only is too difficult for the average consumer to use, it crashes on occasion or gives confusing error messages. My television set always works when I turn it on. I can't boast the same of my computer or that latest line of Java script.

And the convergence of TV and computers won't mean a thing unless we end up with the reliability of television coupled with the customization potential of computing. Not vice versa. But those issues will be ironed out. That's a given. Convergence devices like WebTV and the Network Computer already are gaining a foothold in living rooms worldwide and these two different boxes soon will become one.

The business of transmitting video via the Internet fast is becoming the next battleground for global media companies and already is transforming the way the rest of the world's businesses communicate with their customers, partners, and even with their own employees via corporate intranets.

Choice already is infinite on the Internet. And, marketing, promotion, and advertising dollars aside, users are most often driven to sites featuring the latest bells, whistles, and compelling video-based multimedia content.

But many magazine and newspaper publishers and text-based businesses haven't fully realized that competing on the Internet means running opposite a pack of competitors whose members greatly outnumber their off-line foes. Print vehicles making the move to launch online properties must compete with broadcast and cable network sites, Hollywood studio sites, Internet-only Webzines, Usenet newsgroups, radio station initiatives, advertiser Web sites, and anyone else with a dollar, a dream, and a computer.

It's not the consumer who needs to beware, it's the would-be Internet content provider.

One need only examine the past online moves of a well-known financial magazine to see the perils in the electronic surf. This financial magazine clearly was and is at the top of its print game. It's well-read, well-regarded, and has been profitable for many, many years. Then, not too long ago, it decided to launch a site on the Web. This financial magazine served up a Web site that resembled that of many other periodicals: It digitally repurposed its print articles and those of its two sister publications. And, of course, it crafted that all-too-popular Web panacea—a new daily text-based news feed, exclusive to the Web.

This financial publisher's online problems were obvious: Trying to compete in the general business news race online is serious business. It means competing for mind share online with the likes of old-line traditional business magazines and newspapers, as well as with such cable networks as MSNBC, CNBC, and CNNfn—and even the likes of a small Portland, Oregon, radio station that produces hourly real-time audio business news reports on its Web site.

And remember, broadcast and cable networks, radio outlets, and Hollywood studios all have an added advantage in this multimedia world—wares that actually talk and walk.

This is not to suggest that all sites online can't offer all the multimedia advances of the moment, themselves. Rather, most magazine publishers have configured their business for another key strength: print. And as we all know, acquiring a whole new set of core competencies takes money and time. And these barriers to entry only will rise as video and audio continue to muscle their way onto the Internet.

It's not that everyone is equal on the Web. That small Portland radio station is obviously at a disadvantage when it tries to compete for users with the likes of a Time Warner, whose magazines clearly can afford video, audio, and a surfeit of marketing dollars. Marketing dollars still can aggregate an audience faster than anything else. Key brands obviously will always be ahead in the name recognition game.

But we must remember that Internet users and online gateways are equal. That is, when average users log on to the labyrinthine morass that is the Internet, they bring to this new medium the same interests they've amassed off-line—and that's how they navigate the Web. Users search and surf. They turn to search sites and guide services for guidance and gateways to online sites that will interest them . . . regardless of whether these Internet goods are provided by old-line print publishers, by TV networks, or by newly established Internet empires.

And breaking through to these audiences means more than simply having the marketing budget to do so. It means keeping them glued to your screen after they reach your site. It means delivering the right goods to the right viewers. Audiences online need programming which builds on the strength of the medium—not expanded newspaper or magazine issues or dry, text-based corporate brochures. Audiences need and want video.

As for the fate of that financial magazine I referenced earlier, I can report that they've re-launched their Web presence, having devoted millions of dollars to assemble new teams to craft a truly multimedia experience. It is too early to tell if they will be able to pull it off successfully, and, more importantly, whether or not they will partner with another media company to acquire that core video competency they still are missing.

Clearly, interactive full-motion video is where programming strengths will play out online. And that's what opens up truly mass appeal opportunities. Of course, one needs to boast more than just video capabilities. Breaking through means developing a technologically cutting-edge Website when you launch and keeping abreast of the new media game as it develops. It means giving users the rich media environment they seek.

And that's why at NBC we partnered with Microsoft and with Dow Jones to establish a brand that would mean just this very thing to this new thirsty audience. And this is also why Peggy Miles' *Internet World Guide to Webcasting* is so important.

This book is the seminal work in this nascent but rapidly mushrooming field. Indeed, Miles and her author team have assembled a true "how-to" in every sense of the word, showcasing every facet of the business, from how to choose Webcasting technology, how to develop content strategies to the nuts and bolts of proper marketing and promotion and even how to navigate key Webcasting legal issues. As such, she has written a work that will appeal both to technical and business readers alike.

But most importantly, what you will find within these pages is set against a rich backdrop of case studies and business paradigms, gleaned from the real-life workings of others. *Internet World Guide to Webcasting* does more than tell you "how to" establish a viable webcasting service online, it shows how others already are doing it, my own company included. And webcasting isn't just for computer companies or TV networks. The case studies inside run the gamut from aerospace to news organizations to chocolate makers.

Knowing this world means learning how to target your audience and learn from them. It means discovering how to feed their needs, as well as to market to them. Here, too, Miles and her team shine.

But beyond the world of business and commerce, this book details what fast is becoming a cultural revolution, shaping the way the corporate world communicates and the way families keep in touch across geographic boundaries, the way students learn remotely, and the ways in which we all entertain and inform ourselves.

A future rife with interactivity and full-motion Internet video is a given. In this near future, we all will need to be able to deliver these features to truly compete as full service offerings online. Where the convergence of print, television, and computing really is headed, however, and where the real front-runners will emerge, will be in their ability to personalize and customize this on-demand video content and interactivity.

Video is more than a tool on the Internet, to be dabbed onto a Website like so many colors onto a painting; it rapidly is altering the way we transact, both socially and monetarily from the workplace, the schoolroom, and the home.

To be without video is to miss out on this revolution. To be without this book is to find yourself without a road map telling you how to get there today.

Michael C. Wheeler
President, MSNBC Desktop Video

Robert Silverman
Manager, Corporate Communications, NBC

ACKNOWLEDGMENTS

Dear Webcasters and Future Webcasters!

In less than two years, webcasting has grown from zero to more than one thousand 24-hour webcast broadcast stations! There are now hundreds of thousands of webcast channels on the Internet!

Webcasters, including a 14-year-old with a mike and modem to Fortune 10 businesses and broadcast networks, are webcasting around the clock. We see visions of the future of webcasting from live and recorded channels like www.msnbc.businessvideo.com, www.timecast.com, www.audionet.com, www.hothits.com, and www.playing.com, which showcase news, information, and content from around the world.

This book was impossible to write. The moment we set out to showcase an innovation, a digital genius would make our thoughts obsolete. We did the next best thing; we thought long and hard about the principles of the change taking over the webcasting and the telecommunications industry and compiled in this book instructional and background information and cases that are based on the foundations of marketing and successful business practices. We hope you enjoy. We invite you to be part of future contributions to webcasting by letting us know about your feedback and projects at www.wiley.com/compbooks/miles.

This was a labor of love with contributions from dear friends and colleagues. The true co-author is Jan Wright of Techrite, whose brilliance compiled our thoughts into this book. Without Robert Elliott, the Senior Editor at Wiley, and Brian Calandra, senior editorial assistant, this book wouldn't be here. I was not an easy person to work with on this book. Angela Murphy allowed me to invade her office in New York and make changes to page after page after her deadline. I gave up on this book, and they pressed for solutions to make it possible. They made something I said was impossible, possible, and here it is.

They helped me weave in some contributions from fabulous colleagues from all over the world. They allowed me to include the Foreword from Michael Wheeler and Robert Silverman from MSNBC, who are leading the way in the future of digital broadcasting and webcasting. Bravo to the President of MSNBC Business Video, Michael Wheeler, for carrying this torch!

Please view the bios of the incredible contributors. They went beyond the call of duty and friendship and 3 A.M. e-mails in making this book happen. To Vin Crosbie, John Dickinson, Martin Hall, Doug Mohney, Dean Sakai, Kelsey Selander, and David Wittenstein . . . I can't thank you enough. An additional special thanks to my appendix contributors Peter Chislett, Thomas Edwards, and Noel Moore.

I owe incredible thanks to young webcasters and CEOs of companies who took the time to contribute their experiences to this book. The support of The International Webcasting Association, IP Multicast Initiative, and the National Association of Broadcasters was invaluable. I can't thank enough the brilliant futurist Sr. Vice President of the N.A.B. Rick Ducey. There are many more to name, like the thousands of members of the webcasting lists I run for Intervox Communications, hosted by Broadcast.net, whose expertise made this book possible.

And of utmost importance—thanks to Mr. & Mrs. Francis L. Miles and Ms. Donna Urban, my family who supports my efforts!

Hold on tightly because the Internet broadcasting and webcasting arena with personalized channels is going to change the way we get news, information, and communicate with our co-workers and families. I can't wait to see you on the Net. How great is this?

Peggy Miles

INTRODUCTION

You can't pick up a publication or watch television these days without reading or hearing about the Internet and the World Wide Web. The Internet links computers throughout the world and lets them share information in a variety of ways by sending and retrieving data, text, and graphics. A major advantage of the Internet is its ability to provide nearly instant communication between friends, families, and businesses by e-mail and other communication methods. It is also an enormous information and entertainment source, and it provides new opportunities for sharing information through videoconferencing, group-work sharing, and the like. Webcasting adds the dimensions of audio and video broadcast over the Internet as well as interactivity to make it easy for you to retrieve and interact with broadcast information.

Webcasting opens new opportunities for Internet users. Now, you can send and receive videoconferences from your home or office, automatically retrieve information from the Internet without surfing to find what you need or want, watch live broadcasts of major sporting events—or your grandson's Little League team, and retrieve audio or video tapes for your dinner-time entertainment. All of this information can be sent over the Internet to your personal computer, your TV, your cellular phone, radio, or pager. This book provides lots of examples of webcasting applications and explains how (and why) webcasting is dramatically affecting the way in which we use the Internet.

Webcasting

Webcasting means many things to many people. It can mean a way to communicate, a way to do research, or a way to shop. Today, if you click on a hypertext link, you may retrieve a live broadcast or a recorded program. In fact, the ability to deliver live and recorded audio and video is one of the major benefits of webcasting. In addition, webcasting can deliver information to you based on your previous choices; if you frequently tune in to a cooking program, for example, you may find that individuals or businesses that relate to food or cooking utensils begin to push information to you about their products. Of course, some may just push information about interesting recipes or reminders to tune in again at a specific time. We'll talk more about push technologies throughout the book since it is a major aspect of webcasting.

The programs that are currently being built for webcasting to send you information are designed to act like a TV. You click on a page or a channel and the video, audio, or text and graphics information arrives. Or like a cable subscription, you can subscribe to the Disney Channel, HBO, and Showtime. Push technologies remember your preferences and subscriptions and can push channels to you, similar to those found on your cable system.

The possibilities for webcasting are unlimited, but it is important to understand that we are talking about a technology that is very much in its infancy. It is still far from perfect, but that's pretty typical for all new technologies. When radio was introduced in the 1920s, for example, it was difficult to pick up the signal and, when you did, the sound quality was generally poor. Webcasting faces similar challenges. The audio quality is not nearly as good as a CD and the video is shaky compared to television. Bugs in the software and problems in the hardware and the Net connections require patience and understanding. But, the technology is moving at a breakneck pace to overcome these obstacles and achieve the maximum benefit.

Some of the ways in which webcasting is already being used include:

◆ Long-distance education, enabling students to take courses from notable professors in other states or even other countries

- Sending a video of your newborn child by e-mail
- Remotely checking the security in your home
- Distributing custom videos, radio programs, or interactive stories—essentially, being your own broadcaster
- Training of remote offices by recorded video, audio, or live instructors
- Monitoring by engineers of buildings and homes under construction

This book showcases a number of new technologies. For example, it explains how you can use intelligent agents to pull information off the Web or to take advantage of information that is pushed out to you by other users. It also discusses the leading-edge webcasters and explains how they're already reaping the benefits of webcasting with a wide range of business and entertainment applications. And, this book explains how you can be a webcaster! And why you might want to!

Webcasting is not limited to the large broadcasting corporations that can distribute full-motion audio and video around the world. Your child's fifth-grade classroom could use webcasting to exchange ideas and information with kids on another continent. Doctors can use webcasting to consult about a patient's case and ultrasound results—even if the doctors and patient are all in different states or different countries. You may use webcasting to help train the new overseas sales force, to "walk through" a new home, or to listen to an independent recording artist debut his or her first song. You'll have the ability to produce your own films, videos, radio programs, interactive stories, and games and distribute them to friends and family or to a broad audience around the world—anyone that you can entice to visit your personalized channels. The tools are here to change the face of communications on the Internet. You don't need a broadcast license or a tower. You can rent time or space on the Internet to broadcast whatever and whenever you want.

But, very little of the great information in this book will be relevant if you're not prepared to use the Web. We've tried to include lots of examples of how individuals and businesses are using webcasting now to expand their use of the Internet and effectively share information. We also include information to help you personalize your own news channel or broadcast marketing information to your customers. But, the best source of information for what's happening on the Internet is the Net itself. So, we've also provided lots of URLs that we recommend you check out for the very latest information.

Getting Started

To derive the maximum benefit from this book, you'll need access to the Web and an e-mail address.

If you don't already have a computer, you'll need one with at least a 486-processor, 8 to 16 megabytes of RAM, and a 28.8 bps (or higher) modem. To fully experience the audio and video capabilities of webcasting, you'll also need a sound card.

If you don't want to spend about $1000 to buy a computer, you can buy a set-top box to connect your television set to the Internet. These products, which are still quite new, are available from many TV/appliance stores and computer retailers. The most popular (and most well-known) is Web TV. You can expect to pay about $200 for a basic TV-Internet connector.

Of course, you'll also need Internet access. There are a number of options for accessing the Web; if you subscribe to one of the popular services like America OnLine or CompuServe, expect to pay about $20 for unlimited access to the Internet. Internet service providers (or ISPs) also provide access—often at rates comparable to or below the major services. For a list of ISPs in your area, consult your local telephone directory or borrow a friend's computer and access www.thelist.com.

How This Book Is Organized

The Internet, webcasting, and push technology can be confusing to anyone not familiar with the Internet. In fact, much of the new technology is confusing to those of us who work with computers every day and consider the Internet a basic necessity of life. Hopefully, this book will help to answer many questions about webcasting and its potential application for business and broadcasting. And, while we assume that most readers are generally familiar with computer, communications, and Internet terminology, like home page, URL, and browser, the Glossary at the back of this book defines most of the common terms that appear in the book. If you're new to webcasting or the Internet, you may want to look over the Glossary before you begin reading.

This book is organized into eight chapters, all of which provide actual case studies of businesses that are currently webcasting:

- Chapter 1, an introduction to webcasting, provides an introduction to the Internet and webcasting technology and discusses the three major types of webcasting and current use in the fields of business and entertainment. It also explores some of the market trends that have contributed to the evolution of webcasting and its future potential for a wide range of business and broadcast applications.

- Chapter 2, on business opportunities, discusses webcasting's potential for helping businesses to either make money or save money. It also provides an overview of the various business models that companies are using to reap rewards from webcasting: from banner advertising to subscription and beyond.

- Chapter 3, on webcasting technology, offers an overview of the many standards that presently ensure some level of compatibility among Internet-based products and services, then explains different webcasting technologies and discusses how technology evolution is likely to advance the use of webcasting.

- Chapter 4, on developing a webcast Website, discusses the basic equipment and services that are necessary to establish a low-end webcast Website from scratch—

including the development costs and required personnel—for push and streaming webcasts. The chapter then goes on to explore the continued development of the low-end site into a full-fledged webcast site capable of producing and delivering streaming audio and video.

◆ Chapter 5, on developing content, picks up from the previous chapter and explains how to acquire or develop content for the webcast Website. It provides some guidelines for creating new push or on-demand content that is well suited to take advantage of webcasting strengths and for repurposing existing content from traditional broadcast media.

◆ Chapter 6, which discusses marketing and promotion, offers practical ideas and guidelines for marketing your webcast, beginning with adequate planning and targeting, then ensuring that the correct audience knows the critical when and where factors, as well as the elements of how to tune in and why. It discusses the use of traditional and on-line techniques for promoting webcasting and explains how to invite the target audience to the webcast.

◆ Chapter 7, on managing the webcast Website, discusses the crucial aspects of managing a webcast Website, from identifying and acquiring the necessary staffing personnel to budgeting for the department and making changes all along the webcasting road to respond to audience feedback and take advantage of new technologies.

◆ Chapter 8, concerning legal and regulatory issues, identifies some of the major issues that webcasters face in creating and protecting content or acquiring and re-using content from other sources. This chapter provides an overview of the current regulatory climate for the on-line environment and provides guidelines for buying, licensing, and repurposing content from a veritable maze of agencies and associations.

While we believe all eight chapters are crucial to understanding webcasting technologies and applications, certain chapters will undoubtedly be of more interest to some readers than others. If, for example, you're a Webmaster, thoroughly familiar with the Internet and use of conventional Websites, but you're planning to begin webcasting, you may want to focus on Chapters 4, 5, and 7, which deal with the processes involved in developing a webcast Website, developing content, and managing a webcast Website, respectively. If, however, you're currently involved in the traditional broadcast industry and relatively unfamiliar with webcasting's underlying technology or its application potential, you may want to focus on Chapters 1, 2, and 3, which provide a thorough background in webcasting technology and business applications. If you plan on repurposing existing content from the traditional media, you may also want to spend some time in Chapters 5 and 8 on developing content and the legal and regulatory issues involved in webcasting.

As we mentioned earlier, webcasting is a new and rapidly evolving technology. The best source for information about the Internet and webcasting is, logically enough, the Internet itself. If you haven't already done so, we recommend that you take some time to explore the many and varied Websites that provide current information on webcasting technology, as well as the vendors of webcasting products and services. Appendix A in this book provides a guide to some of the relevant webcasting sites, as do references throughout many of the chapters, but don't forget to search the Web for general references to webcasting as well.

CONTRIBUTORS

Vin Crosbie is President of Digital Deliverance, L.L.C., a Greenwich, Connecticut, consulting firm that advises major publishing companies on New Media issues. He was director of content development at Freemark Communications, Inc., of Cambridge, Massachusetts, and director of media partnerships for Rupert Murdoch's Delphi Internet Services. He also has held executive positions with Reuters, UPI, and newspapers.

John Dickinson has been in the computer publishing business for 15 years, and the computer business for nearly 30 years. During that time he has worked in on-line systems and personal computer systems that did everything from personal finance to large-scale publishing. Currently he is directing the computer editorial products at CurtCo Freedom Group, the publisher of computer and consumer electronic magazines, including Home Office Computing, Small Business Computing and Communications, Mobile Computing Sales and Field Force Automation.

Martin Hall is CTO for Stardust Technologies, Inc., which he co-founded in 1995, and provides marketing, education, and testing services for emerging Internet technologies. Based in Campbell, California, Stardust is the home of the IP Multicast Initiative (IPMI) and Stardust WinSock Labs. Martin is also co-founder of Aventail Corporation, a supplier of Internet and intranet security management software. He is the co-inventor of WinSock and formerly an engineering manager at JSB Corporation.

Peggy Miles, President of Intervox Communications, Washington, DC, is an Internet Pioneer specializing in consulting, content, and execution of webcasting, Internet broadcasting, database marketing, and e-commerce for Fortune 500 companies. She is on the founding board of the International Webcasting Association and has made presentations to prestigious organizations and many broadcast, industry, and Net conferences. She is also a publisher/moderator of the elite on-line lists called Webcasting and Internet Broadcaster whose members include CEOs and broadcasters from leading organizations.

Doug Mohney is the streaming media columnist for BOARD-WATCH magazine and is co-chair of "Video on the Net" for pulver .com. As a speaker, Doug has made presentations at "Voice on the Net," Internet World, ISPCON, and other industry shows. In his day job, he is Director of Marketing for SkyCache, a satellite data delivery company. He's been a guest on the G. Gordon Liddy show and other radio programs.

Dean Sakai is a specialist in Internet and nontraditional revenue for broadcasters. He has served on numerous industry panels regarding affinity marketing and the Internet. As the Internet Business director for a major radio group, Dean pioneered Internet sales and webcasting and helped produce one of the first live broadcasts on the Internet. He created the affiliate relations department for the Internet's premier radio web site network, headquartered in Santa Cruz, California.

Kelsey Selander is Vice President of Marketing at BackWeb, and has been in the world of marketing and advertising for more than 20 years. Previous positions have included Vice President of Marketing at Borland, Vice President of Corporate Marketing at Lotus, and Vice President of Marketing at Bitstream.

David Wittenstein is the head of the Media & Information Technologies practice group of the Washington, D.C., law firm of Dow, Lohnes & Albertson, specializing in intellectual property issues for media and information technology companies. He has long represented broadcasters, television program producers, Internetworks, satellite distributors, and publishers in these areas. David has published articles and given numerous speeches and seminars on media and intellectual property subjects, and writes the Legal Issues column for the New Media Report.

Jan Wright is a technical writer and editor with more than 20 years of experience in computer and communications technology. In addition to researching, writing, and editing for various publications and corporate clients, she manages the Florida office of Tech-WRITE, Inc., a documentation services company that prepares online manuals and training materials.

CHAPTER ONE

What Is Webcasting?

Webcasting means many things to many people. In general, we define webcasting as sending digital information over the Internet for reception, viewing, and/or listening by the public, possibly involving some interaction between the sender and recipient(s). In a technical sense, webcasting is the publish and subscribe and/or broadcast and tune-in methodology for distributing information from one to many recipients. In actual practice however, webcasting can mean a way to communicate, a way to do research, or a way to shop. Essentially, webcasting is the next phase of the Internet—adding new dimensions of audio and video and delivering information on the Internet in unique ways.

Webcasting can be any or all of the following:

1. Broadcasting
2. Videoconferencing
3. One-to-one communications, like an Internet phone conversation

The Internet isn't just text and graphics anymore. With webcasting, it can be used to distribute multimedia content to audiences or communities around the world. Content types include news, business information, and entertainment. Content formats include digital text, graphics, audio, and video. Combined with individual, community, or audience profile databases, webcasting is potentially the most powerful medium yet invented for delivering information and entertainment that people need or want.

Leading-edge companies and major broadcasters are already building Websites that offer a new range of capabilities and services, combining traditional text content with audio, video, database, e-commerce, and personalization features that enable you, through your mouse or remote control device, to access other Websites, videos, information resources, friends, and business colleagues. Many are using audio and video to promote themselves or their products on the Net. While some companies are offering information—text, audio, and video—on a subscription basis much like the cable subscription services, others are using innovative ways to entice potential customers to seek additional information about a product or service. Business applications range from showing new products live on the net to proofing work in progress—whether the work is an inspector checking to make sure that a new $50 million building adheres to the current code or a doctor viewing the sonograms of a child in another country.

Many companies are also using audio and video capabilities to enhance videoconferencing techniques. Internet products like net-Podium (see Figure 1.1) let viewers see the speaker, as well as his or her notes and the whiteboard, in real time on their computer screens. In many cases, the conference participants can even respond to the speaker or to one another by posting text or files on the whiteboard, right with the speaker's presentation, to elicit further questions and comments by all attendees.

There are essentially three types of webcasting:

◆ Streaming
◆ On-demand
◆ Push

We'll talk about each of these in more detail later in the chapter and in subsequent chapters, but for now, it's important to understand the role that each of these types plays in delivering information over the Internet.

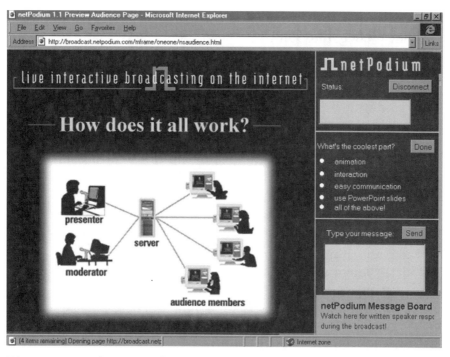

Figure 1.1 The netPodium preview audience page.

Streaming technology refers to the delivery of audio and video signals over the Internet; the signals can be live (in real time), recorded, or delivered on-demand. The term streaming is derived from the fact that audio and video signals are transmitted over the Internet in a series of 1s and 0s that a program converts into broadcast signals much like we're accustomed to seeing on television. The ability to squeeze the audio and video into a stream is the basis of streaming technologies. You may be familiar with some webcasts that use streaming technology, like *Pathfinder* landing on Mars, or the coverage of Princess Diana's funeral, which was webcast live by the BBC, FOX News, ABC News, and Globe News. Similarly, ABC, FOX, MSNBC, BBC, CBC, and C-Span were among the 20 broadcasters from around the world that provided live webcast coverage of the Hong Kong transition.

What Webcasting Isn't!

With all the various meanings and conflicting definitions for webcasting, it's easy to loose sight of what webcasting really is—and isn't.

- Webcasting does *not* originate with the viewer/receiver. It originates at the transmitting/sending station or computer.
- Webcasting does *not* refer to standard Web page access (although webcasting systems may incorporate such access capabilities).
- Webcasting does *not* refer to Internet telephony (although webcasting systems may incorporate telephony capability).
- Multipoint conferencing is *not* the same as webcasting (although webcasting may incorporate multipoint conferencing capabilities).

On-demand refers to the ability to time-shift information that is delivered via streaming technologies. Essentially, it means that you can retrieve the audio/video stream and view it any time that's convenient for you. On-demand is much the same as receiving a program on the television and storing it on your VCR to watch later. Websites like Timecast (www.timecast.com), Audionet (www.audionet.com), MSNBC Desktop (www.businessvideo.msnbc.com), and Netchannel (www.netchannel.net) act much like cafeterias where we can pick and choose the information that we want to receive and play it back any time we want (see Figure 1.2). On-demand technology gives us remote control of a Web page and lets us control our own audio and video choices and delivery schedule.

Push technology, which actually includes both push and pull, delivers information to you—either because you have requested it

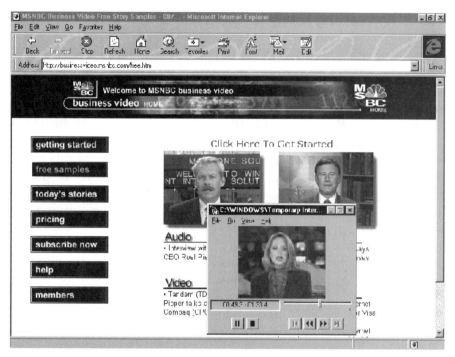

Figure 1.2   The MSNBC business video on-demand page.

or because someone else thinks that you are likely to be interested in it. Push products like BackWeb, Marimba Castanet, and Netscape Communications' Netcaster apply some level of intelligence to determine—based on your needs, interests, and previous information requests—what information is likely to be of interest to you. Push products are available in a wide variety of sizes, shapes, and transmission methods and incorporate both service providers such as PointCast, who supply news content and make their money from media sponsorships, and content providers such as BackWeb and Marimba who make their money by selling enabling technologies. The push product arena also includes middleware providers such as Tibco, who provide a real-time delivery infrastructure for other push companies to use.

How Is Webcasting Likely to Affect Our Lives?

Webcasting offers a different set of capabilities than viewing static pages on the Web. Most of the pages on the Internet today are text-based. They let us view, select, retrieve, and/or buy a range of information resources and services, surfing for related resources and products, and all too often getting lost in the process. Webcasting offers new dimensions of sight and sound. In addition to reading text pages, we can actually experience the sights and sounds associated with products, places, and other people. In many respects, webcasting offers the same capabilities as a TV, radio, or satellite receiver, but it extends those capabilities to support interactive videos and the live transmission of breaking news or alerts sent directly to or from your company. It also extends the traditional concept of the broadcast audience, reaching viewers throughout the world and supporting a variety of receiving devices including TVs, radios, PCs, pagers, telephones, and remote devices that can deliver information right to us, wherever we are.

Webcasting can deliver a 360-degree view of a new car and let us zoom in on the features that we want to examine closely. Or let us act as the director of a TV newscast asking for—and receiving—only the information that interests us, whether that's sports, current events in Ireland, or the weather in Idaho. And, webcasting can offer thousands and thousands of channels, with information provided by small, independent webcasters to huge networks like NBC, CNN, ABC, and CNET, all of whom are currently webcasting on the Internet.

Webcasting is likely to change our lives in many ways. With webcasting, for example, doctors in one continent can watch surgeons in another country or on another continent perform surgery live, asking questions and offering suggestions during the procedure. On a more personal note, webcasting will enable you to watch your new home being built while you're away on vacation or business, and to notify the builder immediately if you don't like the appearance of the tile in the kitchen. We'll be able to review the television news any time of the day or night instead of struggling to stay awake at 11:00 after a hard day of work. If we want, we can have the latest news delivered overnight, ready for us to watch the next morning when we sign onto the PC to retrieve our e-mail. News and relevant information will be pushed to us—not just delivered to our doorsteps like the morning newspaper, but personalized for our specific interests. And it can be delivered to our TV sets, our PCs, or to portable devices that resemble radios, handheld terminals, tablets, and newspapers.

Benefits of Webcasting

With webcasting, we can decide what information we want to receive from the Web, then receive alerts while we're working or playing that let us know that the information is available. Unlike conventional information delivery methods, webcasting technology will be working for us—even while we sleep—retrieving the information we've requested from the Net. It may even retrieve information or programs that we didn't specifically request by predicting, based on previous viewing behaviors, what is likely to interest us.

Right now, most of us have to wait for our favorite TV channel to send a program that interests us (and sometimes that wait is very long!). Similarly, we have to search through our local newspaper for an advertisement on a new car that we're interested in, then ask the dealership to send us a brochure or videotape to review the relevant features. Webcasting offers us the opportunity to eliminate these tiresome tasks; it literally puts us in the driver's seat. The information we want—complete with sound and pictures—is available at any time as close as our receiving device, be it a PC or a television.

Of course, webcasting has a very practical, business-oriented side that is already attracting the attention of business organizations worldwide. Many companies are already using audio and video to promote themselves and their products on the Internet, offering some innovative ways to entice potential customers to seek additional information or order a product or service. Amazon.com (which bills itself as the world's largest bookstore) and competitor

Barnes & Noble are both good examples of showcasing and selling products over the Net. Business applications range from showing new products live on the Net to proofing work in progress. It's likely these companies will add audio and video demos and interviews, as webcasting grows in popularity, to stay competitive.

Webcasting offers a range of very tangible benefits, including:

- Unlimited delivery via the Internet
- Targeted delivery (i.e., for sales training or new product information) to a limited audience via an intranet or an extranet or a subscription basis on the Internet
- Instant dissemination of news and information
- Lower individualized broadcast costs than television, radio, or (with multicasting) cable
- Flexible customization (i.e., personalization) to tailor information delivery for users' particular interests

The Benefits of Internet Webcasting

The content of a Website determines its popularity, but between two sites with similar content, the one that webcasts is likely to attract a larger audience. Not only is moving content more interesting, but also webcasting uses technology that offers immediacy with no long waits for downloads. A user will choose to view a streamed video over the same one that requires a full download before playing.

A survey by Netcraft (www.netcraft.com/survey) reports that there are currently more than 1,300,000 Websites on the Internet. This number is more than four times the amount reported in 1996. Push technology in particular offers many advantages in competing for the Internet audience. Where intranets have a captive audience that will regularly check on their company Websites or notices, Internet Websites are locked in a competitive battle for viewers. Organizations that are serious about building and maintaining a share of the Internet audience are finding that it is necessary to develop a database of their users and to use intrusive, but polite, reminders to encourage users to visit their sites for new programming. With so many new options every day, viewers become understandably transient. This is one of the compelling advantages of push technology; creating a push channel is an outstanding tool to attract and retain a loyal core audience.

CASE STUDY | 1997 SUNDANCE FILM FESTIVAL

Viacom's Sundance Internet Channel used BackWeb technology to deliver updates from the 1997 Sundance Film Festival to PC users' desktops. Subscribers to the channel received daily newsflashes, a photo of the day, words from roving columnists, a diary from the filmmaker of the day, and links to other film-related and festival sites. The channel was open for the duration of the festival.

Viacom Interactive Services designed, produced, and hosted the Sundance Channel Website and the official Sundance Film Festival site. The Sundance channel is a 24-hour, commercial-free cable channel under the creative direction of Robert Redford.

"This is a great example of how quickly a content provider can set up a channel that delivers timely information," said Eli Barkat, CEO of BackWeb. "For those of us who wish we could have been at the festival, it was a vicarious pleasure. For those who are there, it was a way to make sure you were in the loop, keeping up with buzz, and always aware of what happened outside the Egyptian while you were at Prospector Square."

To subscribe to the Sundance Internet Channel, users went to either www.backweb.com or www.sundancechannel.com to download the free client software and subscribe to Sundance. During the festival, Sundance subscribers received content from the Sundance Internet Channel at regular intervals, downloaded in the background during idle on-line time. Users were alerted to the arrival of the content with BackWeb's flash messages, which find users in the application they're using and alert them at the bottom of the screen. If interested, the user simply clicks on the flash to access the downloaded content.

With Internet-based webcasting products, we can attend conferences and presentations without leaving our offices, viewing the speaker, as well as his or her notes and the whiteboard, in real time. As videoconference attendees, we can even respond to the speaker or to one another by posting text or files on the whiteboard, right with the speaker's presentation, to elicit further questions and comments by all attendees.

The accountability of the Internet offers major benefits for webcasters. Unlike traditional broadcasting in which there is no way to know exactly who is watching your TV program or listening to your radio show, the Internet can track your every move: the time you spend on-line, what you do on the Net, how you do it, and with whom. The Internet can track the sites that you access and remember which videos you watch, at what times, and for how long. Proper feedback about your customers and their interests can help you to serve them better, opening the lines of communication for new and improved information products and services.

Of course, the Internet's ability to track usage also has a downside: the potential for invasion of privacy and the release of information to huge databases maintained by companies such as TRW, Donnelly, and Polk. Although all of these companies have been collecting information on consumers around the world for many years, the Internet makes it easier and more cost-effective for them to gather such information. If you're a frequent Internet user, electronic tracking probably provides more and more detailed information about your behavior and interests than conventional data-gathering techniques. Fortunately, there are numerous techniques already in use to help regulate privacy on the Net and to restrict the use of confidential information. Many more methods are under discussion as the legal and regulatory agencies scramble to catch up to this fast-paced technology. We discuss many of these legal aspects in Chapter 8.

Benefits of Intranet Webcasting

Implementing webcasting on an intranet offers the potential for saving money and increasing the efficiency of information distribution. Webcasting can replace instructional videos, tapes, and CDs for a number of applications, including training. Intranet webcasting eliminates the need to distribute information through conventional channels such as mail or to transport people to a common meeting place. It also eliminates many of the expenses involved in establishing and securing a training facility and for lodging personnel during training courses since they can attend the webcast from anywhere in the world. In addition, intranet webcasting eliminates many administrative expenses such as those involved with attendee enrollment and tracking because these processes are handled automatically with the webcast. You know who has, and who hasn't, accessed the information.

With all of these benefits, it's not surprising that a recent International Data Corporation (IDC) study concluded that intranet-based training is the fastest growing segment of the training industry. IDC predicts that spending on intranet-based training will increase as much as 525 percent by the year 2000.

Beyond the cost savings, there are the benefits of increased efficiency and quantity of information available. Employees can access the webcast at their own convenience, 24 hours a day, seven days a week. It allows consistency of corporate messages and lets you get time-sensitive information to your staff immediately. Push alerts pop up on their computers when new and urgent information is available. Webcasting makes complex ideas more compelling and easier to understand. Employees can access video clips of guest speakers, and presentations that might not otherwise have been seen by the employees can be made available. You can even produce and broadcast your own company news program.

The Boeing Company offers a good example of using webcast technology on a large corporate intranet.

CASE STUDY   THE BOEING COMPANY

The Boeing Company has deployed Real Networks' RealVideo (www.real.com) webcasting technology across its corporate intranet to provide its 145,000+ employees with access to a live and on-demand medium for training and corporate communication.

"The ramifications for training using streaming video and audio are truly exciting. This technology delivers a simultaneous increase in accessibility and decrease in program costs that is a rare and valuable combination from an introduction of new technology," says Peter Morton, vice president, Boeing Center for Leadership & Learning.

"Boeing has one of the largest intranets worldwide, making their adoption of RealVideo one of the largest deployments of video across corporate intranets to date," said Rob Glaser, chairman and CEO, Progressive Networks. "This deployment represents a growing desire among corporations to add streaming media to their corporate intranets."

Since the deployment of RealVideo technology in April 1997, more than 3,000 Boeing employees have downloaded the RealPlayer, gaining access to the extensive Boeing library of corporate video programming.

The use of webcasting for training purposes at Boeing is expected to significantly decrease costs in duplicating and distributing videotapes to employees. Prior to the adoption of webcasting, the company was spending significant time and money duplicating and shipping several hundred videocassettes to employees each week.

In addition to the cost savings associated with using webcasting for training, employees benefit from on-demand access to training videos. Employees are currently able to choose from a variety of topics such as, "What Is Cash Flow?," "The Stock Market and the Impact on Boeing," and "Managing for Value." Additionally, employees can access video programs of guest speakers talking about key business competencies.

Boeing has also announced its intention to use webcasting to increase employee communication at the company. Boeing TV, a weekly five-minute internal television newscast about company activities, is now being webcast over the Boeing intranet.

It's All Happening Now!

If our description of webcasting and its benefits all sounds like pie in the sky and Buck Rogers' future stuff, consider how many large companies are already using some form of webcasting, and who's involved in promoting the technology. As we mentioned, most of the major broadcast networks, including NBC, ABC, and CNN are already webcasting. And the computer industry, most notably Microsoft Corporation and Netscape Communications, is taking a very active role in developing and using the technology. According to Microsoft's Product Unit Manager, Jim Durkin, "Microsoft believes the Internet will become the next broadcast network."

The company purchased a leading streaming media company (Vxtreme) in 1997, has invested in Real Networks (formerly Progressive Networks), the leading provider of streaming audio and video on the Internet, bought WebTV, a set-top TV box that includes streaming audio and video, and formed alliances with some 30 other companies that are related to Internet broadcasting. In addition, direct to PC and TV satellite services are sending webcasts via satellite to homes and offices and new remote Internet car radios and portables are now being built. Things are moving and changing so quickly in the webcasting market as we prepare this book for publication that we can almost guarantee that some of the information will be outdated by the time you read this. For the most current information about who's doing what, go to the Internet itself, use one of the good commercial search engines and initiate your own search on webcasting, streaming media, or push technology. You can also visit some of the webcasting and media sites like www.mediacentral.com, www.adage.com, www.news.com, www .webreview.com, www.broadcast.net, www.intervox.com, www .webcasters.org, or www.ipmulticast.com and use their search engines to delve more deeply into the webcasting news updates. Then sit back and wait for the information to pour in.

Although the Internet has experienced phenomenal growth during the past five years, the pace is likely to accelerate in the future as the Internet continues to evolve toward interactive Websites with the capability to deliver high-quality audio and video content. In September 1995, there were an estimated 14.9 million users on the Web. Today, *Business Week* reports there are 40 million users. By 2000, the Internet is expected to have nearly 100 million users.

All things considered, it's easy to understand why so many companies, organizations, and individuals are climbing on the webcasting bandwagon. Even now, in its infancy, webcasting is surpassing the capabilities of traditional television and radio broadcasting, adding a level of intelligence and interactivity that is impossible with traditional broadcasting techniques.

Business Applications

Many businesses are already using webcasting to disseminate information to their employees, suppliers, customers, and potential customers. Webcasting is playing an active role in such diverse fields as medicine, education, advertising, travel, and real estate as well as the broadcast and computer industries. Essentially, webcasting offers businesses the ability to either:

◆ Save money by improving the cost-effectiveness of something they're already doing like disseminating information about a product or service

◆ Make money by launching a new product or service that would not be feasible without the huge market potential and instant delivery afforded by the Internet

◆ Use the Internet as another distribution source for their content rather than, or in addition to, broadcast

McAfee Software is a good example of a company using webcasting to save money and, at the same time, improving its bottom-line service to its customers. The company is using push technology to instantly disseminate new versions of its virus protection software to its subscribers (see Figure 1.3). In this case, the subscribers do not need to request the new software. In fact, they do not even need to be aware that it exists or that it is pushed to their desktops and automatically installed on their PCs. They need only subscribe to the service and trust McAfee to provide them with up-to-the-minute virus protection.

In the broadcast news industry, MSNBC is using webcasting to market a subscription product that would not be practical without webcasting technology and to create a new revenue source at the same time. MSNBC's Desktop Website (www.businessvideo.msnbc .com) broadcasts audio and video by subscription, permitting users to surf both live and recorded programs. The company videotapes news and business programs, including interviews,

Figure 1.3   McAfee software virus protection webcast Website.

commentaries, and major company announcements that are likely to be of interest to business people who have neither the time to watch regularly scheduled television broadcasts nor the inclination to surf the Net to find the same type of information.

Because MSNBC has news and camera crews available around the world capturing events for audio and video broadcast, webcasting was a natural extension for the company. However, they added a new twist with the webcast subscription service by providing unique, and often exclusive, content that is often unavailable on local TV and radio stations since conventional broadcasters edit the news to fit available time slots. For example, a typical video clip of a CEO making a major announcement is shortened to 8 to 20 seconds on most broadcast news programs. While this coverage may be sufficient for the general viewing public, business people are often interested in hearing the complete announcement and possibly listening to a related commentary.

MSNBC asserts that current, comprehensive business information can provide corporate executives with a competitive advantage and predicts that business people are likely to be willing to pay for easy access to such information, especially if such information is going to help them make crucial business decisions in the future. Users can go directly (by audio or video) to major company and government news conferences, speeches, and industry conventions that affect business and the markets, to see and hear the facts behind the numbers. MSNBC offers coverage of more than 300 exclusive CEO and/or company interviews and presentations each month. Their archives include exclusive interviews and analyses from CNBC North America, CNBC Europe, and CNBC Asia.

MSNBC offers its business webcast subscription service for $24.95 per month and is extending the service with additional features that will enable subscribers to customize the information for their particular needs and receive audio and video news by e-mail, push, and delivery through new data channels on your television using the Vertical Blanking Interval (VBI).

CASE STUDY   MSNBC BUSINESS VIDEO SUBSCRIPTION SERVICE

Michael Wheeler, president of MSNBC Desktop, feels that the "delivery of information rapidly is crucial to staying competitive. Knowing what is going on in the marketplace—as it happens—is the name of the game."

NBC had the information and lots of it—hours of live, exclusive, unedited reports of breaking news worldwide that can change stock markets in a second. The question was, how to disseminate it rapidly and cost-effectively. NBC first offered live video to desktop

PCs via two private television channels. Wheeler saw a demand for the service, "but the average price of delivering our TV content to the PC (ignoring our installation costs) was $300 per PC per month. The solution came in the joint venture with Microsoft Corporation. The timing of Internet growth and the partnership created MSNBC Desktop Video and a new Website, MSNBC Business Video (www.businessvideo.msnbc.com), the first site to provide unedited coverage of key market-moving events via live streaming audio and video or in multimedia archives."

"Using the latest technology for streaming media and secure transactions over the Internet, the MSNBC Business Video Website offers live streaming audio and video, an extensive multimedia archive, and transcripts of worldwide events." According to Wheeler, 96 percent of Fortune 1,000 firms are now Internet-enabled. "We have discovered that easy access to our site has enabled us to bring truly important business content to all knowledge workers. Now purchasing agents, brand managers, salespeople, and financial consultants to mergers and acquisitions can see and hear business news live at their PC for less than $25 per month. New technology has allowed us to make our service much less expensive than the $300 price we had to charge just last year."

Also, the MSNBC Business Video Website is easily accessible. The technical requirements are simple: a PC that can play sound, an Internet connection, and Internet Explorer 3.0+ or Netscape Navigator 2.0+. A 486/66 processor (or greater) is needed for audio and video. All major operating systems are supported. Users can download all necessary software from the Website (www.businessvideo.msnbc.com) and install it in minutes. The site utilizes Microsoft Corporation's NetShow 2.0.

Subscribers can view MSNBC Business Video's daily offerings of:

- Market-moving events affecting global financial markets
- More than 3,000 exclusive CEO interviews each year
- Breaking national and international stories
- Analysis and interviews from CNBC North America, Europe, and Asia
- Key governmental announcements
- Corporate presentations at industry and brokerage conferences
- Exclusive New York Society of Security Analysts meetings

In addition, NASDAQ has signed on as a partner, as well as a customer, for its popular NASDAQ.com site and offers daily MSNBC Desktop video reports on its Website, which also offers relevant links to NY Quotes, NewsEdge, BRIDGE, CMP TechWeb, Desktop Data, First Call/Research Direct, and PC Week.

Webcasting is proving its value in a range of industries, from distance learning in education to telemedicine, which uses a combination of computers, communications technologies, and the Internet to provide medical care to patients at a distance. Webcasting also offers some very significant advantages for marketing goods and services over the Internet, and it is in this area that we're likely to see its greatest use in the next three to five years. We'll discuss some webcasting business models in Chapter 2 and provide examples of some organizations that are already using, or contemplating use of, webcasting technology to share information with colleagues and/or promote their products and services on the Internet. Despite its potential for various business applications though, webcasting certainly isn't all business. It also offers great potential for entertainment applications, offering fast, simple access to a virtually unlimited selection of entertainment options, from personalized, animated cartoons to interactive films, radio, and TV channels. Many of the major players in the entertainment industry are already beginning to use the various types of webcasting technology to reach a global audience. Others are developing channels to target a niche audience from baby care to technorock in Belgium.

Types of Webcasts

As we mentioned at the beginning of the chapter, there are three types of webcasting: push, on-demand, and streaming, which can be either live or recorded. Because most of us are probably most familiar with push, we'll begin by describing its underlying technology and application.

Push/Pull

Push technologies (both push and pull are bundled into this term) are audio, video, or textual information, or any combination of the three, that come through the Net to your receiving device. It may be information that you have previously requested (such as a software update or a report on traffic conditions for your route home) or information that someone else (such as your boss or your company's human resource department) thinks you should have. The information may pop up as an alert on your computer, TV screen, mobile devices, or multimedia cellular phones to let you know that the manufacturing plant is closing early or may consist of the latest sales/marketing report that you need to check for accuracy.

Simply stated, push is like a street vendor; information is pushed at you either by choice or because someone else thinks the information is important to you. The town crier may have been the first example of pushing information—yelling out the day's news for the townsfolk to hear—whether they were interested or not. That crier was pushing information using the strength of his voice and people listened (or didn't listen) based on his credibility and their proximity to the crier. Newspapers are a more contemporary version of pushing information. You may choose to subscribe and/or to read the newspaper, but it provides the information regardless of your interest (or lack of interest). It is interesting to note that some of the earliest companies to adopt push technologies were those that were already involved in publishing, such as Ziff Davis and the Wall Street Journal Interactive Edition, both of which started testing a variety of push technologies in late 1996.

Webcasting's version of push technology is somewhat more advanced than either the newspaper or the town crier. Contemporary push technologies apply some level of intelligence to determine—based on your needs, interests, and previous information requests—what information you may want to receive. Push technology relies on your assistance in making this determination. To some extent, the process is intuitive; the computer may track your interest and travels on a Website and notice that you linger awhile on a certain section, or that you purchase products in certain areas. It then takes this information and develops a profile based on your travels on the Internet. Many of the push products ask questions about your interests so that they can send geographically targeted news or business information that is pertinent to your industry only.

Push products come in a wide variety of sizes, shapes, and transmission methods. They may deliver information via scrolling bars at the top of your computer screen, infopaks that flash on a program, screen savers, the wallpaper on your desktop, or a Website designed while you wait or while you're doing other things on your computer. Push is also being added to your TV—new set-top boxes include electronic program guides that can alert you of news or new programs meeting your interests. The simplest form of push is a client-based solution in which the client fetches Web pages and stores them on the local disk for later viewing. This approach can be classified as automated pull since the client is responsible for pulling the information from the server. Both Netscape and

Microsoft support this limited approach to push for free in their latest browsers. Electronic mail, which is unquestionably the most widely used application on the Internet, is another example of push technology. Current e-mail programs from Eudora, CE Software, and Netscape push audio, graphics, and Web pages to you through your e-mail box. Other forms of push require you to download a software package or to receive push information through wireless communications such as AirMedia, NBC Intercast, Wavephore or new multimedia phones and car radios. These companies bundle information and flash it to your radio, portable device, TV, or PC screen via pager or satellite frequencies rather than the telephone lines.

Pull, which is also referred to as agent technology, intelligent database marketing, adaptive processing, or even artificial intelligence, pulls information for you from the Internet. You can set up your own selections, or intelligent software agents can search out information they think you'd be interested in. If, for example, you're interested in a particular aspect of sports or medicine, the software agents look for keywords in information on the Net or other sources, then bundle up the information containing those keys and push it to you according to a prearranged schedule. Although the term intelligent agent was originally applied to search-type programs, current versions of these products are significantly more sophisticated than conventional search programs. They can customize, personalize, and humanize the delivery of content through advanced tracking and demographic analysis. Information that is pulled from the Net may include sports scores from your local teams (if you have requested this information in the past) to the names and phone numbers of singles you may want to meet who fit your criteria for a mate. It may also consist of an alert to inform you that a competitor has just launched a new product or campaign.

Some pull products, such as Open Sesame (www.opensesame .com), use software that actually incorporates reasoning capabilities. This type of software tracks your movements on the Internet (with or without your permission or knowledge) and makes reasonable deductions about the types of information that you have an interest in. Open Sesame (see Figure 1.4) provides personalized information about new books, CDs, TV shows, movies, and upcoming concerts and events that might be of interest to you. To receive this type of personalized entertainment guide, you provide a quick interest profile at your initial sign-on. Then, the Open Sesame software presents choices on a personalized What's New page. The company has arrangements with Atlantic Records, Borders Books, Sony, and MovieFone, Inc. to find information that matches your interests. The intelligent agent software continually learns more about you and your specific interests as time goes by, and you accept or reject the information that it chooses for you. To some extent, these types of products can offer very significant time savings by filtering or sorting through the reams of information resid-

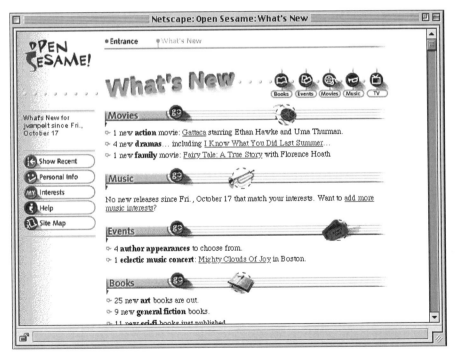

Figure 1.4 Open Sesame webcast home page.

ing on the Internet and delivering only the pieces that are relevant to you. The problem is, of course, they may reason incorrectly or provide too much or too little. Still, they are in their infancy and likely to improve as the Internet continues to expand.

Features and Benefits of Push Technologies

Push technologies allow you to install programs, receive news updates, and interact with the Internet with audio, video, and text sent to your computer—all without actively searching for the information. This represents a significant change from traditional Internet usage, which, until very recently, was limited to a seek model in which users employed search engines to actively locate information that met their needs, such as searching for information about the latest virus software or for stock market reports. While search agents are certainly useful, they still require that users be proactive in seeking information, and they don't solve the problem in which users are typically unaware of exactly what information is available and don't know whether it's been recently updated. In addition, some search engines return too many files as to be practical containing robust content such as multimedia or large bitmaps requiring downloading to their PCs.

Push technologies overcome many of these difficulties. The technology promises to help companies reach the elusive goal of getting the right digital data to the right people at the right time. It brings intelligence and efficiency to the distribution of all kinds of information, giving Web publishers more control over what users see and when. For users, it translates to more productive use of the Internet and intranets/extranets, with less time searching through ever expanding reams of data. For companies, it allows them to develop predictable business models that work on the Web. With push, companies can develop full-fledged electronic commerce systems, replacing or augmenting costly paper-based direct marketing. Or they can develop intranets/extranets that give information technology (IT) and departmental management the centralized control they desire over information flow from company sources, competitive Web sources, customer Web sources, and value-added news sources.

PointCast, one of the first Internet push companies, is classified as a push service provider (see Figure 1.5). The company offers a product that lets users sign up to receive current information on a range of topics including stock prices, weather conditions, and horoscopes, or to receive channels of information from various publications such as the *Wall Street Journal* or *Wired Magazine.* PointCast originally made deals with content providers like the *Wall Street Journal* and chose the information that users could receive via the PointCast channel. The company has since expanded its offering, now giving users the option of building their own channels containing their own content. While the graphics frames and delivery mechanism are the same as the original PointCast channel, the content is different, customized by the provider

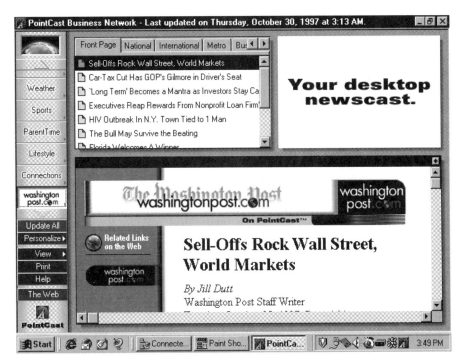

Figure 1.5 PointCast channel home page.

and pushed out to interested users. A public service organization like the Leukemia Society, for example, can create a PointCast channel to push their news releases. Because PointCast is supported by advertising, it pushes the information on its primary channel and the customized user channels free of charge. Its layout is similar to that of a newspaper; users can add information into existing categories on any of the channels as long as they use one of the standard formats (e.g., frames, newsletter, or envelope) but there is no interaction between the PointCast content providers and the users. PointCast sells ads to support its service. Its advertising is a cross between television and print. They provide animated messages over a fixed length of time, like that of a 30-second commercial, in a small box or frame.

Other companies like Marimba and BackWeb, two popular push technology providers, make their money by selling servers or software to their customers who then push their information over their own channels. Marimba and BackWeb can push sophisticated interactive information. Both can incorporate animations, support instant purchase decisions, update user software, or present a virtual walkthrough of a new building, product, or Web site. Their software can use audio and video on demand or links to a live stream. If a public service organization (like the Leukemia Society) chooses to use either BackWeb or Marimba, it has greater flexibility in its interaction with the channel users. It may, for example, be able to determine the amount of a user's contributions to the group or record a user's medical needs and future information requirements. Marimba and BackWeb can both track users' past behavior on the channel and develop sophisticated user demographics and on-line statistics for the various databases that are accessible through the channel.

The popularity of intelligent information that is downloaded and automatically sent out to interested users has opened the doors for more than 60 companies that presently offer push products. These companies distribute a wide range of information products, from children's testing and educational information to the House of Blues, which pushes new music and concert information, and the American Singles Channel (www.as.org), which pushes the profiles of men or women in your geographic area that fit your criteria for a suitable mate (or date).

Future Directions for Push Technologies

Push technologies are becoming more interactive. While the early products represented a publish-only or one-way broadcast environment, the newer products stress interactivity and intuitive, intelligent choice. In the original products, someone had data or content and made decisions about its relevance to users, sorting or filtering the content much like the editors in a newsroom filter the information that appears in a newspaper. Now, the choice of data is largely based on users' past behavior and their response, or lack thereof, to previous information.

Companies like BackWeb and Marimba are already stretching the boundaries of push technology. They currently offer products that show a three-dimensional view of a building or allow the corporate MIS director to remotely update every computer on every desktop within the organization. It's no longer necessary to walk to every machine, kick the user off, and perform the necessary upgrade or repair. Both Microsoft and Netscape have embraced push technology and incorporate the capability in their latest generation browsers (Microsoft Internet Explorer 4.0 and Netscape Netcaster for Communicator). The *Wall Street Journal* and *Business Week* both published articles in 1997 predicting that the browser wars will soon be replaced by push wars. A number of trade publications, including Web Week and InfoWorld have made push a regular feature and others, including *Wired, Network Computing,* and *Internet World* have featured cover stories on push technology. Push technologies are being incorporated as a standard feature in new software. For example, a media planner will decide upon the appropriate mix of advertising or direct mail to use. Push will be selected as appropriate.

The automation and time savings potential offered by push technology is truly incredible. But, while the promise of push technology is great, so too are some of the inherent problems and questions surrounding the technology. How much information is too much?

How much is enough? Do we really want (or need) Big Brother deciding what information we should receive? Certainly, these are still open questions which will not be resolved in the near future. The only thing definite about the future of push is that we're likely to see its widespread use in the next several years until, much like telemarketing, we tire of the onslaught and develop additional technology to select or restrict the information that is pushed to us.

Streaming

Streaming technologies convert an audio or video signal to a digital format and compress it for transmission over a telephone or cable line (the standard means of connecting to the Internet). In many respects, streaming is similar to conventional broadcasting. Events can be either live or prerecorded and can be delivered in real time or on-demand. All live broadcasts—whether for television, radio, or the Internet—incorporate the same basic elements: producing and taping the event, connecting to a transmission signal, and distributing the signal across a network. In television, for example, a live crew may produce and tape an event, then transmit the results by telephone lines, satellite, or microwave link to a television station or network distribution source to broadcast the signal. This program content would arrive at the TV station, be sent to the transmitter, then be sent over the air in waves that you can pick up on your television set.

Although the connection and distribution steps are somewhat different for live webcasting, the production steps and overall concept is very much the same as traditional broadcasting. Two years ago, it wasn't cost-effective for a broadcaster to use precious airwaves for only a few viewers or listeners, but live webcasting makes it possible to pick up a few viewers from here and there all over the world, eventually collecting a sizable audience. The Everest '97 webcast (see Figure 1.6), for example, can assemble an audience for a live or programmed event from anywhere in the world. Similarly, there are a number of niche programs that have fans from around the globe, race fans who want to exchange information on their favorite drivers or replay a program telecast overnight on ESPN at their convenience.

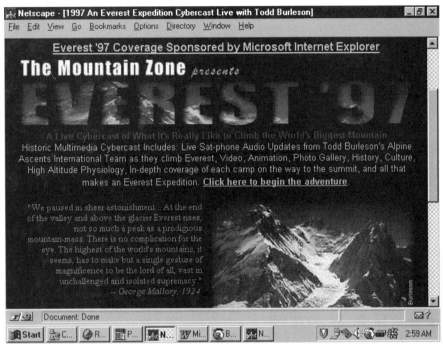

Figure 1.6 The Everest '97 webcast.

In Internet terms, the broadcast of a live or prerecorded live event is called a stream because it uses streaming technologies to send the video signal to you. The Internet is composed of little packets of data comprised of 1s and 0s that a program understands and converts into the normal broadcast signals we're accustomed to seeing on our television screens. These packets have to be continual and in order, in a continuous stream for a live broadcast. The ability to squeeze the audio and video into a stream is the basis of streaming technologies. These technologies use codecs (compression-decompression software) to provide for nearly instant viewing of audio or video. We say nearly instant because there is a buffering factor involved in both traditional broadcasting and webcasting—a few seconds delay when you push enter on your computer or play on your TV. The buffer delays signal reception to enable the streaming technology processor to collect and read the packets. Buffering ensures that all of the audio and video packets are stacked in the right order. The longer the buffer delay, the longer the download time, and the better the quality.

When you receive e-mail, a delay of a few seconds or even a few minutes isn't significant as long as you eventually receive the entire message. But, in streaming technology, if you don't receive the event in the proper order, the sound or video will be garbled. If the packet of digits (1s and 0s) isn't transmitted and received in the correct sequence, gaps occur that make speech and video impossible to comprehend.

Streaming technologies and the companies that support the necessary audio and video products didn't exist until the mid-1990s, and early products were relatively unstable. We've seen significant improvement in product reliability during 1997, with much attention and financing coming from the major technology companies. Microsoft, for example, clearly believes that streaming media is significant to the future of communications.

Live Webcasting

Live webcasting is taking an event that is happening anywhere in the world and placing it on the Internet (or an intranet) in a video or audio broadcast. The event may be a European Union conference on the state of the economy, a live broadcast of a U2 concert, your corporation's shareholders' meeting, or your grandchild's first steps. Broadcasting a live signal over the Internet requires that the signal be transmitted in a continuous data stream to ensure receiving an audio or video broadcast with all of the pictures and sounds in the right place.

A live webcast offers significantly more opportunity for interactivity than a traditional broadcast; it isn't limited to merely receiving an audio or video signal. Webcasting permits users to interact with the event as it is happening, for example, clicking on a model walking down the runway during a live webcast of a fashion show to view the dress in more detail, even spinning the model around to see the back of the dress, or changing the color or length of the skirt. Or clicking on the video of a NASA launch to visit the control tower and hear the controllers' instructions to the astronauts while reviewing the specification details for equipment and fuel.

The July 4, 1997, landing of NASA *Pathfinder* allowed users to interact with history for the first time, selecting the information they wanted to see and hear as the event happened rather than waiting for CNN or other newscasts to replay the videos (see Figure 1.7). While this type of interaction may seem strange to those over the age of 35, just watch your kids as they interact with a CD-ROM video or electronic game. They're used to being in the driver's seat and taking control of the information that they see and hear. In this respect, they're all ready to enjoy the benefits of webcasting. For example, the ability to click on a street sign in a video to access a map of the region, then clicking on a business in the background to view the company profile, is all available today in a Microsoft demonstration for its NetShow product.

Figure 1.7 The webcast of the Mars *Pathfinder.*

How Does Live Webcasting Differ from Traditional Broadcasting?

Most of the differences between traditional broadcasting and webcasting focus on technology issues. For webcasting, we need bigger computers to serve an increasing number of viewers, which might relate to a bigger transmitter for a broadcast station that would cover a larger geographical area. The larger the signal, or the more users or viewers, the more work the servers (computers) have to do to get the signal out to a lot of people at one time. Both also require a means to send the signal over the airwaves (in broadcasting) or over bandwidth (in webcasting).

As you can see in Table 1.1, there are a few more steps involved in preparing content for broadcast over the Internet than there are in traditional broadcasting, but the process is similar.

Two factors affect proper broadcasting on the Internet:

1. The speed of the computers that send out the signal (i.e., the servers). The more people who visit your Website to view your webcast, the more servers or power your servers need to deliver the signal. Imagine 100 people all knocking on your door at one time. This is much like a large audience trying to access the webcast with only one server. If your servers aren't big enough, or if you don't have the proper software, someone will have to wait or won't be able to receive the signal or connect to the Website at all.

2. The amount of bandwidth that you're providing to enable multiple users to view the program. Before everyone knocks on your door to access your webcast, they

TABLE 1.1 Broadcast Technology and Requirements

TV Broadcasting Steps	Webcasting Steps
1. Generate signal	1. Generate signal
2. Transmit signal to TV station	2. Convert signal from analog to digital (encoding)
3. TV station broadcasts signal	3. Compress signal to send over telephone lines or an Internet connection (compression)
	4. Transmit compressed, digitized signal to an Internet service provider (ISP) and replicates
	5. ISP clones the signal (i.e., stream) and broadcasts it over the Internet
Requirements	**Requirements**
◆ Broadcast equipment	◆ Webcasting equipment
◆ Air time (purchased from network)	◆ Communication link to ISP
◆ Program content	◆ Program content
◆ Transmission/tower	◆ Bandwidth (leased from ISP)

have to drive up to your home, request the video, and then find a seat in the audience. This is like the bandwidth: the more people, the bigger the screen, and the more seats. The bigger your event, the greater the bandwidth you will need to provide so that last person at the door manages to get a seat.

Bandwidth is a crucial (and expensive) issue. We'll discuss it in more detail in Chapter 3, "Webcasting Technologies", but for now, we'll just note the technical issues that you'll need to face when you're preparing to webcast. If you don't plan properly, your signal may be garbled or unavailable, and your viewers may not be able to receive any part of the webcast.

There are a number of options to help control bandwidth costs and to send video and audio signals on different levels of the Net.

Multicasting is one of these methods. In essence, multicasting is the ability to take one signal and send it to lots of people through a network or over the Internet. The one signal curves its way across the Net and locates a device (a router and/or splitter) that sends the signal to a number of computers or television sets. This is like a broadcast signal where there is one signal that can be received by many people as long as they are located within the station's broadcast range. In multicasting, many people can receive the same signal if they are on a network that has this capability. The advantage of multicasting is that it is significantly cheaper than unicasting, which assigns a single line (or stream) to each viewer or listener. Multicasting uses only one line (stream) to send the signal.

On-Demand

On-demand webcasting is the Internet version of a VCR that can store hundreds of thousands of programs. In its most basic form, on-demand webcasting allows us to view any event that has been recorded for broadcast on the Internet or an intranet. This is essentially any streaming event, be it audio or video. And on-demand webcasting offers many of the same control features as our VCRs; we can fast-forward through the parts of the event that don't interest us, pause for a cup of coffee, rewind to listen or view something of interest, and replay the event any time we want, as often as we want. On-demand webcasting offers a few additional capabilities; we can also change the size of the picture, modify the audio track, and add captioning or other features to our copy of the event. Actually, you can do just about anything you want; in effect, you become the broadcaster with control of the airwaves. You can even direct the camera or switch cameras to see a sporting event from a different viewpoint or inspect a new car from a different angle. You can also take a subway ride, a train ride, or cruise down the Mississippi River to New Orleans—all at your convenience.

On-demand webcasting offers all of the features and functions of your VCR, with a number of added capabilities, as shown in Table 1.2.

TABLE 1.2 Comparison: VCR and On-Demand Webcasting Features

Typical VCR Features (also provided by on-demand webcasting)

◆ Rewind
◆ Fast-forward
◆ Pause
◆ Stop
◆ Record
◆ Closed captioning

Additional On-Demand Webcasting Features

◆ Instant replay, even during live events; no waiting for rewind or fast-forward
◆ Interactivity: ability to question, respond, suggest, or chat with other participants; view additional selections; or order a product or service
◆ Multiple camera angles
◆ Zoom in and out of the picture (using Webcams and/or robotics)

The term *on-demand* refers to our ability to control the scheduling and appearance of the webcast. This is also known as *time-shifting,* but that sounds a bit Buck Rogerish so it's probably easier to just remember it as on-demand—receiving information, whether it's audio, video, or text, when you want it, as often as you want it. In broadcast television or radio, you have to watch the program when it is broadcast (at a specific time) or tape it on a VCR. On-demand webcasting eliminates the need to plan ahead and tape the event. Instead, we can access Websites that act like cafeterias for webcast events and information, then choose the audio and/or video segments that we want to watch. We can demand (or request) to view a favorite program, the evening news, or the details of the president's State of the Union message at any hour of the day or night. In other words, the information is available on-demand. You can get it when you want it at your convenience simply by clicking on the appropriate channel. (The term *channel* is borrowed from broadcasting and means essentially the same thing as a broadcast channel. On TV, you might click on channel 24 to view the ball game; on the Web, you click on a URL to access a specific Website, which may be a telemedicine channel, horoscope channel, or conventional broadcast channel.)

On-demand viewing is one of the most compelling features of webcasting because it lets us determine our own schedules for retrieving and using information—an important concept in these busy days of telecommuting and collaboration. In this respect, it offers some distinct advantages for disseminating business information. Companies can (and do) schedule training sessions for their staff members around the world (and track which sites tune in to the webcast session and which don't), webcast the shareholders' meeting to owners around the world, and arrange for prospective buyers to walk through new homes in other states or countries.

How to Receive a Live or On-Demand Webcast

When you want to know what programs are available on your television or radio, you probably pick up a TV or radio guide or your daily newspaper and check the program listings or flip through the channels to see if there's anything of interest to you. The process is much the same for looking for programs on the Internet and intranets. You can use your mouse or (for Web TV access) remote control device and tune in to one or more Websites that present a program guide of live events and on-demand webcast programs. These Websites, which are known as link pages or aggregated content pages, serve as the program guides to audio and video webcasts. The new WebTV plus offers their own electronic program guide (EPG). One of the most popular program guides is www.time-cast.com which allows you to go through topic guides and automatically sort programs of interest to you. Audionet.com offers a jukebox of on-demand CDs, talk programs, and industry meetings in both audio and video formats. In addition, there are a number of program guides and e-mail lists that tell you of upcoming events, and many of the Internet search engines are adding live events to their programs. Yahoo! for example, is a popular Internet search engine that lists live-event and chat webcasts as well as audio news on-demand. Ultimate TV is another webcast directory and lists all TV and internet-only webcasts (see Figure 1.8).

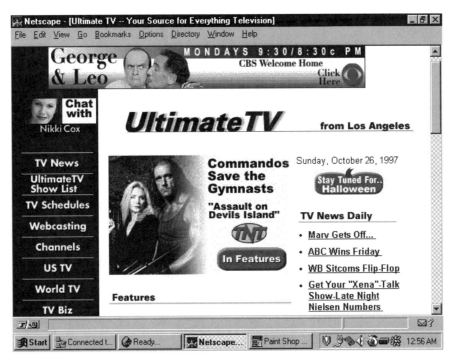

Figure 1.8   The www.ultimatetv.com home page.

Who Is Webcasting?

Webcasting isn't limited to large broadcasting corporations like NBC or to huge manufacturing companies like General Motors. Your son's or daughter's fifth-grade classroom may already be using Internet conferencing to exchange ideas and options with a similar classroom in New Guinea. We'll discuss the requirements for developing your own webcast Website in Chapter 4, but for now, it's important to understand that virtually anyone can become a webcaster. In fact, thousands of individuals, businesses, and organizations are already webcasting. It doesn't require either a broadcast license or a tower. You can rent time or space on the Internet to webcast whatever and whenever you please. Webcasting technology is essentially the same for an individual involved in a low-end, family-oriented webcast as it is for a major corporation like MSNBC. Only the scale of the webcast—the amount of time and money spent developing the content and the size of the audience that it reaches—differs.

Low-End Webcasting

Virtually any individual or organization can use push or streaming technologies to webcast. In fact, many organizations are already webcasting on a low level by pushing information via e-mail. Unfortunately, most of us are all too familiar with junk e-mail— those unwanted messages that pop up on our screen when we sign on to our Internet account. The organizations that send those messages are actually pushing information out to us. And, as most of us know, it's very easy to delete that type of information without ever investigating the message. To avoid the appearance of junk mail or information overload, many companies restrict their e-mail campaigns to customers, suppliers, or business associates that have actually requested information. This type of direct e-mail marketing can be a highly effective method for sending new product information, pricing details, and/or notices of sales or special offers to customers and prospective customers. Because many e-mail products and browsers allow you to attach audio and video files or animated graphics, e-mail push campaigns are popular marketing tools for retailers such as automobile dealers, computer outlets, and furniture and appliance stores. Effective e-mail marketing campaigns combine the capabilities of Internet push technology with a good list of prospective customers and/or individuals who have previously shown an interest in their products.

To establish a direct e-mail marketing campaign, you need a database of customer information that includes as much data on the customer interests and preferences as possible. This information can be invaluable if you decide to move beyond e-mail to some more sophisticated types of webcasting. A car dealer, for example, might want to record customers' preferences for particular automobile models, years, or colors. An accounting firm may record information about their clients' investment preferences or account balances. At some point in the future, this type of information can be used by mid- to high-level push application products to enhance the marketing campaign, automatically notifying the prospective car buyer of a car on the lot that meets his or her preferences or warning the accounting client when an account balance falls below a prespecified level.

The cost for setting up an effective e-mail marketing system ranges from $500 to $5000, depending on the size and complexity of the database, the frequency of the mailing, and the sophistication of the message. Obviously, an automobile dealer who sends a snazzy video of the latest model cars to a list of 2000 prospective customers is going to spend considerably more than an accounting firm that sends a text message out to its top 100 clients. The expense lies largely in preparing the database and the message rather than delivering it. And the auto dealer has a number of options for preparing the content which may substantially affect the overall cost.

For example, the auto dealership can stream a videotape of the latest models, either creating the videotape on-site using the manager as spokesman or hiring the services of a professional video firm and using a local celebrity to tout the benefits of doing business with the dealership. A streaming program does not have to use multiple cameras, a studio stage, or advanced programming. Self-producing a streaming video typically requires renting a digital camera, buying or renting an audio/video editing program that is compatible with your computer, and hiring an Internet service provider (ISP) to place your video on a Website—either your own Website or one provided on a temporary basis by the ISP.

The camera rental and editing program is likely to cost anywhere from a few hundred dollars to a few thousand dollars, depending on the sophistication of the hardware and software and whether you need to hire a cameraman and editor or have personnel that can handle those tasks. The ISP charges may range from nothing— if you currently have a Website and a provider that can support streaming—to $100 a month. To some extent, the charges will depend on the popularity of the site; the more popular the site, the more expensive the monthly charges. But obviously, higher charges would not necessarily be bad news in this situation.

A Penny Saved . . . Isn't Always a Good Thing!

With apologies to Ben Franklin, we just want to mention that although it is very possible to create a reasonable-quality streaming video on a shoestring budget, it's not a good idea to cut too many corners in making or buying a webcast video. After all, the video will present your image to both existing and prospective customers. High-quality graphics, copy, text, audio, and video can give your organization a real competitive advantage. But a sloppy production can severely damage your company's image and your customers' perceptions of you. Remember, the video will be appearing on the Internet—the world's largest fishbowl. It's not a place where you want to make mistakes!

If you don't have personnel who are experienced in video production, you should look into hiring professionals to handle the filming and editing chores. Better yet, look into hiring the services of a video consultant, preferably one who is familiar with webcasting and the specific advantages and disadvantages of streaming video on the Net. If you can't hire a competent professional to assist you in the production, look into buying a suitable video and tailoring it for your needs.

If all else fails, consider holding off on a streaming video for the time being. More and more small businesses and consultants are addressing the specialized needs of webcast production. Whatever you do, don't take a chance on presenting a poor-quality video on the Web. An attempt to economize or rush is likely to be very costly in the long run.

Mid-Range Webcasting

Nearly any company that has audio or video archives may find webcasting an easy and natural extension of its day-to-day operations. Placing video on your Website is one method of providing your customers and business associates with 24-hour access to current events and information about your product or service. It's simple, effective, and they don't have to wait for your latest videotape to arrive in the mail or go to your location to gather information or view your products. Video dating services, comedy clubs, training centers, and speakers' bureaus are just a few businesses that can (and do) benefit by placing their videos on-line. Swiss Connection (www.swissconnection.com) is an example of a manufacturing organization that is using webcast streaming to disseminate information about its products to prospective customers around the world. The company enhances its webcast (see Figure 1.9) by adding instructional and entertaining videos.

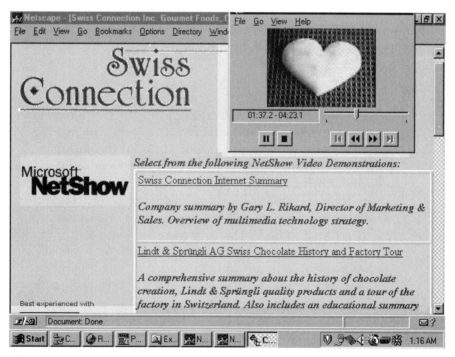

Figure 1.9   Swiss Connection webcast Website.

CASE STUDY SWISS CONNECTION ON-DEMAND WEBCASTING APPLICATION

Swiss Connection manufactures chocolate confections, coffee, and dessert ingredients. Established in 1984, the company delivers its products and services across international borders. Prior to the Internet, Swiss Connection had difficulty in reaching its vast audience of potential customers. Now, the company uses Microsoft's NetShow software for streaming media.

According to Gary Rickard, director of Marketing and Sales, "Microsoft NetShow uses a new concept for delivering media over the Internet protocols. The streaming technology signals a new era of delivering audio, video, and text to the mass market. It allows a growing company like Swiss Connection to communicate information about our concepts and quality brands to a larger audience."

The Swiss Connection Website allows viewers to tour the factory, watch the production process, and learn about the company history. The site also provides educational videos, including information about how to use its freeze-dried mixes and a step-by-step description of the process used to make its Alaska Express Cream Cheese. "We have found that value is added by having a more educated consumer. Providing customers with this type of information helps to turn them into repeat customers."

"NetShow enhances our Website because consumers can rely on getting quality information in a form that meets their changing needs. Our site provides on-demand demos of products and recipes to shoppers and customers. If, for instance, someone wants to make a Black Forest cake, they can find a list of the ingredients on-line in our outlet store. Even though we pride ourselves on the simplicity of using our products, you still can see a step-by-step demo by a professional chef."

"Many of our customers do not have the time or opportunity to travel to trade shows or conferences, but they still want to learn about our new products or events that we participate in. By implementing Net-Show, we reinforce the message that Swiss Connection is dedicated to new and innovative ways of servicing our customers."

Rickard also believes that using NetShow has contributed to an improved level of service to its customers. "New employees can learn about our products and their many uses, thus reducing training and organizational costs. This directly contributes to our profitability."

Swiss Connection plans to further explore training and education options on their Website. "We envision using NetShow to deliver educational content to schools specializing in culinary education. We may also use NetShow to deliver live presentations from industry trade shows.

There are a wide range of features available to let businesses enhance their Websites. These range from search engines that help viewers to find specific information, to captioning and cued slides or diagrams that can be displayed along with the audio or video. For example, a comedy club may want to webcast weekly live broadcasts and archive the rest of their presentations on their Website for viewing at other times.

If an organization, like the Comedy Club, decides to webcast a live show each week, they need to get their audio or video signal to an Internet service provider (ISP). This may require high-speed telephone lines, satellite delivery, or other ways to transmit the signal to the Net connection. They also need to purchase sufficient bandwidth for the live webcast. The webcaster pays per viewer for a live webcast and the costs are twofold: The Comedy Club must purchase enough bandwidth necessary for many people to watch at one time and must license the software service that they use. The bandwidth is a recurring cost per event. The software isn't. Some audio or video Net software is sold per user or per stream. The club has to order the number of streams necessary to support viewers of the live broadcast. Telephone lines, bandwidth, and access costs range from $1000 to $10,000 a month for a program that reaches 200 viewers at a time. The software cost (streaming) is typically a onetime cost which ranges from free to $5000. These costs will decrease as multicasting is implemented on the Net and it becomes cheaper to broadcast to hundreds of thousands of people.

Additional costs to consider for live webcasting include special graphics, ad banners, chat room programs, and/or a database of available guests to appear on the webcast. A chat room program adds a level of interactivity, allowing visitors to ask questions of the guests or trade reactions and information with other attendees.

Placing the tape archives on the Website for on-demand viewing is a considerably simpler—and cheaper—process. If an organization has videotapes available, the cost to encode and digitize those tapes for presentation on the Web typically ranges from $100 to $500 a tape, depending on quality and any editing services required to place the video on their Website. Many sites provide a video database or program guide to help viewers find specific events or information. Providing this type of service is essentially free but may add to the administrative overhead for the site.

In general, the costs for establishing a fairly low-volume streaming Website capable of supporting both live and on-demand webcasts range from about $5000 to $10,000 for the basics. Adding interactivity features like chat room programs increases the costs by anywhere from a few hundred dollars to $5000. Similarly, the costs associated with special graphics and captioning can range from a few hundred dollars to a few thousand dollars. Databases and the data entry fees can range from several hundred to thousands of dollars.

High-End Business Applications

High-end webcasting applications may be either push or streaming, or a combination of the two. In many respects, high-end streaming audio and video can serve as an alternative to traditional broadcasting. A number of businesses are using this form of webcasting to disseminate information to remote office locations or to reach prospective customers or investors. Of course, the entertainment industry is also beginning to use high-end streaming audio and video to reach a global audience via the Internet. One feature that differentiates high-end streaming webcasting from traditional broadcasting is the availability of an instant video library, which is accessible on-demand, 24 hours a day. High-end streaming webcasting applications can, and usually do, include a combination of live events and access to an archive of past events.

A number of companies, including Boeing, Cisco, Digital Equipment, KPMG, MCI, Oracle, and Sybase are using RealAudio and/or RealVideo to stream information over their corporate intranets. We'll discuss the Boeing webcasting application in detail in Chapter 5, but all of these companies use streaming media in much the same way—to provide users with access to live events (e.g., shareholder meetings, major corporate announcements, and so on, on-demand training, and employee benefits information. Similarly, a number of major corporations including AT&T and Allied Signal Corporation are using high-level push applications to deploy new product and training information internally via their intranets.

There are many applications for streaming media in the entertainment world. We've already discussed MSNBC and its video subscription service which is certainly a prime example of a high-end business application, but high-end does not necessarily mean something on the scale (or budget) of MSNBC. Streaming media can also be used to present special events such as festivals, parades, and/or sporting events that are of interest to people around the world. A company in New Orleans (www.neworleansweb.org), for example, specializes in streaming live events such as the Mardi Gras and riverboat cruises. Mark Weitz, president of New Orleans

Web, emphasizes the need for a broad range of experience for streaming live webcasting, including expertise in broadcast production, filmmaking, and videography as well as Internet technology. And he warns that webcasting live events necessarily involves a tight margin for error. (Refer to the New Orleans live-event webcasting case study in Chapter 4 for details on New Orleans Web and some very practical suggestions from Weitz for webcasting live events.)

The majority of expenses for high-end live webcasting are involved in production and presentation—storyboarding to build the event webcast and bandwidth to broadcast it on the Net. There are, of course, also miscellaneous personnel and postproduction expenses, but production and presentation probably account for 80 percent of the total, which can easily run into hundreds of thousands of dollars, depending on the event, the equipment required, and the size of the audience. And, of course, that price goes up if you add such special features as two-way videoconferencing or other real-time tools to enhance the webcast.

State of the Webcast Market

There is little doubt that webcasting is likely to mirror the phenomenal growth of the Internet. Studies by BRS Radio, UltimateTV, and Intervox Communications indicate that the number of webcasters has increased by more than 1000 percent during 1997. There are now more than 800 webcasters sending signals 24 hours a day from radio, TV, and net-only broadcast stations, with a new webcast station or show launched on the Net every day. While there is no way to count the audio or video programs available on the Net, estimates begin at hundreds of thousands of audio and video files ranging from TV programs to instructional videotapes to class reunions. According to Real Networks, there are now more than 45,000 hours of live content broadcast each week and hundreds of thousands of hours of archived audio and video content accessed each day.

So, what are all of these programs and webcast messages? Again, studies show that much of the growth is business-oriented. In fact, Forrester Research predicts that business-to-business commerce on the Net will grow three times faster than business-to-consumer. Similarly, CommerceNet predicts that business-to-business transactions will represent 25 percent of all Internet commerce by the year 2000. Of course, some areas of business are likely to use the Internet and webcasting technology more than others. An Emerging Internet Market report by Find/SVP Web predicts that Web advertising will soar to $1.5 billion by the end of 1997 as Internet use shifts from a technical-education audience to a consumer- and business-oriented marketplace. And, this doesn't even take into consideration the vast number of products and services whose sales are influenced by users seeing a product in action or listening to information on the Net.

In addition, while all three types of webcasting are experiencing phenomenal growth, streaming and push seem to be finding the greatest application in the business arena. Patrick M. D'Acre of www.growyourbusiness.com reports that his company has experienced a 200 percent increase in quarter to quarter sales with the use of RealAudio streaming technology which allows his company to display products live on the Internet. According to Brian Ratzlif of ESPNET SportsZone, streaming media adds a uniqueness to Websites that attracts people and increases site traffic: "Certainly during our real-time broadcasts, we have people staying on-site for two hours because they're listening to the final rounds of play at a premier professional event or a world championship. That increases the amount of time people are spending on our site."

William Kelly, general counsel for Silicon Graphics believes that video "does a better job of grabbing your attention and conveys an awful lot more information . . . than you're going to get with a banner ad that blinks at you." In fact, studies confirm that the human mind develops and learns by association and reinforcement. According to Professor Fred Hofstetter, director of the University of Delaware's Instructional Technology Center, "multimedia allows the same information to be reinforced using sound, images, and text." He cites a report which found that people remember 20 percent of what they see, 30 percent of what they hear, 50 percent of what they see and hear, and 80 percent of what they see, hear, and do simultaneously.

Companies of all sizes are beginning to use push technology. Although the early adopters tended to focus on information publishing applications, companies that do business on the Internet are now embracing the technology to give themselves a competitive advantage in building market share. Examples include companies like McAfee Software, which is automating the distribution of new software releases to their subscribers; PC Quote, Inc., which provides financial updates on stocks on a regular basis; Lufthansa, which offers travel updates to customers and agents; and Heineken, which is rolling out a push channel to promote its brand awareness through the Internet.

Large enterprises such as AT&T and Allied Signal may look first at adopting push technology for their intranets and/or extranets. These companies typically test the technology internally for several months before moving ahead to full-scale deployment. They want to be able to collect all of their corporate information into a customizable information management center and to enable individual departments to publish and push content to and from this central information center. As push technology becomes more established, it is also becoming an increasingly important part of existing work flow. For example, the U.S. Department of Agriculture is using push technology to replace a satellite broadcast system, reportedly saving more than $1 million by doing so, and the U.S. Department of Defense is using push technology to deliver virus software updates to approximately 5000 system administrators throughout the country.

Market Trends (What's Driving the Growth?)

Of course, no new market, especially one based on new technology, expands without a few hiccups along the way. This is as true of webcasting as it is of the Internet and the computer industry in general. In many respects, webcasting resembles interactive TV, the new technology of the 1980s that was a precursor of webcasting. Interactive TV, which has largely disappeared due to hitches in the technology and the popularity and accessibility of the Internet, offered many of the same capabilities as webcasting. Like webcasting, interactive TV offered the ability to purchase a product or service on the air and conduct a transaction through a television set. It also pushed information or programming to viewers based on their earlier selections or previously specified interests. In fact, much of the personalization and customized media delivery for which businesses are now using webcasting was originally tested via interactive TV.

CASE STUDY TIME WARNER INTERACTIVE TV*

Have you ever flown on the Concorde? Has anyone?

The Full Service Network, Time Warner's $200 million plus interactive television project near Orlando, is a lot like the Concorde. Not many people have flown on it, and not many will get the chance.

The Full Service Network is sleek, fast, and gorgeous. It was intended as a flagship for its owners. But it's not commercially viable. And just as pundits once predicted that the supersonic transport would be the only way to travel, many experts believe that someday everyone will watch television the way FSN subscribers watch television. But that day may be a long way off. Time Warner announced in May 1997 that the project, which serves about 4000 subscribers in the northern suburbs of Orlando, would close by the end of the year.

Full Service Network
Time Warner chairman Gerald M. Levin launched the Full Service Network with great fanfare in December

* By Peter M. Zollman, excerpted from "Interactive News: State of the Art."

1994, predicting that it would revolutionize television and interpersonal communications, "providing people with unprecedented access to information and entertainment," and be a "turning point for the communications industry."

Reporters swooned over the drumbeat of "choice, convenience and control" that Time Warner's public relations machine banged out. Cable television users and operators from around the world called asking when they, too, would be able to get interactive television on their block.

Unfortunately, reality was more difficult. Six months later, the FSN was in fewer than three dozen homes. It took a massive installation blitz at the end of 1995 with installation crews of up to eight cable installers at each home and dozens of marketing representatives and FSN executives pitching in as customer trainers before the company announced the completion of 4000 installations.

The complex and sometimes frustrating system was powered by a big, noisy set-top box, operated only by a remote control. Customers were not charged for use of the $5000-plus box, which was as high-powered as a Silicon Graphics Indigo computer with loads of extra software, chips, memory, and a Scientific Atlanta cable converter thrown in.

Movies on-demand were by far the most popular service on the FSN, but they were far from the only service. The FSN started with ten venues, or areas of interest. Although they evolved slightly during the trial, the initial venues were:

◆ Movies
◆ News
◆ Sports, offering NFL and NBA sports videos, bloopers and shorts, along with an interactive statistics overlay during NFL games

- Controls, which included such things as channel lock, VCR setup, personal favorites settings, and more
- Games, which offered free and later pay-per-use and subscription interactive video games
- Services, including an Orlando-area entertainment and restaurant guide, classified ads for homes and autos from *The Orlando Sentinel,* home banking, and Pizza Hut
- Shopping, with stores like Spiegel, Eddie Bauer, and Horchow
- Smart Living, planned (but never launched) with health and education programs
- Custom TV, including the Interactive Preview Guide, which resembles a cable television preview guide with 24-hour search capability, and on-demand reruns of soap operas and prime-time shows on a pay-per-view or à la carte basis
- Music videos on-demand

The ambitious plans for the Full Service Network—indeed, the reason for the name—also included Time Warner providing alternate local-access telephone service to the home; a Time Warner Internet-on-television service through the set-top box; and other services such as driver's license renewal, Seminole County library catalog access, grocery shopping with regional supermarket giant Winn-Dixie, and more. None of these services ever came to pass, although Time Warner still hopes to roll out the Internet-on-TV service before shutting down the FSN at the end of 1997.

What Time Warner quickly found was that the technology was too complex to roll out easily, from both a consumer perspective and a cable television network perspective. Early in the venture, the network developed the annoying habit of crashing almost every Saturday night. Later, after that problem was overcome, network engineers struggled with the return path— the signal coming back to the network operations center from the home. The Silicon Graphics servers and software used to operate the four-terabyte operations center underwent several revisions and upgrades, but several key elements for commercial success (such as the ability to scale the network beyond 4000 homes and the prices of the set-top boxes) remained well beyond reach for rolling it out beyond suburban Orlando.

The News Exchange

Although movies were the most popular service, The News Exchange, or TNX, was also very popular. FSN executives proclaimed that, when they began charging for The News Exchange in some FSN homes in late 1996, it was the first time in the history of broadcasting that people were paying specifically for TV news on a subscription basis—$1.95 per month in some neighborhoods, $3.95 in others. Consumers have been paying for CNN and Headline News for years, of course, but only as part of their basic cable subscription, not à la carte.

If you've ever come home from work at 7:15 P.M. and wished you could watch the 6 o'clock news, you can appreciate the logic behind TNX. In a very elegant and simple fashion, TNX offered more than 100 newscasts, news clips, headline packages, and long-form programs—all on-demand, whenever viewers wanted them. And like FSN movies, you could fast-forward or rewind, pause and play or replay them to your heart's content.

The News Exchange content included local, national, and international news with dozens of clips from the local ABC and NBC affiliate stations and major news shows like *Nightline, 20/20, PrimeTime Live,* and *Dateline NBC.* It also included CNN's *Sports News Tonight* and local prep, college, and pro sports coverage from the *Orlando Sentinel,* as well as CNN Headline's *Dollars and Sense* segment, and a twice-daily *Fortune Business Report,* as well as weather updates from The Weather Channel, movie reviews from *Entertainment Weekly,* a variety of science and technology news clips, and The Democracy Network, an interactive video voter guide developed for the 1996 presidential election.

The TNX subscription buy rate exceeded 10 percent according to FSN. Viewers particularly homed in on TV news magazines like *20/20* and *Dateline NBC* that they had missed earlier in the week. But just as with the FSN itself, some of the most attractive interactive features promised for TNX never materialized. A personal stock portfolio, similar to those you can create on AOL or any one of a dozen Websites, was scrapped, as was a Custom Scoreboard made up of a viewer's favorite teams and players. Both required software that never worked properly. And the feature that was initially touted by TNX as its most valuable benefit—indexing or bookmarking of newscasts—also fell by the wayside. With indexing, viewers would have been able to review a rundown of a newscast or program like the local 11 P.M. newscast, or *Dateline NBC,* and jump directly to the stories that they wanted to see. It was too complex to launch.

Has I-TV Already Arrived?
Despite the demise of the FSN and the unclear future of interactive television, new-media expert Paul Sagan contends that I-TV is already available (albeit in limited form) to diehard computer users. To demonstrate, Sagan played several Chicago Bulls clips

downloaded from ESPN SportsZone on his laptop computer, cheering along as Michael Jordan made one of his trademark dunks. "This is the year interactive TV starts a comeback," Sagan said. "Last year it was bashed, but this is the year it returns in a different way—like the Internet on steroids."

Sagan, former president of Time Inc. New Media, helped develop The News Exchange and is now on the board of VDOnet Corp. (www.vdo.com), a provider of technology for streaming video over the Internet. Sagan thinks proprietary closed systems like the Full Service Network have been overtaken by the open systems of the Internet.

Streamed television's video quality is spotty, and the images are still postage-stamp sized, but major TV networks including NBC and CNN are now offering full-length streamed TV programming regularly on the Internet. "Interactive television as it was envisioned two years ago was way too far ahead of its time and too far ahead of the technology," says analyst Ken Lim of The CyberMedia Group. Lim thinks full-motion, full-screen, on-demand digital interactive video is absolutely inevitable. He predicts it will develop slowly, first through Internet access on TV screens, followed by two-way digital cable and two-way digital broadcast satellite services.

Webcasting offers many of the same capabilities as interactive TV through cable, satellite, and on-line services. And, increasingly, our television sets are beginning to take on the capabilities and characteristics of our PCs, just as our PCs begin to emulate our televisions. As the two technologies converge, so too are push and streaming technologies coming together in webcasting, with push taking on the characteristics of streaming and streaming taking on the characteristics of push. The Sundance Film Festival channel and the

Clinton/Gore Inaugural channel are both examples of combining push and live-event webcasting. In both instances, an event notifier pushed webcast information to a potential audience and directed people to sign up to attend the live-event webcast. Then, real-time audio and video broadcasts were streamed to users' PCs during the live event.

As webcasting continues to evolve, audio and video are likely to become tools for push, and push to become a tool for audio and video streaming. You may view the items that are pushed to you on- or off-line, saving them if you're away, or having them instantly forwarded to you, wherever you are. Again, these capabilities resemble interactive TV, but the capabilities are built onto the Internet, which offers worldwide access and a fast-growing global network that wasn't available and may have doomed interactive TV in its infancy.

Certainly, of the various trends that are contributing to the growing popularity of webcasting, the widespread and increasing use of the Internet, intranets, and extranets in business is the factor that is most likely to determine its ultimate success. At the same time, however, webcasting is being driven by the ever increasing sophistication of users, who are accustomed to browsing the Internet for business and entertainment purposes and who demand faster and faster access to the information they seek. This desire for instant gratification is in turn contributing to continuous improvements in computing and communications technology, ensuring widespread access to larger, faster PCs and modems, all of which further fuels the use of the Internet in a huge (some would say vicious) circular pattern of growth and usage that is likely to continue at an ever accelerating rate.

So, where is all this likely to lead and how can it affect your business in the short term? As we'll see in Chapter 2, many organizations are already beginning to take advantage of the benefits that webcasting offers over traditional Internet business techniques. To a great extent, its potential is limited only by imagination, but it is important to recognize that webcasting still isn't suited for everyone or every type of business application. It is still a new and evolving field that requires careful consideration and considerable knowledge before jumping in.

CHAPTER TWO

Business Opportunities for Webcasting

There is little argument that the Internet has changed the way in which many organizations conduct business. Websites are now a common means for dispensing information about business products and services for virtually all types and sizes of companies—from the mom-and-pop grocery store on the corner to major corporations like IBM, General Motors, and (of course) Microsoft. But what can webcasting offer that conventional Websites don't? And how can you determine if webcasting is appropriate, now or in the near future, for your particular industry and organization?

Websites Literally Don't Deliver, or Do They?

Webcasting offers all of the advantages of Internet marketing and conventional Websites: It can reach a global audience or a targeted group of users with common interests or concerns; it offers immediate access to news and information, with easy updating to ensure that information stays fresh for delivery; and it offers easy access via a standard PC or, with new technologies, an appropriately equipped TV set or mobile devices. But, in addition to these advantages, webcasting offers the added benefits of sight and sound and satisfies our desire for instant gratification. While we turn on the radio or TV today and immediately receive some type of news or entertainment, the programming is restricted to linear time schedules. Similarly, libraries and video rental stores offer a variety of content on-demand, but we need to physically retrieve that content. None of these options provide the vast amount of information that is readily available on the Internet. But webcasting goes one step beyond conventional Websites: With streaming technology, we can experience audio and video content almost immediately without waiting for the content to download. Push downloads this content to our receiving device while we're doing other things so that it's ready when we are.

Webcasting does what Websites don't: It delivers. Websites quite literally don't deliver your product, service, information, or brand information on-line. To ably use on-line media or technologies effectively, you should understand the following mathematical equation: Web ≠ Internet.

In other words, the Web is not the Internet. Nor is the Internet the Web. The word *webcasting* itself is a misnomer. It doesn't cast throughout the Web; it casts throughout the Internet. Many people think that Web is another word for Internet. It isn't. In fact, the Web is only one of four media on the Internet.

Confused? Let us explain and tell you why anyone who is considering using webcasting may need to know the difference: A medium is a means used to put someone in touch with what or who they want (information, products, services, etc.). The Internet comprises four identifiable media:

◆ *Browsing medium.* This medium takes various forms, such as Web pages, Usenet Newsgroups, and bulletin boards. The hallmark of any browsing medium is that consumers must navigate to its content. Like a library or kiosk, it doesn't deliver its contents. Consumers must remember to go to it.

◆ *Broadcasting medium.* You'll recognize this from traditional media. It's any application in which information, data, or entertainment content is broadcast live or prerecorded to consumers. In traditional media, it is TV and radio. On-line, it uses technologies such as PointCast, RealAudio, VDO, and cameras that snap pictures of exploding volcanoes every minute to broadcast content. Broadcast media is publicly available to everyone. On-line broadcasting is the most identifiable and easiest-to-utilize form of webcasting.

◆ *Conferencing medium.*   This on-line medium comes in three forms: alphanumeric, such as any commercial on-line service's or Website's chat rooms or Internet relay chat; telephony, in which two people use a computer to hold a private audio or video conversation; and conferencing and announcements, in which someone uses a PC to hold an audio or video meeting, conference, or announcement. The primary difference between this medium and broadcasting is that conferencing is most often private, by invitation, or by subscription.

◆ *Delivery medium.*   This is both the oldest and newest form of on-line media, and the most popular. It's so popular that people who use it tend to forget that it is a fully functioning medium in itself. Its oldest form is *electronic mail.* If you are on-line, you typically have an e-mail account; you can't really go on-line without one (unless you're sitting at someone else's desk). E-mail is universal on-line. Each and every survey of on-line usage ever taken has shown it is the single most popular on-line activity. E-mail delivers. And a new form of delivery—push—has recently joined this oldest form of delivery media. The newcomers are software programs (like those offered by BackWeb and Marimba) that automatically deliver information to your computer desktop. The hallmark of delivery media is exactly that: Content is regularly and routinely delivered to consumers.

Browsing (the Web being the best example) requires that your customers and consumers must remember to visit your Website before they can even see your product or service. They must not only remember but also use their increasingly scarce time and effort to navigate to your Website. They must come to the content. The new features of webcasting allow information, audio, video, text, and personalized Web pages to be sent to you by using push or streaming media.

Each of us, every individual, obtains information, products, services, even food, by either of only two ways.

- Sometimes we don't know what we want, or we might have time on our hands, so we browse. Website. Bookshelves. Video racks. Department stores. Restaurant menus.

- Other times, we don't have spare time (and who does nowadays?) or we know what we want, and we want it immediately. Mail. Magazines. Newspapers. News. Refreshments. Aspirin. Pizzas.

We all use both ways, at different times, even for the same things. These are the two universal modes for obtaining information, products, services, and things. Browsing and delivery. Or as these are known on-line, pull and push. Having a Website satisfies one of the two universal modes of human behavior, but Websites are only half the answer. Webcasting satisfies the other mode. A Website is a place where people can find information about your products and services, but Websites don't deliver the information. Webcasting does. Can your business survive without delivering its product or service? In most cases, the answer is no. Successful products and services cater to people's behavior and habits.

Would the *New York Times, Chicago Tribune,* or any other daily newspaper have gained household circulation, attracted advertisers, and become viable businesses if the only way in which a consumer could receive it at home was to call the newspaper's circulation department daily to request home delivery? Would consumers make that call *each and every day?* They would not. Newspapers succeed because of delivery.

Expanding Website Capability into Webcasting

Unlike their catalogs, L.L. Bean's and Lands' End's Websites aren't delivered yet. The two companies can heavily promote these Websites, but nevertheless depend upon consumers seeking them out. By using webcasting, however, these companies could deliver their Websites' information directly to customers. Here are two simple ways:

1. The simplest is e-mail casting. Whenever a customer telephones an order to these companies' operators, an operator asks for the customer's e-mail (in addition to postal) address. Then whenever L.L. Bean or Lands' End offers new merchandise to their Websites, or seasonally changes them, the companies can send e-mails notifying customers of the updated information and suggesting that customers visit the refreshed Website.

2. A similar method can redirect near sales into new sale opportunities. Next to each item of merchandise offered on their Websites, the companies place a graphical button that says, "Would you like to be informed whenever our company offers items similar to this one?" or "Would you like to be notified if this item is offered at a reduced price?" or even "Would you like to view additional selections that are similar to this item?" When a consumer presses the yes button, the Website either displays the alternate selection or requests the consumer's e-mail address and records it in a database along with information about the merchandise item and price. Then, the consumer receives an e-mail message whenever similar items are offered on the Website or when the

item goes on sale. The e-mail message can even offer a direct link to the relevant Web page to facilitate ordering. This application pushes information to the consumer and offers a twofold benefit to the merchandiser: providing updated product or pricing information and keeping the company brand name fresh in the consumer's mind.

Would ABC, CBS, NBC, Fox, UPN, CNN, or Warner Brothers television networks be viable businesses if their signals weren't automatically delivered directly into consumers' homes? They would not. Broadcasting succeeds because of delivery.

Would L.L. Bean or Lands' End, Inc. be viable businesses if their catalogs weren't automatically delivered, often unsolicited, into the mailboxes of millions of consumers nationwide? Direct marketing succeeds because of delivery.

Companies that operate on-line *solely* via a Website don't automatically deliver anything; they rely on Internet users seeking out the information. And, the fortunes of such companies depend almost entirely upon consumers, customers, and prospects finding their Websites, remembering to visit them, and periodically returning to the site for updated information. No matter how much content a Website contains, how many animated graphics, video or audio files, and other whiz-bangs it has, Websites are *passive*. They depend entirely upon consumers coming to them to seek information.

Should you wait and hope that customers and prospects will seek out your Website and remember to visit? Or should you deliver information about your products or services directly to them?

The real allure of webcasting is that it turns passive on-line media, such as Websites, into *active* media. Companies that use webcasting literally deliver. And delivery keeps your brand—your products and services—in the minds of your prospects and customers.

Waging the Battle for Mindshare

How can you keep your product or service in the minds of your existing and prospective customers when there are more than 1.3 million Internet domains competing for their attention? (And that number is growing by approximately 67,000 per month.)

An active medium can be heard over the noise of millions of passive media. A webcast service can cut through the clutter of Website services. If information about your product and service is delivered directly to the computer desktops of your customers and prospects, they are much more likely to be aware of that information and to keep it in mind than if they are forced to seek out your Website and periodically revisit it to gather new information. In short, although people forget to revisit Websites or lack the time or inclination to revisit, webcast content arrives nonetheless.

Even the two dominant manufacturers of Web browsing software have realized these advantages of webcasting. Both Microsoft and Netscape Communications have built webcasting channels into the most recent releases of their Web browser suites: Internet Explorer 4.0 and Netscape Communicator. And other savvy media companies are already taking advantage of these capabilities. ABC News and Federal Express, for example, have opened channels on Netcaster, Netscape's webcasting application.

Preventing Brand Deconstruction

As the Internet continues to grow and encompass an ever increasing wealth of information, it becomes more and more difficult to find specific information within the maze. Search engines help, of course, as do cookies, but finding new information in unfamiliar topic areas can still be frustrating and time-consuming, even for fairly knowledgeable users. This is probably one reason that consumers love to bookmark Web pages. Bookmarks let them jump directly from a Web search engine to a specific Web page, thereby avoiding the need to travel from the top of the Website to the specific page to view the information they're interested in. Similarly,

Web search engines link consumers directly to specific Web pages within a Website that the search engine has indexed. These Website technologies are wonderfully convenient for consumers, but they can contribute to a loss of brand identity or, at the least, allow companies to lose control of their brand identities. For example, no matter how carefully a company designs its Website, consumers may skip over all of the carefully presented product and company information to directly access a specific Web page that is of interest to them. No matter how attractive or logical the sequence of information on the Website, consumers—even those who frequently revisit the Website—may never see anything but that particular bookmarked or indexed Web page unless the site uses advanced software to send new pages. Consider these examples:

◆ A consumer, interested in a Ford Contour, can walk into a Ford showroom and see the entire Ford automobile product lineup. However, if the consumer shops on-line, he or she may bookmark the Contour web page and not see any other Ford models.

◆ People almost always read a printed magazine from front to back. Editors, publication art designers, and layout artists carefully lay out, format, and bind a printed publication with that front-to-back linear flow. When someone reads it, he or she will likely see most or many of the advertisements and other articles in that magazine while turning pages to reach the article they seek. Advertisers generally pay higher rates for their ads to appear toward the front of the publication, not because the best stories are necessarily at the beginning of the publication, but because they know that is where most people start reading. On-line, however, linear publications unbundle. A reader might start at the front or top of the Website, but can then instantly jump to anywhere in the on-line publication and bookmark it for return visits. That reader never has to see any of the other stories or ads in the on-line publication, stymieing any linear flow of the Website.

The carefully designed linear publication in print, and with it the publication's brand name, deconstructs on-line.

When brands directly compete in traditional markets, the tactic that owners of those brands most often use is to control locations or store shelves. McDonald's may locate a restaurant at the only available site on an important highway junction, denying that junction to Burger King. Wonder Bread might pay a supermarket a stipend to lease triple the normal amount of shelf space for its bread, denying that space to other brands of mass-produced bread. These business tactics work because location is scarce. However, location isn't scarce on-line. The second peculiar problem that brands face on-line is that there have been no locations or shelves to control. Everywhere and anywhere is local and equally accessible on-line. The old business adage of location, location, location doesn't work when your brand controls only one of 1.3 million equally accessible Websites.

The consumer who is interested in a Ford Contour can receive a steady stream of information about all Ford models—including new features and price changes since the last time he or she visited the Ford Website—streamed directly to the computer desktop. On-line publications and broadcasters can webcast urgent, late-breaking stories or events directly to an individual's hard disk or computer desktop. The traditional function of an editor—telling people what they didn't know, and hence didn't search or bookmark—is maintained through webcasting. And a marketer can webcast brand information directly to the consumer. Every Website may be local on-line, but there is no more local on-line location than the consumer's own computer desktop.

And fourth, the first three problems combine to level the competitive playing fields. Established brands in traditional marketing and media have always had advantages of extensive distribution, control of location, and reinforcements among the brand product line. However, with universally equal distribution, universal location, and lack of brand reinforcement, a well-managed start-up

Sometimes, Location Does Matter!

There are exceptions to the rule that location doesn't matter on the Web. These exceptions include intermediaries on the Web like Netscape Communications and Microsoft or on-line services like America Online or CompuServe. Each provide Web browsers in which the default settings automatically force the users to see their Websites whenever these browsers are started. These default settings can be changed to show a blank Web page or any Website's Web page. However, tens of millions of users don't know this, haven't figured out how to change the setting, or just don't care. As a result, the main Web page of Netscape, the dominant browser manufacturer, is now the most frequently accessed site on the Internet. Advertisers have taken notice. Netscape reaps millions of dollars each year by selling ads on this (by default) popular Web page. Microsoft has followed suit with its main Web page. In addition, push software uses flashes, desktop wallpaper, and screen savers that change with new information. These locations vie for your attention and are important in the new Internet real estate market of location, location, location.

company can compete successfully against a titanic, established brand.

An April 1997 panel in Boston brought together the chief on-line industry analysts from a number of major research companies including Forrester Research, Yankee Group, Gartner Group, and International Data Group. What companies were the big success stories on the Web, the panelists were asked. Their answers: Netscape, Yahoo!, C/NET, AOL, and Amazon.com. What were the distinguishing characteristics of these companies, the panelists were asked. They are all well-managed, fleet start-up companies that sensed a commercial need on-line. The panel was then asked to name the notable failures on-line. Their candidates: the old Prodigy (Sears and IBM), CompuServe (H&R Block), GENIE (General Electric), and iGuide (Rupert Murdoch's News Corporation). What were these companies' distinguishing characteristics, the panel was asked. All were backed by well-established brand-name companies with a wealth of resources, but these companies didn't understand this new medium.

Webcasting can keep brand names intact when used in a company's on-line marketing strategy. A brand such as Heineken Brewery (see Figure 2.1), can create an active channel directly into prospects' and customers' computers. This means that a marketer can determine what among his brand line to show to people. A company can decide what order in which to provide editorial content and advertising to readers. And a webcaster can decide what consumers will see and when. Webcasting restores some of the tra-

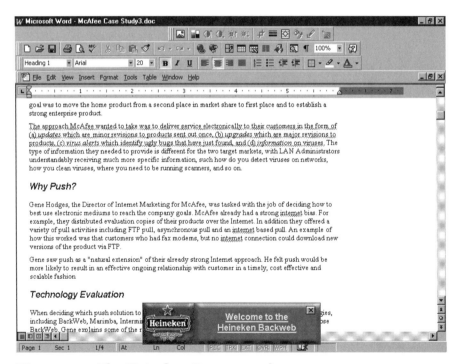

Figure 2.1   The Heineken Brewery webcast.

ditional control that businesses have had over their own products and the way in which consumers see those products and brands. The challenge for companies like Heineken is to develop content in

CASE STUDY HEINEKEN PUSHES BRAND AWARENESS

Heineken Brewery has teamed up with BackWeb to roll out a push channel to promote its brand awareness through the Internet. The company is using webcasting to deliver content directly to users' PCs. The campaign includes all of the following components:

1. Regularly scheduled flashes delivering news about special offers, promotions, and history of the Heineken brewery
2. Screen savers and wallpapers branded with Heineken art
3. Special pieces about events and selected pubs and other establishments where Heineken is served

The promotional content that Heineken delivers through its webcast channel possesses the same elements that are associated with the brand's traditional advertising: rolling bottle caps, floating bottles, red star symbol, and other associated works, along with a friendly, informal tone that invites the viewer to relax and enjoy the presentations without feeling as if they were watching a commercial. Heineken emphasizes the need to develop custom content for webcasting rather than merely repurposing existing TV advertisements and believes that these efforts at innovation are likely to be well rewarded with brand awareness and recognition.

their push channels that is compelling, reinforces the brand, and provides value to their consumers.

Determining if Webcasting Is Feasible

There are no long-term direct precedents or examples to study webcasting effectiveness since the field is new. This makes determining business opportunities that much more difficult. Identifying a business opportunity, the single most critical moment for any business, is a challenging task for a webcaster.

Logic

Unfortunately, the two most common criteria that companies use when deciding whether to webcast are (1) whether everyone else is doing it and (2) what do market research surveys show.

That first criterion is the lemming effect. Animal behaviorists have marveled at the Norwegian rodents called lemmings whose herd instinct is so great that they follow each other to their deaths over sheer cliffs. The same effect occurs when a business does something simply because everyone else is doing it. A company sees its competitor begin webcasting but doesn't really understand how webcasting can help its business. Nonetheless, the business begins webcasting simply because it doesn't want to be left behind. When the competitor, who may have begun webcasting simply because doing so is in vogue or because the CEO's kid loves computers, sees the competitive organization also begin to webcast, it redoubles its own webcasting efforts. The two companies begin a fervent competition to build the best channel. They may engage in a headlong and expensive competition without clearly understanding their own goals. Their behavior becomes self-reinforcing. This effect can take over entire segments of industries. Don't follow the example of the lemming. Don't webcast simply because your competitors are. If you are going to webcast, you should have your own solid business reasons for doing so.

The second common criterion—what do market research surveys show about Webcasting—will someday be a valid tool for deciding whether or not to webcast. However, not yet. Most webcasting research is less than one year old. Some on-line research companies have predicted that push or webcasting will result in billions of dollars in revenue by the year 2000 (the Yankee Group, a Boston-based firm, predicts over $6 billion).

Moreover, webcasting is so new that market research questions or respondents don't yet understand it. A similar example of this occurred over a decade ago when CBS, Sears, and IBM were forming the Prodigy on-line service. Researchers for those companies asked consumers how many letters they wrote each month that didn't have to do with paying bills. None or hardly any, consumers said. They told the researchers they used the telephone nowadays to communicate with friends. How many conference calls do you make each month? Few, if ever, consumers responded. Armed with this research, Prodigy initially launched its on-line service without much, if any, provision for electronic mail or chats, missing two of the subsequently most popular on-line features. Consumer e-mail and on-line chats were unknown when Prodigy conducted its research. Likewise, many of what might prove to be the most popular features of webcasting are only now being invented, and consumers are too unfamiliar with them to provide reliable research.

For now, any company that is considering whether or not to webcast must rely on solid business principles and be aware and evaluate research studies with caution.

But, that's not to say that there aren't some guidelines to follow. The following sections present some questions and considerations that should be useful in determining if webcasting is feasible for your particular organization.

Migrating or Starting Anew?

Does your company plan to migrate an existing or traditional business to webcasting, or does it plan to develop something totally from scratch? The latter is far easier. Products or services can be created especially to take advantage of the benefits and technologies of webcasting. Many existing or traditional businesses that are based upon physical delivery aren't easy (or practical) to migrate to webcasting. Either the content or current on-line delivery technologies aren't yet amenable. The Norfolk News Shipyards, the sole manufacturers of American nuclear aircraft carriers, probably wouldn't be able to use webcasting to promote its product to its sole customer. The Pentagon might have the communications bandwidth to receive the information, but webcasting the details of a presidential-class nuclear carrier would probably sink the personal computers on admirals' desktops. More realistically, the Hollywood studios may see great benefit in webcasting new movie clips directly to consumers who are interested in seeing those films. The Weather Channel (see Figure 2.2), however, which can webcast your local weather

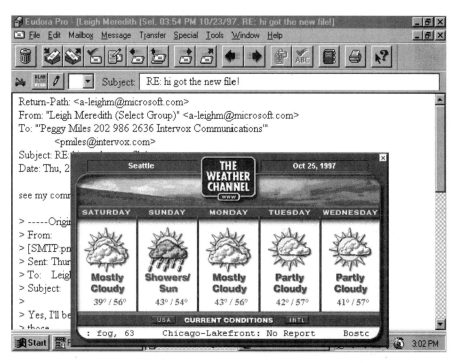

Figure 2.2   An example of a Weather Channel webcast.

charts and simple graphics directly to your desktop, can ably use webcasting technology.

If you plan to develop a webcasting service from scratch, build it to take advantage of webcasting's ultimate benefits and current bandwidth and technology.

Information That Is Sensitive or Critical to Time.   If the product, service, data, or information is time-sensitive, it is well-suited for webcasting. What's the latest news? Is there an unexpected problem? Is a tornado or major hurricane bearing down on your geographic area?

A good example of a need for webcasting is a newspaper that operates on-line solely via a Website. Newspaper readers are used to having a complete printed product automatically delivered to them each day, a habit that has been ingrained for generations. They need do nothing but pick it up on their front steps and read it. In most cases the expectations are for readers to remember to navigate to the newspaper's Website each day, in effect delivering their own newspaper. Will people change their habits and deliver their own newspaper each day? Will they prefer to download only one page at a time, rather than have an entire newspaper intact? Select newspapers are using webcasting to deliver personalized newpapers to their consumers and getting back into the delivery business using the Internet.

Products or Services That Can Change without Customers or Consumers Knowing It.   Similarly, data or information that can change without people knowing it is ideal for webcasting. Has the corporate health plan changed? Has a bug been found in the company's software? Will the company be changing to a new shipping service due to a strike? This type of information is ideal for webcasting; it can be pushed out to users over the Internet or a corporate intranet to update users' desktops without the users ever needing to be aware of a change in the information.

Information That Constantly Needs to Be Updated.   Any product or service that deals in constant progress or improvements can immediately benefit by webcasting. The technology's ability to constantly update customers creates customer reassurance and loyalty.

Federal Express has created a business channel using Netscape's Netcaster software. The channel notifies customers where their packages are as they move from pickup, trucking, air shipment, trucking, and delivery. With webcasting, a customer can always know the exact status of their order.

McAfee Software, which we mentioned in Chapter 1, is one of the world's leading antivirus software manufacturers and a leader in online distribution. Over 80 percent of its sales involve producing or distributing packaged antivirus software diskettes. Now, webcasting allows customers to download McAfee's antivirus software electronically through the Internet (see Figure 2.3). Eliminating the costs

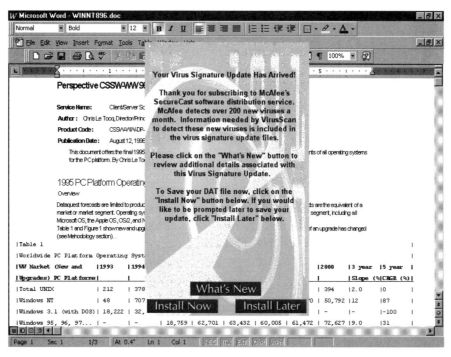

Figure 2.3   The McAfee virus software update page.

of physical packaging and shipping greatly reduced McAfee's costs and enhanced its revenues. But, it also introduced some new problems. New computer viruses are constantly arising, but McAfee's customers generally remember to download the latest version of the software only once or twice a year. All too often, they discover the need to update their software only when they become infected with a completely new computer virus. McAfee solved this problem by webcasting. The company automatically sends updates—inoculations against the latest computer viruses—directly into the personal computers of people who have bought McAfee software. The users don't have to remember to check for updates or run the risk of new infections.

A number of major software publishers have begun webcasting updates of their software products. For example, the user of a particular software package no longer needs to seek out and buy a new version when it is released, just subscribe to a software update service. During the term of that subscription, the software publisher automatically delivers any updates or improvements to the program directly to the user's computer. Both the company and the consumer benefit from such an arrangement. The consumer can continually use the most up-to-date version of the program without the inconvenience of seeking out the latest release, and the company derives ongoing revenues from the updated subscription along with a certain level of enforced customer loyalty.

Customer service organizations are also using webcasting to reduce costs. If, for example, a company discovers that a significant or growing number of customers need answers to the same questions, it can use a webcasting channel to push the necessary information to all customers. With this approach, the company eliminates the expense of answering the customers' questions individually and, hopefully, builds good customer relations by providing information before the customers discover the need for it.

Information That Is Enhanced by Sound, Video, or Graphics.   A picture can actually be worth far more than the proverbial 1000 words. Even an incredibly imaginative and thorough description of how something or someone looks can't compare with actually *seeing* the object or person. That's why webcasting, with its versatile audio and video capabilities, is beginning to attract attention from a variety of businesses that need to show their products in order to market them effectively. Viewing the webcast video of a new automobile (see Figure 2.4), for example, is literally the next best thing to traveling to the dealer showroom and walking around the car. And, with on-demand webcasting, you can view as many automobiles as you want, at your convenience, from the comfort of your own home.

Leading-edge businesses are already using webcast audio/video to display a range of products, from automobiles to high-fashion

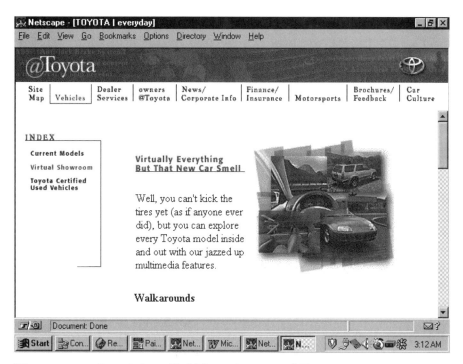

Figure 2.4   Omniview Bubbles pictures of Toyota.

clothing to new building designs. In July 1996, for example, the French couturier, Yves Saint Laurent, teamed up with World Media Live (WML), a pioneer in webcasting and on-line journalism, to show its haute couture collection live in video format on the Internet. The two companies followed up the highly successful event by launching Fashion Live, a web magazine that delivers exclusive presentations of the couturier's latest collections.

Business-to-Business versus Business-to-Consumer Considerations

Companies considering webcasting also need to determine whether their primary use of the technology will be internal (i.e., limited to an intranet), business-to-business, or business-to-consumer. This subtle difference can make major differences in the success of any webcasting endeavor. The problem is that there aren't yet any clear interoperability standards for webcasting software programs, and your company may or may not be able to dictate which program your customers use.

Businesses that plan to limit their webcasting to an internal audience may have an advantage in this area, especially if they are webcasting over an intranet or extranet. In this situation, the company has a captive audience and can dictate precisely what software the viewers will use and what will appear on their desktops. If the company is webcasting to a relatively limited number of other businesses, it may be able to suggest what software the users should have to access the webcast. If, for example, a company plans to webcast product or service information to its business partners, it can contact those companies and determine what software they're using, then try to match their webcasts to the majority of software users or convince some business partners to use a compatible software. If the executives of those companies decide that the webcast product or service is beneficial to their businesses, they might mandate that their businesses use the suggested software. However, the company might already be using software that is compatible with another business partner's webcasting software and which conflicts with the suggested software.

Finally, businesses that plan to webcast to a general business and/or consumer market over the Internet have virtually no control over what software their audience will use. If the webcast product or service is valuable to those consumers, they might agree to download and use that company's webcasting software. A consumer who wants to receive webcasting from *USA Today, Sports Illustrated,* and the *New York Times* needs to run the Incommon, Berkeley Systems, PointCast software, and Real Networks, all without crashing that consumer's computer.

The situation in the webcasting consumer market today is akin to the on-line browsing consumer market in 1994. Back then, a consumer who wanted to browse *USA Today, Sports Illustrated,* and the *New York Times* on-line needed to have subscriptions to Prodigy, America Online, and CompuServe. Yet, hardly anyone subscribed to all three services. When the common standard of HTML arrived, content providers realized that by using it they could allow all consumers to access their content from a single place, and consumers realized it as well. That single place is the Web.

Webcasting vendors have similarly realized the need for common standards. We'll discuss the existing and emerging standards and the so-called push wars in more detail in Chapter 3, but you should understand that standards play a key role in the evolution of webcasting and may determine its ultimate acceptance by the business and entertainment industries. Microsoft has proposed a Channel Definition Format (CDF) that can be used by any company or software that wants to webcast. Netscape and Marimba have allied to use Marimba's Castanet technology as a common standard, and Microsoft is considering adopting this proposal. Until the various software providers adopt common standards, however, you'll need to decide which webcasting software format best suits your particular requirements and clientele.

Choice of Media

Earlier in this chapter, we mentioned the three on-line media that can utilize webcasting: broadcasting, conferencing, and delivery.

Each has its own advantages and disadvantages. The choice of which to use depends upon:

◆ The service, product, or information you are providing
◆ How your customers or consumers want to obtain that service, product, or information
◆ Your revenue model, if any

Some products, services, and information obviously lend themselves better to either broadcasting, conferencing, or delivery.

Traditionally mailed or delivered goods such as catalogs, magazines, and newspapers are ideal for the delivery medium. In the case of news, financial information, or weather, if the news is urgent, then it might also be ideal for webcast. For example, news that the president has been shot, your stock has just filed for bankruptcy, or there is a tornado approaching your house is something that you may want to appear on your computer or TV screen as soon as possible.

The most popular Internet delivery mechanism—electronic mail—is undergoing a transformation. Most people know e-mail as just alphanumeric text. However, e-mail is now becoming graphically rich. The Web also once contained only alphanumeric text, but the addition of graphics in 1993 catalyzed the Web into a wildly popular mass medium. Now, a number of software vendors, including Netscape, Microsoft, and Qualcomm, are introducing programs that allow people to receive e-mail that contains the same graphical richness. An e-mail message can now contain graphics—photos, sounds, and video—along with the message. Clicking on an embedded icon in the e-mail message can invoke a live webcast or a recorded audio or video stream (see Figure 2.5). What will happen when e-mail, already the most popular of all on-line activities, is further enriched by graphics capabilities? The development should transform e-mail into an even more formidable delivery medium, one that can be used to push an even richer variety of information to consumers.

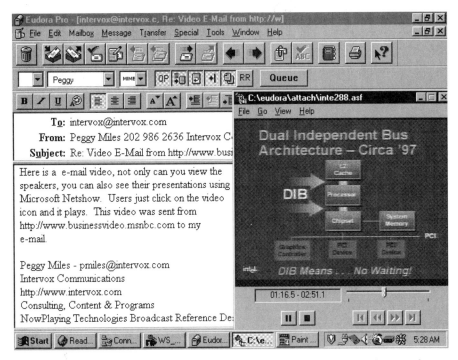

Figure 2.5 Example of e-mail message with embedded icon for audio/video stream.

CASE STUDY NEW CENTURY NET-WORK'S E-MAIL WEBCAST PROJECT

One of the problems with maintaining a Website is that most consumers don't visit every day. If you're a daily newspaper, this problem can hobble your online efforts.

To solve this problem, the nine major U.S. newspaper publishing corporations that comprise the New Century Network on-line consortium (New York Times

Co.; Washington Post Co.; Tribune Co.; The Hearst Corporation; Gannett Co.; Advance Publications; Cox Newspapers Inc.; The Times Mirror Co.; and Knight-Ridder, Inc.) are using e-mail for webcasting. Web pages on the consortium's 130+ newspaper Websites feature buttons asking consumers if they would like that Web page's contents delivered to them daily or whenever the content changes. A parent might like school lunch menus delivered daily. A Chicago Bull's fan might like the *Chicago Tribune*'s game story and box scores delivered the moment a game ends. A businessperson searching for stories about the insurance industry might want new search results automatically delivered every day. The Website buttons will, in effect, allow people to subscribe to that part of the newspaper's Website that they might want to see on a daily basis. These people will receive those Web pages by e-mail, the single most popular and frequently used on-line activity, each day.

The on-line newspapers will get daily home delivery of their content directly into the consumers' computers. Consumers will have their choice of receiving the e-mail in plain text or in rich graphical HTML format. The HTML e-mail will carry the same banner advertising as the original Web page. This delivery of advertising is particularly important to on-line newspaper publishers who depend upon advertising revenues. A consumer might remember to visit their Websites only two or three times per week—generating ad revenues only that many times. However, daily e-mail delivery of news and ad banners generates advertising revenues daily—the same way a print newspaper does.

It is likely that on-line newspapers may incorporate audio and video, once limited to broadcast sites. USA Today has added sports webcasts through audionet.com and the New York Times has added audio author interviews in their book section and a video of the TWA plane crash investigation to their news section.

Live or prerecorded video and audio entertainment, press conferences, and teaching are ideal for the broadcast medium. You might want a series of movies to download to your computer in the background during the day so that you can view them later that night. The House of Blues Inc. has begun using delivery technology to send multimedia clips to subscribers (see Figure 2.6), who, when they subsequently listen to them, can order the full recordings through the same channel.

If the broadcast event, press conference, or teaching is live, it might be better suited to the conferencing medium. This way, it becomes truly interactive. You can ask questions of the presenter via your computer and share insights with other attendees.

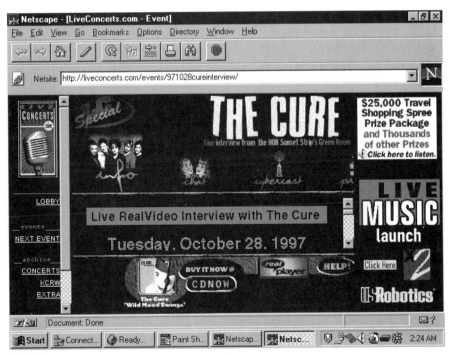

Figure 2.6 A House of Blues webcast.

Certain webcasting media better lend themselves to some revenue models than to others. If your company plans to webcast its products or services for free, then these considerations might not matter. Nevertheless, only governmental and nonprofit organizations generally provide such products or services for free. If your company is such an organization, free webcasting will give it the most widespread and objective reach possible.

CASE STUDY   HOUSE OF BLUES BUILDS BRAND AWARENESS

House of Blues Inc., a worldwide entertainment company, uses push technology to deliver the blues to music enthusiasts around the world, thereby building a community of interest around the House of Blues brand. The company initially developed an Internet Website that allows surfers to participate in activities taking place at clubs and restaurants sponsored by the House of Blues. The company's next step was to reach out to the worldwide music community by using push technology to pull community members in, rather than waiting for them to visit the Website. The company's marketing managers believe that push technology delivers a programming experience that is more compelling than radio or television.

In the process of selecting a push technology, House of Blues evaluated products from BackWeb, PointCast, and Marimba. According to Nick Wild, the associate director of technology, they chose BackWeb because it gives them control over the look and feel and delivery of the channel, allowing them to be more creative. The company uses that creativity to assign a variety of delivery attributes to the content. For example, their first content displayed a car speeding across the bottom of the screen and dropping a house in the middle. A smokestack emerged from the house and morphed into the House of Blues logo, accompanied by music. That got people's attention!

House of Blues serves the channel on a Sun Ultra-Sparc workstation running Solaris, which is also used for all of their Web hosting. The company creates their content using Windows NT. Everything is done in-house.

The company was able to launch its channel after one or two days of training by the vendor, by repurposing existing content. "Frankly," says Wild, "I was surprised to see how quickly we could put the channel up. One week after attending training, we were rolling."

House of Blues carefully chooses the content it sends. The company's goal is to send valuable, stimulating material that is significantly more appealing than can be delivered through other media, such as e-mail. Therefore, they frequently send sound and multimedia clips, ensuring that not only is the message memorable, but so is the delivery. In addition, they set up a customizable framework to make the content highly meaningful to users.

Says Wild, "The best way to make the content exciting and relevant is to make it very specific, so we set up content to correspond to the geographic region of our clubs. For example, you can sign up for the House of Blues channel and get pushed the schedule of events for the club nearest you. So, if you are in Chicago, you can get the content for the John Fogerty show that is taking place only in that region. Or if you live near the Myrtle Beach Club, you get pushed schedules and promotions for that club only." In addition to push, their Website also streams special concerts from their clubs around the world.

Generating Revenues

Profitable companies, however, need revenues. The most common webcasting revenue model today is advertiser support. It is occasionally used in internal company and business-to-business webcasting but is almost always a function of business-to-consumer webcasting. Recognizing webcasting potential for reaching consumers, some companies are beginning to target corporate intranets, such as IBM's, to advertise products and services. In addition to generating revenue through advertising, webcasting can generate revenues through subscription.

Advertising

There are many forms of potential advertising revenues: exposure or sponsorship, per inquiry, and per sale or transaction.

- *Exposure sponsorship.* Some advertisers are now webcasting much of their Website's contents in the background behind the banner ad. When a consumer clicks on these types of banner ads, he or she instantly sees the advertiser's contents that are otherwise on the Website. The advantage to this background information webcasting is that the consumer can instantly see the advertiser's information without then being on-line. The rates for webcast banner ads currently run between $35 and $150 per thousand viewers, with the exact price dependent upon how focused or targeted the ads are for the specific viewer audience. The advertiser is responsible for paying for the ads regardless of whether anyone actually responds to them.

- *Advertising banners.* Advertising banners are the most common element on a Website (see Figure 2.7). They are priced at $35 to $150 per thousand viewers, with the exact price dependent upon how focused or targeted the ads are for the specific viewer audience. The advertiser is responsible for paying for the ads regardless of whether

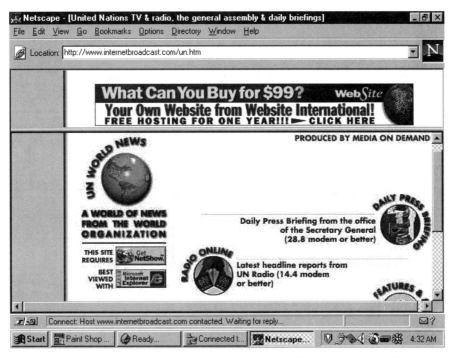

Figure 2.7 A sample ad banner with clickthrough to a webcast Website.

anyone actually responds to them. Some ad banners or webcast (audio and video-enabled ads) can be forced to be viewed before a user can access a page. This is called interstitial advertising.

◆ *Sponsorships.* You are probably familiar with the sponsorships of golfing or charity events. Advertising messages are integrated in other graphics or text (advertorials) on the Website. This is another way to make money on the Internet.

◆ *Audio- and video-enhanced banner ads.* New advertising banners and sponsorships include audio and video to enhance the experience. The audio or video can start playing when a visitor arrives on the Website or when the visitor clicks on an ad banner.

◆ *Webcasting commercials.* You can place advertising (like TV or radio commercials) when someone clicks on an icon to watch a streaming media program. Commercials can also be inserted in streaming media at regular intervals, randomly, or programmed by you to appear at certain times of the day. These are priced at the same rate as banner ads.

◆ *Per inquiry.* A per-inquiry advertiser pays the webcaster only when someone actually clicks on a banner ad or otherwise requests information. Webcast providers generally run these ads for free, recouping to make up the revenues whenever an ad triggers a response. In doing so, the webcast provider takes a risk that no one, or not enough people, will respond. However, responses generally generate much higher individual revenues than do exposures or sponsorship ads. Webcast per-inquiry respond rates generally range from a few pennies to an average of $5 to $20 *per clickthrough,* not per thousand, depending on the product.

◆ *Per sale or transaction.* A per-transaction advertiser pays the webcaster only when someone actually buys something, not just when someone responds to an ad or requests information. Ads run free, and the webcaster earns revenues only when a sale actually results from a response. This form of advertising carries an even greater risk for the webcaster than the per-inquiry form of advertising: If no one buys, or not enough people buy, as a result of the ad, no revenue is generated. But, this type of advertising also generates the greatest revenues. Per-transaction revenues can start at $20 per individual and may run to several hundred dollars per individual.

None of these advertising revenue models are without other, associated costs. All successful webcasting ads require that a company hire or manage an advertising sales staff, or at least subcontract such sales to other agencies, preferably agencies that are familiar with webcasting and the unique requirements for successful advertising on the Web.

Subscription

Subscription is the second most common means of generating webcasting revenues. It has proven effective in business-to-business situations, but is not enjoying as much success in business-to-consumer webcasting situations largely due to control issues. (The Internet sex industry is an exception to this statement; it is reaping huge profits through user subscriptions.) In a subscription arrangement, a customer pays an hourly, daily, monthly, quarterly, or annual fee to receive a webcast. Companies that can make money from the information or data received from such a webcast are usually willing to pay for a subscription. For example, brokerage houses are generally willing to purchase a subscription to receive constant updates of stock market information and prices. Consumers may also be willing to pay a subscription fee to receive some types of information on a timely basis, particularly if they, too, can make money from the information. But, in the incredibly competitive consumer market, consumers are generally unwilling to pay a subscription fee unless the webcast delivers a premier brand of a particular type of content or a live event performance such as a rock concert. The *Wall Street Journal* and ESPN (see Figure 2.8), for example, can charge consumers subscription fees to access their Websites or receive a webcast, but this doesn't mean that your small town newspaper or the local soccer league can successfully charge for its versions of such information.

Subscription models have the advantage of receiving payment in advance for that month, quarter, or year.

Microtransactions

Microtransactions are a promising form of webcasting revenue that are gaining popularity. With microtransactions, people pay piecemeal (generally in pocket-size amounts) whenever they receive a webcast or download prerecorded audio or video webcasts. Because

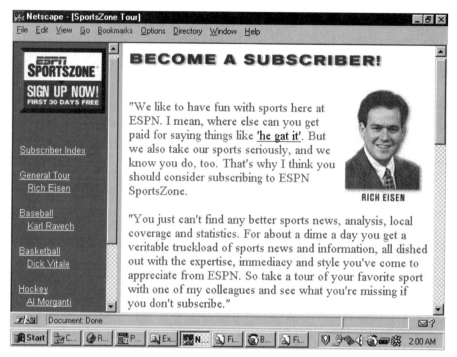

Figure 2.8 The ESPN webcast Website.

the cost per transaction is relatively low, most customers have no hesitation about agreeing to pay for the webcast. However, when those pocket-size transaction fees are collected from a large audience, they can add up to handsome revenues. One problem with microtransactions, however, is that the traditional credit card companies have resisted (to date) processing the tiny transaction amounts. This is changing, however, as a number of the traditional credit card companies including MasterCard and VISA and new credit agencies such as Cybercash and Digicash have begun to experiment with microtransaction processing systems. Most analysts believe that such systems will be in commercial use before the end of the decade. Microtransactions have a potential to be a valid revenue model for a webcaster.

Database Marketing

Another method to success on the Internet is collecting information on your clients and consumers and using that information to better serve them. This qualitative data, psychographically targeted, is valuable, both to you and possibly to other companies. This method should not be overlooked and is extremely valuable. This should be in your long-term strategic marketing plans, as database marketing use will increase as information on consumers drives product sales in the Internet Age.

Hybrids

There are also hybrid revenue models. Webcasters may use advertising revenues to subsidize subscription or microtransaction revenue systems. Similarly, they may build a revenue model based on a minimum guaranteed subscription rate or microtransaction fees, whichever is higher. Or they could base a revenue model on microtransactions but offer a discount to guarantee subscribers. Any revenue model may accommodate the particular type of webcast and its audience. A hybrid revenue model can be unique to a particular company, designed to benefit both it and its customers.

Free

Consider that webcasting that promotes awareness of your brand can increase your traditional business. So, is it worth it to webcast without any webcasting revenues? The answer very often is yes. Heineken's webcasting project, for example, won't generate any direct revenues; Heineken will not be charging a subscription fee to receive the webcast nor will it earn advertising revenues from other firms. But if the webcast helps people to think about Heineken, collect a database, and, as a result, to buy more Heineken beer, then the webcasting effort will surely be worth the effort.

Cost Justifying Webcasting

The basic costs of webcasting include the content production and delivery equipment, staff to compose the content and operate the equipment, and recurring costs such as those required for Internet connection and communications facilities. Obviously, the expenses involved with implementing and managing a webcast Website will play a major role in determining whether webcasting is practical for your organization. Chapter 4 provides details about webcasting production and delivery expenses, but you need to begin projecting the cost for your webcasting project early in the implementation decision process, at about the same time that you establish goals for the project and forecast the revenues, if any, that you hope to gain from it. Staff costs will vary according to your region of the country or world and current market conditions. Recurring costs vary according to whether or not you use proprietary technology to webcast. Some proprietary technology vendors charge fees for the volume of content you deliver through their equipment. Such costs can have a direct effect on the financial success of a webcasting endeavor. Other methods of webcasting, such as utilizing a nonproprietary channel definition format (CDF) using Web browsers, normally don't incur any recurring costs.

A Caution Signal

Whatever webcasting business model a company chooses, it should always observe an important general concern about on-line media. Namely, that these new technologies have more closely shifted the balance of control in media into consumers' hands more now than was ever true in traditional media. This is the most significant difference between traditional and new media. Most companies that are launching on-line products or services don't yet recognize or understand that shift, even when they see its nearly universal signs: Consumers object much more vociferously to junk e-mail than they do to postal junk mail and protest vigorously when their behavior and purchases are tracked by central agencies on-line but have grown accustomed to huge credit agencies tracking their purchases and behavior in traditional markets.

Has there really been such a shift in control? Every evolutionary progress in media technology has shifted control further from the hands of the people who previously controlled the media into the hands of media consumers. This historic fact is visible over centuries. Consider that the aboriginal media were state- or religion-authorized public theater, sermons, and town criers. Control of these media was in the singular hands of church or state. Johannes Gutenberg's invention of commercial printing presses fractured this singular control and began shifting control into the hands of the people who could afford to buy presses, beginning a 500-year-long period in which control began shifting from the one to the many. Marconi's invention of broadcasting further accelerated this control shift. In our own century, a variety of predigital analog technologies have had similar effects. Clandestine underground news periodicals often produced through xerography upset Eastern European Communist dictatorships 20 years ago. And information disseminated by facsimile machines rattled the Chinese Communist government during the Tienanmen Square uprising a decade ago. Each evolution in media technology always further fractures centralized control by state, church, estate, corporation, publisher, or broadcast house bringing more individual choices and shifting control closer into the hands of consumers. On-line media are no different.

Indeed, the propagation of digital technologies has shifted media control more suddenly and further than at any time in the past—the largest and most remarkable control shift in history. The abrupt rise of the Internet as a mass media has taken almost every traditional publisher, broadcaster, marketer, advertiser, media system operator, and government by surprise. No corporation invented it as a consumer product or service. No media company invented the Internet as a mass media. No advertising agency created consumers' demand for the Internet. Even the major proprietary on-line services (America Online, Prodigy, CompuServe, and GENIE) and Microsoft were caught sleeping. Consumers spontaneously embraced the Internet and did so because of the newfound control it gave them. It satisfies their latent need for better access to the information that they feel they need to better live their lives.

Consumers aren't going to surrender their newfound control. An evolution in media technology has given consumers the ability and freedom to satisfy their individual needs without the limits traditional media had imposed. No state, church, or corporation will ever again have as much control over its citizens, congregations, or consumers as it did in traditional media.

What does this shift in control mean to companies that plan to webcast? Webcasting is the on-line technology that allows traditional publishers, broadcasters, advertisers, and marketers to try to reassert control over on-line consumers. Many companies are embracing webcasting primarily for that reason. They want to brand consumers' computer desktops or channel consumers back into systems where the consumer sees only the company's service. These services save the webcaster money and attempt to reassert control or channel consumer behavior back toward the ways of traditional media.

Companies that want to use webcasting successfully need to devise their on-line business practices and models to provide tangible benefits to consumers. Successful on-line products and services benefit both a company and its customers, not just the company. Given the choice of a webcasting service that benefits only its purveyor and another that also benefits the consumers, consumers will choose the latter every time. No amount of money, alliances, publicity, or goodwill can indefinitely keep alive a business that serves itself but fails to serve its customers.

CHAPTER THREE

WEBCASTING
TECHNOLOGIES

There are a huge number of technologies, some new and some old, which enable people to implement webcasting solutions. This chapter attempts to identify and describe the current landscape of webcasting technologies, standards, products, and systems. Since the technology is evolving so quickly, it also attempts to pinpoint some of the trends and things to watch for as we continue our journey into the communications future at warp speed.

This chapter is designed to help create context and structure for an understanding of how various technologies relate to one another, and what you need to consider in designing and implementing a webcasting system that works for you today and will be relevant and useful tomorrow.

At the highest level there are probably two things to bear in mind as you start to make sense of webcasting technology. First, terms can be confusing. As we discussed earlier, the Web and Web technologies are actually a subset of the Internet and Internet technologies, but webcasting technologies include both pure Web and broader Internet technologies. Second, it's no accident that webcasting and its revolutionary personal and enterprise potential is moving forward hand in hand with the so-called move from pull to push technologies.

Accessing Web pages or other information from a Web browser is the traditional pull model. First you decide what you want. Then you try to find it via your bookmarks or search engine. Finally, you try to access the particular location/Website and hope that it's not too busy to let you in and that it has valid information.

Webcasting and the push revolution is all about combining a whole series of different technologies so that users can tune in to information that is served up to them based on information they need and want. It's about the marriage of Internet, telecommunications, satellite, cable, broadcasting, and publishing technologies. It's about information from content vaults being married with databases of individual and community profiles and making its way to those people and populations that want and need that information. It's ultimately about removing redundant information from and adding relevant information to the streams of content that barrage everyone today.

Fortunately, although there are a zillion relevant technologies, many of the concepts are already familiar to us from our exposure to radio, TV, and hard copy publications such as newspapers and magazines. We're all familiar with tuning in to channels. We're all familiar with subscriptions to newspapers and magazines. Some of us are familiar with the dreams and false starts in Interactive TV. Most of the technology covered in this chapter ultimately fits into these categories and is designed to add value to the ways in which we presently receive our information.

Technology Standards and Protocols

The Internet is a collection of hardware and software products that are interconnected and communicate with each other based on a common protocol called TCP/IP. Successful communication in any situation depends on some kind of agreed-upon protocol: a standard. Without standards, life would be awfully complicated. Actually it would be just awful! Without standards there would be no Internet. There would just be CompuServe and America Online. The holy grail of standards, and the most significant benefit to users of official standards-based webcasting products, is interoperability. In other words, standards allow users to communicate without concern for compatibility. They allow you to buy products and services with some assurance that they'll be relevant in the future. This section is designed to provide background to the relevant organizations and to the protocols and standards prevalent in today's and tomorrow's webcasting products and systems.

The way Internet standards are defined and agreed upon has historically been through standards bodies. The governing standards body for the Internet is the IETF (Internet Engineering Task Force). However, with the pace of change and opportunities created by the Internet, we've seen two new significant trends in standards for the Internet. First, standards created by other organizations such as the ITU (International Telecommunications Union), MPEG (Motion Pictures Experts Group), and W3C (World Wide Web Consortium) have become much more important. Second, because standards are so important, many companies set out to establish their technology as a de facto standard and then submit it to a standards body for official ratification.

When new technology and business opportunities burst onto the scene, as is the case with webcasting, there is usually a parallel explosion in new protocols. These protocols are often proprietary, and therefore the products that include them are not interoperable with other vendors' products. This is very much the situation with webcasting products today. There is only partial interoperability between different vendors' audio/video streaming products. Push applications suffer from the same problem. However, the standards consolidation phase has begun with Darwinian consolidation through acquisitions, mergers, and bankruptcies as well as through the various standards bodies. This is one reason why paying close attention to standards bodies is so vital for companies with webcasting products, services, or content. It's very easy to head down a particular vendor track only to find that progress in a particular standards organization has left you and your organization completely out in the wilderness.

IETF Standards

There would be no Internet without the IETF and no future for it. The IETF is an open, international community of network designers, operators, vendors, and researchers concerned with the evolution of the Internet architecture and the smooth operation of the Internet. The IETF is such a significant and revered community that, rather tongue-in-cheek, the introduction to how it works is sardonically entitled "The Tao of the IETF." (For more information on the IETF, visit its Website at www.ietf.org.)

In addition to its many tasks concerned with routing, transport, security, and so forth, the IETF defines protocol standards. A protocol defines the way that one hardware or software component interacts with another with respect to specific functionality. The webcasting software applications that we discuss in this chapter all transmit information over the Internet by interacting with TCP/IP through a programming interface. TCP/IP protocols are basically transport mechanisms that allow internetworking devices such as routers, switches, and operating systems to communicate with each other. In other words, they create the highways and byways of the Internet. Software applications are the vehicles by which information is transferred between two points. These vehicles have their own protocols, too. If one piece of software puts some information inside a vehicle at one end, and the software at the other end doesn't know how to take it out, then there isn't much point to the communication. So standards are important to the way in which information is transmitted by one software application and received by another.

As we'll see later in the chapter, there is still work to be done to enable webcasting software applications to work with each other, so standards are not a given where these software applications are concerned.

IP Multicast

There are essentially three ways to transmit from a source to multiple recipients on the Internet:

- Unicasting is a point-to-point transmission requiring the source to send an individual copy of a message to each requester. This is inefficient for a large number of requesters because it requires the sending computer to retransmit a copy of the information for each recipient. More importantly, the network has to transmit duplicate copies of the information, which clogs up precious bandwidth very quickly as the audience size increases. (See Figure 3.1.)

- Broadcasting is a one-to-all transmission method where the source sends one copy of the message to all systems, whether they wish to receive it or not. This technique on the Internet is largely undesirable because it often leads to network disruption or flooding.

- IP multicasting is an efficient, standards-based solution to the problems of unicasting and broadcasting. IP multicasting is the Internet broadcasting technology standard, an extension of IP, the internetworking protocol that is used on the Internet. With IP multicast, applications send one copy of the information to a group address, reaching all recipients who want to receive it.

Unlike unicasting, IP multicasting allows small or large amounts of digital information to be sent to large audiences. IP multicasting involves groups of receivers that participate in multicast sessions; only those group members actually receive the webcasts or data for that group's session or program. IP multicast technologies tell the hardware, software, and data at different levels in the network and internetworking infrastructure to efficiently handle one-to-many group communications.

The following example may be useful for illustrating the difference between unicasting and multicasting: A T1 connection, which is still considered a relatively big and fast connection on today's Internet, permits data to flow at a rate of 1.5 Mbps. (That's enough of a throughput or data flow to handle 53 users.) If we transmit an audio-based webcasting session at a rate of 28.8 Kbps from a single

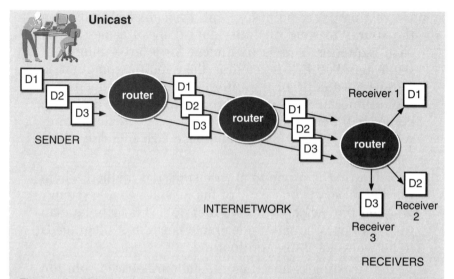

Three copies of the same data (D) are sent point-to-point as D1, D2, and D3 to Receivers 1, 2, and 3 in a shared conferencing application. These are "unicast" transmissions, sent point-to-point from one sender to one receiver.

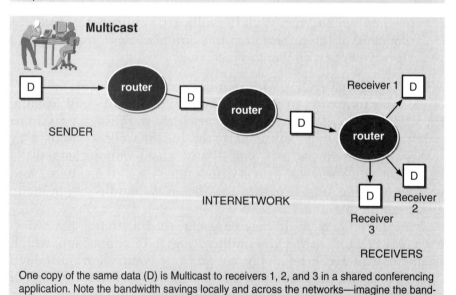

One copy of the same data (D) is Multicast to receivers 1, 2, and 3 in a shared conferencing application. Note the bandwidth savings locally and across the networks—imagine the bandwidth savings for hundreds of recipients.

Figure 3.1   Unicast versus IP multicast.

source over a T1 connection using unicast, the T1 connection is full after 53 users are concurrently tuned in (i.e., listening) to the session. If we transmitted the same audio session using IP multicast, however, thousands and thousands of users could access the single audio stream being transmitted. Since webcasting's popularity is demanding the transmission of large amounts of data to many people, IP multicast is an increasingly important technology standard.

Despite its many apparent advantages, however, IP multicast is not yet widely available on the Internet or across corporate intranets. Two multivendor organizations are currently attempting to encourage the widespread adoption of IP multicast: the IP Multicast Initiative and the International Webcasting Association (IWA). Both organizations focus on building awareness and knowledge of multicast capabilities and count among their membership a number of significant and well-established vendors from the communications, cable, broadcasting, publishing, and movie industries. (For more information on these organizations and their various programs, visit their respective Websites: www.ipmulticast.com for the IP Multicast Initiative, www.webcasters.org for the International Webcasting Association (IWA) which has chapters around the world.)

ReSerVation Protocol (RSVP)

Quality of service is the phrase used to describe a network capability that protects the integrity, end-to-end predictability, and bandwidth utilization of data transmission. For broadcasters, it means turning on the radio or TV and getting good quality audio or video. Quality of service becomes much more important when we're transmitting multimedia content across a network than it is when we're transmitting straight text, for example. RSVP, the ReSerVation Protocol, enhances the current Internet architecture with support requests for a specific quality of service (QOS) from the network for particular data streams or flows.

RSVP is designed to allocate network resources appropriately for the requirements of the data being sent. To optimize transmission for particular types of data such as audio and video, an application requests special services (to assure quality) from a network using RSVP. RSVP defines several classes of network traffic depending on the application's tolerance for variations in network response times. RSVP can be used to control both quality of service and resource management for unicast and multicast sessions. RSVP is an emerging Internet technology. Companies such as BBN, Cisco, Intel, Microsoft, and Precept Software have RSVP-based products available. (For more information, refer to the Website at www.isi .edu/div7/rsvp/rsvp.html.)

Real-Time Transport Protocol (RTP) and Real-Time Control Protocol (RTCP)

RTP provides end-to-end network transport functions suitable for applications transmitting real-time data, such as audio, video, or simulation data, over multicast or unicast network services.

Audio and video webcasts (comprised of packets) transmitted over the Internet experience variable delays and are subject to loss. RTP is intended to enable synchronization and recovery from delays and packet loss. RTP also defines a format for a variety of audio and video encodings to promote interoperability among different computer platforms, operating systems, and application software products. RTP is an application-layer software protocol.

In order to provide robust, quality audio/video delivery on the Internet, the RTP protocol has specific data fields that contain time stamp and sequence information. These fields can be used by a receiving computer to reconstruct the time-specific properties of RTP packet streams.

A related protocol to RTP is RTCP, which checks the status of your webcasts from time to time. This is a monitoring and management protocol in which sender and receiver reports are transmitted from time to time so that applications using RTP can get RTCP reports on how well RTP packets are being delivered, end-to-end. Host computers can then potentially adjust transmissions to adapt to network conditions.

Reliable Multicast Protocols

Reliable IP Multicast's goal is to offer 100 percent data integrity over a network when needed. Reliable IP multicast protocols overcome the limitations of unreliable IP multicast datagram delivery and expand the uses of IP multicast. Transmitting audio and video via IP multicast is acceptable because human ears and eyes can tolerate and compensate for certain loss or interference in sound or pictures. However, when we need 100 percent data integrity, such as when we're transmitting databases or software across a network, absolute reliability of data transmission is of paramount importance. This is where reliable IP multicast protocols come in. One example of the increasing importance of reliable IP multicast is NetShow, Microsoft's audio/video software solution. Microsoft has licensed reliable IP multicast software from StarBurst Technologies and other companies in order to enable completely reliable one-time transmission of audio/video files.

ISO (International Standards Organization)

The international organization for standardization (ISO) is a worldwide federation of national standards bodies from some 100 countries, one from each country. The mission of ISO is to promote the development of standardization and related activities in the world with a view to facilitating the international exchange of goods and services, and to develop cooperation in the spheres of intellectual, scientific, technological, and economic activity.

The ISO's work results in international agreements which are published as international standards. (For more information, refer to the Website at www.iso.ch/.)

Motion Pictures Experts Group (MPEG)

MPEG, the Motion Pictures Experts Group, is probably the most widely used group of standards for audio and video. MPEG is a group of people who meet under the ISO to generate standards for digital video and audio compression. The three main steps of MPEG are:

MPEG-1 Coding of moving pictures and associated audio for digital storage media at up to about 1.5 Mbps

MPEG-2 Generic coding of moving pictures and associated audio information (MPEG-3 was originally to be a high-definition television standard but was merged into MPEG-2.)

MPEG-4 Coding of audio-visual objects

The MPEG-1 video standard is primarily aimed at video on CD applications at bit rates of 1.5 Mbps, although smaller bit rates are possible due to the generic approach of the standard. MPEG-1 starts with a relatively low resolution video (such as 352×240 pixels at 30 frames per second). The image is then converted into two chrominance and one luminance channel, and the chrominance channels are further reduced to 176×120 pixels.

MPEG-2 targets digital television applications in the range of 4 Mbps. It is, therefore, of little interest to Internet cybercasters.

MPEG-4, a standard that is currently not finished, targets very low bit rate applications, defined loosely as having sampling dimensions up to 176×144 pixels of 10 frames per second (fps) and coded bit rates between 4.8 and 64 Kbps. MPEG-4 will be a very complex set of coding tools for audiovisual objects capable of providing support to different functionalities such as object-based interactivity and scalability, and error robustness, in addition to efficient compression. It will also have a syntactic description of coded audiovisual objects, providing a formal method for describing the coded representation of these audiovisual objects and the methods used to code them.

MPEG audio compression comprises three coding techniques: Layer-1, Layer-2, and Layer-3. These layers provide increasingly higher compression ratios at equal audio quality. To reproduce CD quality audio, Layer-1 requires 384 Kbps, while Layer-3 only requires 112 Kbps. MPEG Layer-3 audio is capable of further reducing bandwidth (and quality) of the audio signal from 128 Kbps (best quality) all the way down to 8 Kbps (telephone quality) with several steps in between (96, 56, 32, and 16 Kbps).

MPEG has been extremely important in many non-TCP/IP digital video environments as a means for the digital encoding and transmission of audio and video. Today, however, it's becoming increasingly important for Internet audio/video-based webcasting software. In higher bandwidth environments and as broadband Internet connectivity reaches the home, support for and use of this standard in software applications will become even more important. (For more information on MPEG, refer to the Website at www.mpeg1.de.)

ITU Standards

The ITU (International Telecommunications Union), headquartered in Geneva, Switzerland, is an international organization within which governments and the private sector coordinate global telecom networks and services. As numerous industries converge at warp speed, the role of the ITU with respect to the telecommunications and Internet industries is becoming more significant.

The ITU has played a large standardization role for the videoconferencing industry with the H.320 suite of audio/video compression and communications standards. The H.320 standard was designed to be used with equipment from different vendors and linked in the same audio/video conference. In particular, it was optimized for circuit-switched media such as fractional T1, Switched 56 phone lines, and ISDN.

Two more recent and significant H.320-style ITU standards are H.324, for POTS (plain old telephone service) videoconferencing, and H.323, which standardizes conferencing over packet-switched networks, such as Ethernet and token-ring.

The ITU has also worked on standards for multipoint document conferencing and is currently working on standards for electronic program guides (EPG) that will affect webcasting and the listing of

webcast events on the Internet and television. The T.120 rec-
ommendation lets users collaborate in multivendor data-only
conferences and add document-sharing capabilities to any H.32X
videoconference. DataBeam, Intel, Microsoft, and PictureTel's use
of these standards is particularly important. (For more information, refer to www.itu.ch/.)

H.323 Specification

The H.323 specification, which was approved by the ITU in 1996,
describes terminals, equipment, and services for multimedia communication over local area networks (LANs) that do not provide a
guaranteed quality of service. H.323 terminals and equipment may
carry real-time voice, data, and video, or any combination, including video telephony. Since these types of networks, especially
TCP/IP, dominate today's corporate environment, the H.323 standards are important building blocks for a broad new range of collaborative, LAN-based applications for webcasting products.

The H.323 standard is broad in scope and includes both stand-
alone devices and embedded computer technology as well as point-
to-point and multipoint conferences. It addresses call control,
multimedia management, and bandwidth management for point-to-
point and multipoint conferences. H.323 also addresses interfaces
between LANs and other networks.

H.323 is part of a larger series of communications standards that
enable videoconferencing across a range of networks. Known as
H.32X, this series includes H.320 and H.324 which address ISDN
and PSTN communications, respectively.

T.120 Standard

The T.120 standard contains a series of communication and application protocols and services that provide support for real-time, multipoint data communications. These multipoint facilities are important
building blocks for a whole new range of collaborative applications,
including desktop data conferencing, multiuser applications, and

multiplayer gaming. T.120 is a comprehensive specification that solves several problems that have historically slowed market growth for applications of this nature. Like the H.32X standards family, T.120 resolves complex technological issues that apply to the Internet and telecommunications industries.

The T.120 standards were defined by leading industry enterprises. Over 100 international vendors, including Apple, AT&T, British Telecom, Cisco Systems, Intel, MCI, Microsoft, and Picture-Tel, have already committed to implementing T.120-based products and services.

World Wide Web Consortium (W3C) Standards

The W3C is an international industry consortium founded in 1994 to develop common protocols for the evolution of the Web. For webcasting, the most significant projects underway in the W3C today are the efforts on synchronized multimedia and Extensible Markup Language (XML). (For more information, refer to www .w3.org.)

Synchronized Multimedia

The Synchronized Multimedia project in the W3C is an effort to address some of the looming dangers of multimedia product interoperability on the Internet. This project is attempting to bring together and facilitate communication between the Web community, the CD-ROM community, and the community working on Internet-based audio/video on-demand.

Since webcasting content can be an amalgamation of text, graphics, animations, and audio/video streams, there is a clear requirement to enable synchronization so that a text and graphics presentation can be enriched at a certain well-defined point with an audio or video stream. This is what the concern with synchronization is all about. This ties in with two other protocols mentioned: RTP and RTSP.

XML (Extensible Markup Language)

XML is significant because vendors are starting to examine and rally around it as a way to deliver richer information using a standard definition language. Many push vendors are presently looking at this standard for their product development efforts. Microsoft and Marimba, for example, are both using XML for their open software distribution (OSD) proposals as a way to standardize mechanisms for software delivery.

XML stands for Extensible Markup Language. It is extensible because it is not a fixed format like HTML (HyperText Markup Language) which is used for building Web pages. XML is specifically designed to enable the use of SGML (Standard Generalized Markup Language) on the Web. A regular markup language defines what you can do in the way of describing information for a fixed class of documents (like HTML). XML goes beyond this and allows you to define your own customized markup language. XML is often referred to as a metalanguage—a language for describing languages.

SGML is the Standard Generalized Markup Language (ISO 8879), the international standard system for defining, identifying, and using the structure and content of documents. This standard development is one of the most significant things to watch for as well as its impact on the Web in general and on push-style webcasting applications.

Proprietary Protocols and De Facto Standards

Some of the protocols being used in webcasting products today are proprietary. However, some of them are on their way to becoming de facto standards and others are being formally presented to particular standards bodies. This section covers some of these protocols.

Real-Time Streaming Protocol (RTSP)

Defined jointly by Real Networks, Netscape Communications, and Columbia University, RTSP is an application-level protocol for control over the delivery of data with real-time properties to enable controlled, on-demand delivery of such data (audio and video). It is designed so that sources of data can include both live data feeds, such as live audio and video, and stored content, such as prerecorded events. It works with established protocols such as RTP, HTTP, and IP multicast to enable streaming media over the Internet. RTSP has been submitted to the IETF for standards consideration.

Advanced Streaming Format (ASF)

Microsoft has introduced and is supporting ASF as an industry standard for defining the storage format for streaming media. It is intended to replace a variety of separate file formats, such as WAV and AVI. According to its Website on the subject, www.microsoft.com/asf, ASF is the open standard file format in which multimedia content will be stored, streamed, and presented by the tools, servers, and clients of multimedia vendors. Their vision is that digital multimedia content is gradually trickling onto the computer desktop. "The digital seers, Negroponte (Being Digital), Gilder (Life After Television), Gates (The Road Ahead)—all say the same thing . . . this trickle is about to turn into a flood, and that flood will engulf not only your computer desktop, but also your television, your telephone, your toaster, your fridge, probably even your tennis shoes." They note the differences between RTSP and ASF: RTSP is a control protocol used to control (e.g., rewind, fast forward, play, record) the streaming of media stream(s). ASF is a multimedia file format especially tailored for media streaming. Thus, media streams stored within ASF may be played and controlled by RTSP. Microsoft has submitted ASF for standards consideration with the International Standards Organization (ISO) and the Internet Engineering Task Force (IETF).

Synchronized Multimedia Integration Language (SMIL)

The World Wide Web consortium (W3C) has a new proposed markup language, Synchronized Multimedia Integration Language (SMIL), designed to allow the easy mixing of simple media objects in different formats, such as audio, images, text, and streaming audio/video. The coding would be with simple tags, a method to designate elements on a Web page. If this is approved, the streams and images would be scheduled together to make it easier for the average person to design and add webcasting elements to their Web pages. This would be in addition to Microsoft's NetShow ASF submission. An appeal of this submission is that multimedia productions could be created to use less bandwidth. SMIL is only a proposed language, and not a media format in itself. One common problem with streaming media is precise synchronization of the audio to the video. Long video files have "time drift" problems. SMIL and RTSP address drift (latency) problems in their proposed protocol.

Reflectors/Splitters/Exploders

As an interim solution to the scalability problems of unicasting on the Internet (i.e., reaching large audiences), several companies have developed proprietary (broadcast-like) fan-out server products. When these fan-outs—also known variously as reflectors, splitters, or exploders—are strategically placed across a network or internetwork, they can reduce some of the data replication and bandwidth utilization required within the network. There are disadvantages to this approach, however. Adding these components to the network typically increases the overall cost, and the solution is generally vendor-specific. So, to deploy both push and streaming (audio/video) webcasting, for example, you need separate reflector products for each type of webcasting. More specifically, if you want to deploy a Real Networks solution and a PointCast solution, and reach a large audience, you'll need to purchase a reflector from each vendor. This may be a necessity until multicasting becomes widespread.

In situations where IP multicast is available, it offers a more general and architecturally desirable solution in many cases than the fan-out server products. This is because IP multicast can be used by any Internet application that has been programmed to take advantage of it. There are an increasing number of such products available as the vendors involved in developing and delivering webcasting products and services—hardware and software product companies, network service providers, and content providers—begin to view IP multicast as a way to deliver more and more data to increasingly larger audiences. Major hardware and software product vendors including IBM, Microsoft, Hewlett-Packard, Sun Microsystems, Silicon Graphics, Cisco Systems, 3Com, Ascend, and Bay Networks already incorporate IP multicast support in many of their products. And many new webcasting software products are programmed to take advantage of IP multicast. Similarly, the network managers that control technology deployment within enterprises and in ISPs across the Internet have been testing and in many cases implementing IP multicast as a means of taking advantage of the new webcasting software applications without bringing their networks to a grinding halt. But until IP multicast becomes widely deployed on the Internet and corporate intranets, the fan-out products offer a feasible interim solution to reaching many users simultaneously with acceptable data replication and bandwidth requirements.

Webcasting Transmission and Content

The content broadcast through a webcasting system may originate from one or a set of sources including people, radio, TV, VCRs, professional production systems, newspapers, and so on. However, all the data transmitted within the webcasting network itself is digital. If content starts out nondigital then it has to be digitized before being transmitted.

Although many people equate webcasting with multimedia content, there are many scenarios in which webcasting pure text data is valuable. One of the most compelling early uses of the Web was the retrieval of financial information and stock quotes. Real-time distribution of financial and/or news information via pure text to multiple individuals, organizations, or audiences in the financial market has obvious appeal. Easy access to stock prices and news via webcasting products has been popularized by products such as PointCast and small news-alert add-ons to existing Web browsers such as the news receiver made available by MSNBC.

Transmission Types

There are essentially five types of webcasting transmissions that fit under the general classifications of streaming, on-demand, and push. Differences in webcasting transmission types are characterized by the information source, when the request for the information occurs, when the download occurs, and when viewing takes place. Table 3.1 summarizes the different types of webcasting transmissions.

- *Live event.*   The webcasting transmission of a live event has as its information source a real-time happening such as a music concert. User access to a live event webcast is via a request that happened anytime up to the present. The download (or streaming) and viewing of the content is in sync with the event taking place.
- *Periodic event.*   A periodic webcast differs from a live event in that the information being requested is periodically sent to the requesting user. Push applications that provide stock quotes are driven by and supply informa-

TABLE 3.1   Webcasting Transmission Types

Transmission Type	Information Source	Request	Download	View
Live event	Live feed	Previously or now	Immediate	Immediate
Periodic event	Live feed	Previously or now	Periodic	Continuous
VOD	Archive	Now	Immediate	Immediate
NVOD	Archive	Now	Delayed	Delayed
View later	Live feed or archive	Now	Periodic, immediate, or delayed	Later

tion to users based on periodic downloads to the desktop computer. This transmission type is actually analogous to a magazine or newspaper subscription.

◆ *Video (data) on demand.* Video (or actually any digital data) on demand (often referred to as VOD) usually provides immediate access to archived information such as a movie. This is analogous to putting a video in a VCR and watching it.

◆ *Near video (data) on demand.* Near video (or data) on demand (NVOD) is very similar to VOD. Many hotel room TV sets provide access to the same movie which is repeated on a scheduled basis. This is near video on demand. In a computer-based webcasting environment, another example of NVOD is the collection of requests by a server computer over a certain time period which are then satisfied with a single transmission to all the users who requested that information.

◆ *View later.* In a view later transmission, information such as Web pages or video files are downloaded to a desktop computer based on some predetermined profile or request. Since the digital result is a file on the desktop computer, this can be viewed at some later time or date.

Streaming

As we mentioned in Chapter 1, the term streaming refers to the technique used by audio and video software to make audio and video transmission appear to be continuous. There is a continuous feed of digitized audio or video transmitted by the server computer. Because the Internet was originally designed to handle text and graphics rather than to support audio or video streams, the mechanisms first used for audio and video playback on the Internet were quite complex and not altogether satisfactory. They typically involved downloading a file, waiting for the download to complete, and then opening and playing a file with a local software viewer. As the commercial Internet and Web explosion took place, a number of companies started to work on and deliver products based on streaming technology to provide a more direct and continuous link between the audio/video source and viewing software. The client software component of contemporary streaming products typically employs a buffering technique to transparently accommodate any delays introduced by the packet-switched Internet.

Audio and video fidelity continues to be a significant problem and ongoing challenge for digital audio and video streaming products. There is a direct relationship between available bandwidth and the quality of audio and video. One way to think about audio quality is that 14.4 and 28.8 Kbps modems deliver approximately AM quality audio. In other words, you simply can't get high fidelity audio quality over a modem in real time. ISDN transmission rates improve audio to the approximate equivalent of FM quality sound, and CD quality sound is possible at transmission rates of about 1.5 Mbps, the equivalent of a T1 connection.

Fortunately, digital audio compression techniques are improving all the time. Combined with streaming techniques that buffer audio and video data to smooth out the bumps in transmission over the Internet, we will see continuous improvements in audio and video fidelity.

Compression and Decompression (codecs)

The word *codec* is short for compression, decompression. The job of a codec is to encode audio and video data into a form appropriate for digital transmission, and then to decode it back into audio and video signals (and hopefully reproduce the original with some amount of fidelity). Not only must a codec turn analog data into digital bits, but it usually must also perform compression to fit the data into communications channels of limited bandwidth (like a 28.8 Kbps dial-up Internet connection).

Compression is achieved by reducing redundancy in a signal. This means replacing multiple copies of the same pattern of information in a signal with a single copy of that pattern. Both temporal (across time) and spatial (across an image) redundancy can be reduced. A trivial example is a representation of a black screen. It could be represented by tens of thousands of zeros (one for each pixel), or it could be represented by a handful of bytes which signal "insert 120 lines of 160 zeros here." The repeated pattern of black is replaced with a count and a single example of the pattern. GIF image coding uses this simple method called run length encoding to encode long runs of the same color along a row of pixels. Compression techniques also use knowledge about peculiarities of the human visual and hearing systems to reduce the number of bytes required to encode information that the sensory system doesn't pay as much attention to.

When popular Internet audio was introduced, proprietary compression techniques delivered relatively poor quality. Since 1996, however, professional audio techniques such as perceptual audio coding have been introduced into Internet streaming media systems. This is the same technology used in DirecTV satellite and Sony MiniDisc players.

There are different methods used to encode audio and video. These three coding methods showcase how different codecs are constructed.

Bandwidth Issues and Requirements

On one level the issue of bandwidth is simple: There is never enough! There is no such thing as unlimited or infinite bandwidth. What bandwidth is available is quickly used up by increasingly data-intensive Internet and intranet software applications. Webcasting systems are almost always both data intensive and focused on efficient distribution to as large an audience as possible. Since audio, video, and push applications appeared on enterprise and ISP networks, they have eaten up larger and larger portions of the available bandwidth. They are literally bringing existing networks to a grinding halt. Many enterprise network managers are now limiting (or removing completely) webcasting software components based on unicast.

Time Domain Coding

The simplest type of audio encoding is linear pulse code modulation (PCM). PCM simply samples the analog audio signal at regular intervals and converts the analog samples to a binary code. PCM makes no assumptions about the audio signal and requires the highest bit rate to encode audio. Audio CDs are encoded in this way.

Frequency Domain Coding

Frequency domain coders split the signal into a number of separate frequency components and encode these independently. The number of bits used to code each frequency component can be varied dynamically.

Vocal Tract Models

Vocoders and linear predictive coders (LPC) model the way we produce speech in our vocal tract to minimize transmission bandwidth.

The Mbone

The Mbone is an experimental, cooperative volunteer effort spanning several continents. In many ways, it is a webcasting network that predates current discussions by several years. The Mbone (Multicast BackBONE) is a virtual network layered on top of the physical Internet to support IP multicast. It has been in existence for about five years. The Mbone, which originated in an effort to multicast audio and video from the IETF meetings, has been used extensively for testing multicast protocols and services. As a result, the number of participating sites has grown significantly. Technical meetings, NASA space shuttle launches, a Rolling Stones concert, and many other live meetings and performances have been multicast over the Mbone. (See Figure 3.2.)

A related venture, the Internet Multicast Channel, is a pilot project being run by the IP Multicast Initiative. The project, which involves the MBONE community along with numerous ISPs, telecommunications companies, and broadband carriers such as cable and satellite vendors, is intended to stimulate commercial IP multicast network services and business broadcasting services on the Internet.

HTTP versus TCP/UDP versus Multicast

As we discussed in Chapter 2, the Internet and the Web are not one and the same. The beauty of the Web is that it essentially reduces every bit of communication to three elements: an address (URL), a

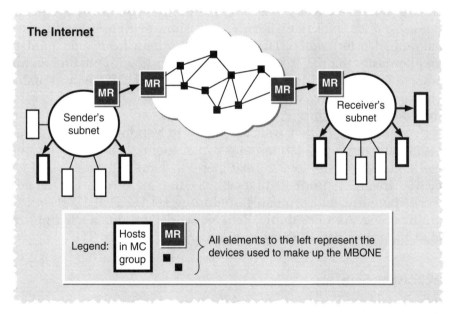

Figure 3.2   Mbone virtual network.

standard protocol layered on top of TCP/IP (HTTP), and a page layout language (HTML). All of these elements have their technical drawbacks. When it comes to audio and video, HTTP probably has the biggest drawback. Without significant enhancements to this protocol, it is unlikely that it can be used for high-quality, large audience webcasts—including audio and video—in the future.

The HTTP protocol actually employs TCP, the protocol on which reliable data transmission over the Internet is based. By contrast, UDP is an unreliable protocol, meaning that it does not guarantee that data will arrive in the right sequence or at all. Without getting into details, the price of a reliable protocol is complexity and bandwidth utilization. Therefore, UDP is often used where data loss can be tolerated by either the software itself or the human being exposed to this loss. This is particularly true where audio or video transmissions are concerned. People can implicitly or explicitly compensate for loss in audio or video transmissions; if a few data packets are lost during the transmission of an audio or video data stream, it doesn't really matter since the human ear or eye either doesn't notice, makes up for the omission, or puts up with some amount of interference. UDP also moves data from one point to another faster than TCP, so its speed, combined with the human tolerance for audio/video packet loss, makes UDP an acceptable choice for streaming webcasting applications. This choice is reinforced by the fact that IP multicast uses UDP.

Because audio/video webcast software vendors are striving to create software applications that can respond to a variety of network situations, the logical next step for them is to offer adaptive media streaming products that can use one, many, or all of the network standards and protocols, including HTTP, TCP, UDP, and/or multicasting. As an example, Real Networks' products attempt first to use IP multicast, then try simple UDP, and finally, TCP.

Webcasting Software

Webcasting software products fall into two categories: audio/video streaming products and push products. Although we're likely to see increasingly blurred lines between these product types over time, it's currently quite easy to distinguish between audio/video products and the so-called push products.

Audio/Video Streaming Software Products

When audio and video capabilities first came to the Internet, the limited bandwidth of the Internet itself and the prevalent use of dial-up modems made pure audio transmissions a much more attractive proposition than the introduction of video. This is still the case for low-bandwidth Internet connections, such as those supported by 14.4 or 28.8 Kbps modems. The allure of Internet video and increasing bandwidth in consumer and enterprise Internet connections is, however, driving continued innovation and deployment of video webcasting products.

Although Microsoft continues to provide the most prevalent desktop computer operating environment, there are still enough Apple Macintosh and UNIX workstation computers in use to make cross-platform audio/video software program availability important. Many audio/video webcasting software vendors, including Real Networks and Microsoft, offer multiplatform implementations of their desktop webcasting software, thus highlighting the ongoing importance of platforms beyond Intel-based Windows.

There are essentially two different categories of audio/video streaming software products: highly specialized digital video products and Internet-specific products. Most of the latter category of products have come onto the market since 1995. Since the Internet streaming video market is still relatively new, there is a lot of change, innovation, and consolidation happening very quickly. Table 3.2 lists some of the vendors of Internet video streaming products.

Push Software Types

Push software products are still relatively new, and there is still considerable confusion about precisely what characterizes push products. As with any new technology term that appears to have sizzle and market opportunity written all over it, the term has been abused, refined, and subdivided. Several vendors simply don't want

TABLE 3.2   Audio/Video Streaming Software Vendors and Products

Company	Product(s)
ICAST	The Company Channel
Microsoft	NetShow
Precept Software	IP/TV
Real Networks	RealAudio and RealVideo
Starlight Networks	StarCast and StarWorks
VIVO	VivoActive
Vxtreme (Pending acquisition by Microsoft)	Web Theater
VDONet	VDOLive
Xing Technologies	Streamworks

to be called push vendors, and others claim the terminology even though their products lack some of the pertinent characteristics. For the sake of clarity, it may be better and easier to think of these software products as webcasting systems that focus on distributing text, graphics, and/or software. As time goes by, lines between these and audio/video webcasting products and systems will inevitably blur. Table 3.3 lists some of the vendors and products to consider and watch.

TABLE 3.3   Push Software Vendors and Products

Company	Product(s)
BackWeb	BackWeb
DataChannel	Channel Manager
GlobalCast	Reliable Multicast
Marimba	Castanet
Microsoft	Internet Explorer 4.0 (Active Desktop)
Netscape Communications	Netcaster
PointCast	PointCast Connections
StarBurst	Multicast File Transfer
TIBCO	TIBnet
Vxtreme (Pending acquisition by Microsoft)	Web Theater

Implementing a Webcasting System

When implementing a webcasting system, network managers and enterprise professionals must decide whether they are going to be transmitting text, graphics, and audio and/or video data. They also have to decide whether the data is going to be made available for on-demand retrieval or will be broadcast live or near-live. These system requirements determine the type of webcasting system to be implemented and the vendors from whom to choose a solution.

Audio/Video Webcasts

Audio/Video webcasting transmission systems can be divided into two categories: live and recorded. In a live system, the audio/video feed is continuously encoded and transmitted. In a recorded system, the audio/video feed is encoded and stored prior to transmission. There are therefore four key roles performed by a webcasting system:

1. Capture
2. Encode
3. Store (for nonlive systems)
4. Transmit

Since unicast-based systems have a huge impact on the transmitting server with substantial stream replication requirements, a fifth function is often added to unicast-based webcasting systems: replication.

Getting Video onto the Internet

The first step in getting a video segment onto the Web is the sampling or digitizing of the video source. This is achieved by using a video capture board. This hardware component, usually a device that you simply plug into your computer, takes the video in through a typical NTSC, PAL, or S-Video source and converts it to either a digital stream or file. This is a CPU-intensive process requiring a high-end computer and *lots* of space to store the result if it's being written to a file. A few minutes of video stored in one or more files can consume megabytes, gigabytes, and even terabytes of disk space.

Editing and Compressing Digital Video

After a video segment has been digitized, you can edit and modify the result using a software tool. Products available for this process range from free (i.e., available for download from the Internet) to those that are bundled with full-suite professional webcast publishing systems that allow sophisticated editing. As the audio/video webcasting software market matures, we can expect to see an increasing number of these sophisticated publishing/broadcasting products with high-level editing and compression facilities.

Where digital compression is concerned, the process can be either explicit or implicit. This is one of the points at which trade-offs between data size and quality are introduced. A smaller file is bandwidth friendly but usually results in lower quality audio and/or video. The ultimate size and quality of the image and audio delivered to and rendered on a desktop computer depends on a combination of product/vendor, bandwidth, and target image size. The most prevalent video on the Internet today typically shows up postage-stamp size on the target computer. This is because of the size of the data being transmitted and the capacity limits of the Internet—especially 28.8 Kbps modems.

Capturing Audio and Video

Transmitting audio or video from the Internet or an intranet requires a mechanism to get the audio and video into the server computer. This is achieved using sound cards and/or video capture boards. Many multimedia computers now include relatively high-quality sound cards. Video capture boards are a newer technology and typically not included as standard components in off-the-shelf computers. The role of a video capture board is to convert the NTSC, PAL, or S-Video output of a VCR, cable, or satellite TV feed into a digital file or feed. These cards are increasingly available from computer retail stores and require 100-MHz CPU-based machines or faster. If audio or video data is going to be stored before transmission, the other requirement on the server computer is a generous amount of storage space on a relatively fast device such as a hard disk.

Encoding Audio/Video

The encoding component is usually hosted on the same computer as the audio or video capture. They are typically dedicated hardware or software components that often require a large amount of the host CPU's processor to perform effectively.

Storing Audio/Video

The amount of storage space for audio and video varies depending on the compression ratio used/achieved by the encoding component. Compression ratios are usually between 12 : 1 and 48 : 1. No matter how good the compression ratio, you are going to need a large amount of storage space. Even with a high compression ratio of, for example, a mono quality audio stream, you will use 120 Kbps of space for only a minute's worth of audio! Dedicated storage systems or devices are and will become much more significant components of webcasting systems as organizations deploy increasing amounts of audio and video.

Transmitting Audio/Video

The server computer used to actually transmit the digitally encoded audio or video stream is sometimes the same system on which the computer Website is hosted. As users demand better quality and more specialized audiovisual webcasting systems are constructed, it's becoming more usual for the audio or video data stream to be served up by a dedicated computer device.

Replicating Audio/Video

Serving up only one stream of audio or video is a CPU-intensive process. When unicast is the transmission mechanism (instead of IP multicast), there is a huge impact on the transmitting computer.

This often means that multiple computers have to be used to serve the number of viewers or listeners that want to tune in to a particular transmission. Where replication systems are employed, they are sometimes located at the same point in the network as the first transmitting server. Other times, however, they are located strategically within an intranet or the Internet so that one stream can be accepted from the original source which is then replicated or split into multiple streams (see Figure 3.3).

Text and Media Webcasts (Push and Software Distribution)

As with audio/video webcasting systems, push and software distribution webcasting systems will transmit either real-time information feeds or publish stored information. Again there are multiple components of a text or media webcasting system:

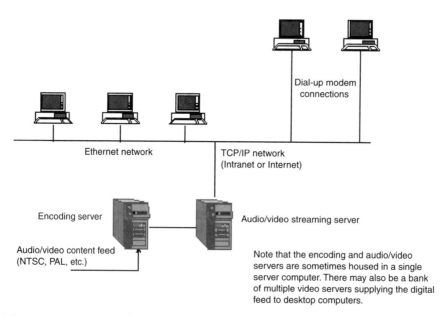

Dial-up modem
connections

Ethernet network

TCP/IP network
(Intranet or Internet)

Encoding server

Audio/video streaming server

Audio/video content feed
(NTSC, PAL, etc.)

Note that the encoding and audio/video
servers are sometimes housed in a single
server computer. There may also be a bank
of multiple video servers supplying the digital
feed to desktop computers.

Figure 3.3   Typical A/V streaming schema diagram.

1. Capture
2. Translate
3. Store (for nonlive systems)
4. Transmit
5. Replicate

Capturing and Translating Data

In a live text media webcasting system, data can make its way into the transmission system in a number of ways. There might be a line feed that is sent via ISDN, cable, or satellite feed. Sometimes the receiving device is connected to a PC which performs some kind of intermediate data and format translation in order to convert the data and pass it on to another translation device for TCP/IP-based transmission.

Storing Data

As with an audio or video webcasting transmission system, if data is not being served up in real time or if it's being archived, data storage becomes an important part of the system. If the data is only text, then the storage requirements are much smaller than if the information is graphics, animations, audio, or video. High-volume file system–based storage devices are becoming increasingly popular as storage servers.

Transmitting Data

In a text, media or software distribution webcasting system, the data is usually served up by a computer server running a push or software distribution server component. (See Figure 3.4.) Popular push applications such as PointCast are computer-intensive since they deliver text and graphics and only use unicast transmission techniques. Where unicast is the delivery mechanism, there is usually a requirement for additional (potentially numerous) replication systems located close to the original content source or distributed strategically through the network between the content source and receiving desktop computer-based users.

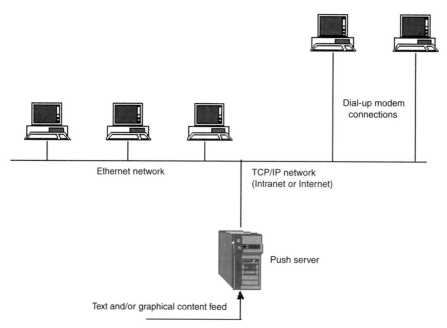

Figure 3.4   Typical push schema diagram.

Receiving a Webcast

To receive an Internet webcast, you need an appropriate Internet device and some level of Internet connectivity. The type of device and the speed of your Internet connection directly affects both your ability to receive an Internet webcast and the quality of the transmission you receive.

Connectivity

Connectivity to the Internet is important for receiving a webcast because it has a direct bearing on the quality of your experience. Historically, the vast majority of Internet connectivity has been through directly connected devices (such as PCs and Macs at home) and networks (in the enterprise). The explosion of the Internet has created further opportunities and innovation in indirect Internet connections. There will be further changes in both direct and indirect Internet connectivity—from cable and satellite to phone, TV, radio, pager, and set-top box—in the near future.

Direct Internet (IP)

On one level, receiving a webcast of any kind is simply a question of Internet connectivity. Whether you're connected by telephone-based modem, cable modem, satellite, wireless, frame relay, ISDN, or something else, you will be able to receive webcast data. However, depending on your connectivity, headlines or pictures will trickle or zoom in. If you have a slow modem, you simply cannot expect to see anything but jerky and postage stamp–sized video. Compare that with any TV you use every day and you soon realize that higher bandwidth and broadband connectivity through satellite, cable, or xDSL technologies are becoming much more appealing.

Indirect or Interlaced Internet

In some cases, viewing or listening devices have not yet been enabled for direct Internet connectivity. This has been historically true of televisions, radios, and telephones although this is changing today. Interim solutions are being developed that enable these devices to receive Internet information. Systems such as Web TV have been developed that enable TVs to access the Internet and display webcast channels.

Indirect or interlaced Internet devices are one of the most complicated technical areas since they are hybrid devices. Many innovations in this area are being worked on and developed. One example is Intercast, a technology designed to use the vertical blanking interval (VBI) of traditional TV signals to transmit data. Existing Intercast devices and transmissions are focused on HTML-based Web pages. This is changing as we incorporate Internet protocols as needed, such as TCP/IP and IP multicast. (See Appendix A for hybrid devices.)

Receiving Devices

Desktop computers are currently the most typical devices for receiving webcast transmissions today. Webcasting systems are employing more and more CPU cycles, bandwidth, and software on both the serving computer and the desktop computer receiving the webcast. Current debate revolves around the traditional PC running Windows, Mac OS or UNIX—employing fat client software programs—and the emerging Network PC-based on thin client software programs. Since software is the key technology enabler, and bandwidth can be limited, the network PC has restricted functionality and capabilities today.

A much more significant debate is between the TV and the PC. Will the PC become the dominant communications device in the office and at home receiving and responsible for telephone conversations, TV broadcasts, Internet connectivity, and interactive information services? With the rate of innovation and momentum being applied to Internet technologies across multiple industries, it's hard to see how the TV device will be able to sustain its position. It is, however, the incumbent home device. However, the race is on for the TV to become intelligent like your computer. The deciding factor may be cost. Will an Internet PC be cheaper than an Internet TV? The United States is undergoing a federally mandated transition to digital TV termed HDTV (High Definition Television). Consumers will be forced to buy new digital TVs in six to ten years. Both computer and TV manufacturers are racing to come up with multi-use TVs and PCs, both receiving webcasts.

Several interesting trends are adding Internet value to the traditional TV device. New capabilities, including keyboards, being added to set-top boxes are now enabling couch TV viewers to access the Internet and webcasts. Microsoft's acquisition of WebTV is particularly noteworthy as a clever way to influence technology, content, and branding via the TV.

An interesting TB/Internet hybrid technology is Intercast. It is focused on enabling PCs and TVs to receive data and Internet Websites. There are also mobile Internet radios by www.audible.com and www.audiohwy.com, and car radios and handhelds in production.

Telephones, Pagers, and PDAs

The mantra being recited and invoked across communications companies and device manufacturers across the globe is *IP everywhere.* Traditional telephone and pager manufacturers are not standing still when it comes to receiving Internet-based information including webcasts. The holy grail of telephone, pager, and personal digital assistant (PDA) manufacturers is an integrated communications device capable of receiving and sending e-mail, receiving and making phone calls, receiving and sending pages, and (of course) receiving Internet webcasts. For example, new multimedia color cellular phones receive e-mail and Web pages. With reductions in form factors and standards-based Internet protocols, we are within sight of a new class of integrated, mobile communications devices based entirely on Internet technologies.

Technology Futures

It's certain that by the time you read this, the Internet and webcasting world will have been enriched and changed by new technology, products, acquisitions, and further industry convergence. There are a number of key areas to watch that will undoubtedly impact the world of webcasting.

One of the least known groups of individuals in the world is, in many ways, at the heart of the change and opportunities created by the Internet. The IETF and associated groups and forums continue to drive technology innovations and new opportunities. This is one of the key barometers for patterns of change on the Internet. This is where technology infrastructure advancements are discussed, refined, and standardized. No matter what industry you're in, ignoring this group and the technologies it's working on is a perilous approach. Many technologies at the heart of webcasting are being worked on in this forum. Particularly significant in this group is further work on IP multicast such as security, billing, and reliable multicast protocols.

Another key area to watch is the growing battle for dominance between the PC hardware and software manufacturers and TV manufacturers. Sledgehammer and subtle technology enhancements to these devices will increasingly blur the line between them. We are likely to look back in five to ten years and realize that momentum was the key. We're much more used to change and improvements to computers than to TV. This is a battle that the TV industry starts with a clear lead but will have to fight hard to preserve. This battle continues with the addition of high definition television (HDTV) which can deliver multiple channels or enhanced picture quality.

With respect to key infrastructure technology changes, we should expect changes in two areas. First, audio and video streaming standards will happen. You don't go to a consumer electronics store today and choose between TVs based on what content you'll be able to view or not be able to view with a particular vendor's product. You expect to be able to plug in, turn on, and consume information. We're already experiencing some level of consolidation among vendors of streaming products. There will be much more consolidation, and a standard framework or protocol will emerge that is supported by multiple vendors whose products will interoperate.

Overall, the biggest area to watch is software. There is untapped power in software that we simply haven't seen realized. Software powers databases. Software powers digital encoding. Software powers our view of anything that happens on a computer screen. Java is a software thing. So software is the key enabling technology for the future of many industries and certainly for the future of webcasting. Marry digital information carried by software products with sophisticated indexing and searching software technologies with individual and community profiles utilized by software distribution mechanisms and you get what you want—not want what you get. Software agents will rise, and subtle indexing and hypermedia capabilities built into content transmitted through webcasting systems will create information systems that we've dreamed about; they will happen sooner than we think.

CHAPTER FOUR

Developing a Webcasting Website

So, you've decided that you want to set up your own Website and begin webcasting. That's great! But before you get started webcasting, you're going to have to decide what type of webcasting you want to do (i.e., streaming, on-demand, or push) and make sure that you build a Website capable of supporting that type. Of course, you can also modify your webcast Website and add features and capabilities as you become more familiar with the technology or your goals change. If you plan carefully now, you should be able to build onto your original Website hardware and software, as your webcasting requirements change. Webcasting sites vary widely depending on their application and the amount of money that you spend initially to get the site up and running.

We define a simple broadcast Website as one that can support a maximum of 20 to 40 people at a time viewing live, real-time video and/or audio. It can also be one that supports a smaller number of on-demand viewers. A typical simple webcast site uses off-the-shelf hardware and software for encoding and server duties, and uses a T1 communication connection (1.54 Mbps) to the Internet. We'll describe the required components for setting up this type of webcast Website a bit later in the chapter and estimate the basic costs involved in establishing such a site.

Websites that are intended to push information to users go through essentially the same steps to capture, encode, and transmit information as Websites designed for live streaming or on-demand webcasting. Although programs in most cases have been placed under the care of information technology departments, it is important to consider the features that fall outside this department. These features may include graphics, database marketing, and public relations. Internet webcasting requires the talents of a diverse group outside of the programming field. The method to success will be the selection of a proper manager who has the authority and talent to work with many departments. But the administration and content of push Websites is likely to differ significantly from the other types. In many cases, for example, the responsibility for developing and managing a push Website falls to the information technology (IT) department rather than to PC technicians and audio/video specialists or an outside consulting group, as is often the case with streaming and on-demand webcasting. We'll discuss the differences in more detail later in the chapter, but for now it's important to understand that there are two emerging format standards for push—one from Microsoft and another from Netscape Communications. (These are the so-called push wars that we mentioned in Chapter 1.) At some point during the planning process, you're going to need to decide which of these two standards to use to push information. Alternatively, you may want to follow the example of companies like The Wall Street Journal Interactive Edition and Ziff-Davis and participate in multiple channels that support both formats as well as those of independent suppliers. And of course, you're going to need to determine what type of information you're going to be pushing through your webcast Website, to whom, and by what medium (i.e., an intranet, an extranet, or the Internet).

Who Can Webcast?

Anyone with the appropriate equipment to capture, encode, transmit, and (optionally) store audio and/or video data can do live-event or on-demand webcasting at a basic level. Essentially, you need only three ingredients for basic webcasting:

◆ A recent (i.e., purchased within calendar year 1997) multimedia PC equipped with a sound card, video capture board, and Windows 95 to capture and encode the audio/video data

◆ A server PC running Windows NT or UNIX to transmit the digitally encoded audio/video stream

◆ A high-speed Internet connection

Installing the basic webcasting hardware and software can be completed in one day's time by a technician.

High-end webcasting requires significantly more hardware and software than a basic system, as well as considerable expertise. At the high end of the streaming and on-demand webcasting spectrum are the large-scale networks designed to support live event audio/video broadcasting to anywhere from several hundred to many thousands of people at once. Large audience broadcast Websites aren't *sites* in the true sense of the word. Instead, they are typically based on a high-speed network of multiple, geographically distributed servers that use T3 (45 Mbps) communications connections. The broadcast Websites run by AudioNet (www.audionet.com) and itv.net (www.itv.net) are good examples of large-audience broadcast Websites. (See Figure 4.1.) These two companies—AudioNet of Dallas, Texas, and itv.net of Vancouver, Canada—broadcast many events over the Internet, including concerts, sporting events, and awards ceremonies. These events attract tens of thousands of viewers over the course of a few hours. Because of the bandwidth and engineering requirements necessary for these types of large-audience live events, there are less than a dozen broadcast webcasters with the reliability and technical infrastructure to support webcasts that reach thousands of users.

Figure 4.1   AudioNet webcast Website.

Push Technologies and System Requirements

In a simple push system, the software on the user's PC (the client) fetches Web pages and stores them on the local disk for subsequent viewing. This approach is sometimes classified as automated pull since the user's PC is responsible for pulling the information from the server. Both Microsoft and Netscape incorporate this type of push capability for free in the latest versions of their browsers. Functions that are common to both the Microsoft and Netscape push systems include (1) the ability for users to sign up for something of interest and receive regular updates, (2) the ability for users to get headlines and links or locally downloaded HTML pages that contain the full articles from the headlines, and (3) the ability to view the information sent to them either on- or off-line.

Content control is very important in push technology because the provider is generally targeting specific information for delivery to an identified—often captive—audience. Push systems that are designed to give IT maximum control of the content actually separate the presentation of the information from the download phase. When the download phase is complete, a scheduling agent checks the user's settings and the properties of the content to determine when and how the content should be displayed. Some basic push systems do not provide facilities for controlling either the user notification or content delivery, so they are a poor choice for use with intranets or extranets, or for software distribution or electronic commerce applications.

More sophisticated push systems that can deliver virtually any type of content (e.g., graphics, audio or video, plugs-ins, or software) to users' desktops obviously require more complex hardware and software but allow shared control between the user and the channel provider. These systems, including those from BackWeb and Marimba, typically use (platform-based client/server) architectures that are designed to provide a range of tools for developing, distributing, and managing content. In these architectures, the client software can maintain a persistent connection for querying the server for new information or can periodically connect to the server and ask it for updated information. The server checks whether there is information to send, and, if there is, it instructs the client to start downloading it. In these systems, the content can be narrowcasted or filtered, which enables users to select a subchannel (e.g., their city) for delivery of local weather information, or personalized, which develops the personal distribution model for content on the fly from a combination of information on the corporate database and the Web server.

Most mid- and high-level push systems also incorporate some type of a user notification facility. Some allow users to set up separate windows that display information that is pushed to them, such as news or stock price updates. Others use a flash or animated graphic to notify users when new information of interest to them is delivered. (See Figure 4.2.) These flashes, which are persistent and invasive, alert users to the information delivery regardless of the user's location or current task—even interrupting or appearing above an active application that is maximized on the screen. A lim-

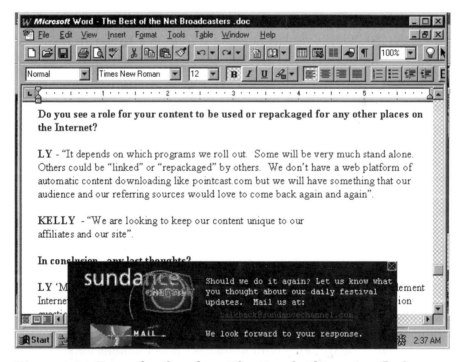

Figure 4.2 Example of push notification facility using flash arrangement.

ited number of push systems also offer screen savers or wallpaper as a display mechanism for pushed information and some others allow users to set up a new application for displaying pushed information from the Start menu.

Many of the high-end push products offer significant scalability (that is, the ability to push content to a large number of viewers) and security features that make them suitable for a range of applications including electronic commerce, software distribution, and work flow management.

Who Can Receive Webcasts?

Receiving webcasts is easier than sending them. As we discussed in Chapter 3, there is very little specialized equipment required to receive most webcasts. Live, on-demand, or push webcasts are best viewed on a multimedia PC equipped with a 100-MHz Pentium (or better) processor and Windows 95, or a 100-MHz (or faster) Macintosh PowerPC equipped with the appropriate sound card and speakers. At minimum, you'll need a 28.8K modem connection to receive decent sound and some moving pictures, but the faster the modem and connection to the Internet, the better your chances for receiving high-quality audio and video. Many live event and on-demand webcasters offer video and audio at two speeds, 28.8 Kbps for modem users and 56 Kbps for ISDN and cable modem users.

In addition, you'll need a software player such as Real Networks' Real Player or Microsoft's NetShow to receive most audio and video live event webcasts. You can download most of the available software players (including those from Real Networks and Microsoft) from the Internet, but you should be aware that the download will take at least several minutes, even with a 28.8K modem connection. To download, you go to a software Website and select the audio or video player for download. Upon clicking on your selection, it saves (downloads) your file on your computer. In most cases, you will need to find this file on your computer and select Run or double-click to install the software. Here are the locations for download of the common audio and video players:

Microsoft NetShow, www.microsoft.com/netshow

Real Networks, www.real.com

Xing Streamworks, www.xingtech.com

Telos Audioactive, www.telos-systems.com/

VDOnet, www.vdo.net

Vxtreme, www.vxtreme.com

In addition to the audio or video webcast software for streaming media, users typically will need to download push software from companies like PointCast, Backweb, and Marimba.

Although a 28.8K modem connection to an ISP is adequate for receiving a push broadcast, many companies that are using push technology to deploy information and/or software to their employees on a regular basis are using dedicated connections provided through high-speed leased lines or cable modems. This type of connection is generally more convenient for the user and sender alike, facilitating sending large amounts of information and ensuring the immediate delivery of such time-sensitive information as stock quotes and news reports.

Selection Criteria: Choosing the Right Vendors and Components

After you've determined which type of webcasting will be most effective for your particular application and audience, the next step in establishing a Website is determining which (if any) components you already have and what components you'll need. Then, you will need to select the appropriate equipment and vendors.

Sending Live Video

Video is taken from an analog source, such as a video camera, and then translated into electronic form for shipping over the Internet to a distribution server.

Live video encoding requires a high-speed multimedia PC. Depending on the software that you choose for live encoding, you'll need a PC equipped with a Pentium 166-MHz processor at a minimum. A Pentium II 266 MHz (or higher) is preferable given the ever increasing demands of live video encoding software. RealVideo encoding software, for example, recommends the use of a 200 MHz Pentium at minimum for live encoding, and either a dual Pentium Pro or a Pentium II machine is preferable. A machine equipped with a standard hard disk and 32 or 48 Mbytes of RAM should be adequate for live video encoding. Video encoding software can run under Windows 95 or Windows NT. Some encoding programs also run under the Apple Macintosh operating system.

Most off-the-shelf multimedia computers include a good quality sound card as a standard component, but you'll probably have to add a video capture board to act as an interface between the analog information supplied from the video source and the computer's. Typically, the video interface card will use the computer's PCI bus for desktop machines or PCMCIA for laptops and will have a port to plug in a composite video source. Higher-end cards may also accept S-Video, which can be supplied by high-quality video cameras such as newer versions of the digital video cameras.

Another alternative uses the high-speed universal serial bus (USB) interface, currently being incorporated into laptop and desktop computers, in combination with digital video cameras built with the USB interface. In this case, video will be transferred from a digital video camera in digital form directly to a PC without having to be translated into analog form as an intermediate step. Such solutions are still new, however, and composite video and its S-Video big brother are going to be around given the millions of VCRs and camcorders in use.

Sending Video On-Demand

Video on-demand has several conveniences that live-event webcasting doesn't. First, the video to be turned into digital form can be cleaned up and edited using software tools such as Adobe Premier to cut and paste different clips together, add titles, and effects such as animated logo sequences, as well as sound tracks. In many cases, the video source is a videotape played on a VCR or from a feed. Several tapes can be used to supply content in order to create a final product.

Further, since the conversion from analog video signal to digital form isn't occurring in real time, you can use a slower, less expensive machine to encode the video and/or encode video at several different replay rates. For example, you may want to optimize one on-demand version for playback at 28.8K speeds and create a second version for playback at 128K ISDN speeds.

The planning and logistical requirements for video on-demand archives are less strenuous than live video. You can, for example, create, review, and edit a video clip at a relatively leisurely pace; once it is digitized, it is available around the clock for playback. If the server goes down, viewers may be disappointed, but they can return at a later time to see the video.

Video on-demand provides a perfect complement for live-event webcasting. If viewers were unable to watch the event as it occurred due to time considerations, technical difficulties on their end, or overloaded distribution servers, they can return to the webcast Website at their convenience to view the event. Video on-demand provides the means to create an archival history of events that can be stored and conveniently reviewed with the click of a mouse button.

Determining Bandwidth Requirements

The biggest single resource for live-event webcasting or large-scale, on-demand video/audio is bandwidth. How many streams (i.e., viewers watching at the same time) do you expect to support? A good rule of thumb to remember is a T1's worth of bandwidth (1.54 Mbps) for every 50 viewers of a 28.8K video or audio stream when information is sent in unicast mode. So, if you're expecting 150 viewers to come in across the Internet, you'll need three T1s worth of bandwidth.

On-demand video or audio clips have a distinct advantage over live-event webcasts because they don't have the overwhelming immediacy that attracts viewers. Because people can listen to the audio or watch the video at their leisure rather than as it is actually happening, the Website may support activity at all hours of the day and night. This means that, depending on the popularity of the content, several thousand people may visit your Website over the course of a few weeks to access the audio/video that is stored there. Consequently, you don't need the same amount of bandwidth as you do to support a few hundred viewers tuned in for a live event for an hour or two. However, if the content is popular, you may still experience heavy bandwidth use at peak Net hours.

Evaluating Live-Event/On-Demand Webcast Vendors

Evaluating live-event webcasting vendors (i.e., the organizations that broadcast audio and video over the Internet in real time as an event is taking place) is a challenging task, since the whole field of webcasting is very new and few companies have acquired a wealth of experience. The marketing of video webcasting by Microsoft and Real Networks has encouraged many companies to jump into the field. Some are traditional Web shops that are moving from static presentations of pictures and text on a Website to adding sound and motion pictures, while others consider themselves new media start-ups and have one foot in standard journalism, video film production, or traditional broadcast and the other in the Internet.

We've included a list of major webcasting vendors and consultants in Appendix A of this book, but we recommend that you use this list only as a starting point in your search for a webcasting vendor. Things change quickly in the webcasting field. For the most up-to-date information on webcasting vendors in your area, we suggest that you visit the Websites for the major product and service vendors. You may also want to check with the webcasting forums and professional associations.

Live-event webcasting is a demanding project. PC encoding hardware has to work properly when the event starts, a high-speed Internet connection has to be running (and stay running) during the duration of the event, and the event server or servers have to be able to handle the number of people estimated to tune in to view the event. Some of the benchmarks that you can use to evaluate live-event webcasting firms include:

- Event marketing
- Project management
- Broadcast experience
- Internet experience
- Technical expertise
- Defining responsibility
- Corporate resources

The more documented live events the webcaster has done, the better, especially those who have broadcast events from challenging event locations such as stadiums or stages. The webcasting firm should have a producer as part of their staff or hire an independent producer or project manager. Further, the webcasting firm should have a solid mix of equipment technicians and administrative coordinators who can work with you.

Knowing how to deal with the telephone company and debug phone lines, whether they're ordinary analog lines, ISDN, or high-speed leased lines, is a necessary skill. Experience in satellite transmission may be essential to the success of your project.

A live-event webcaster should be prepared to spell out exactly what parts of the project it is willing and able to handle and to recognize *your* responsibilities as the event planner. If the webcasting firm doesn't have a list of questions to ask you about who, what, when, how, and where's the electrical and telecommunications going to come from, start looking for someone else. Due to the number of technical and logistical pieces that have to come together on time and on target, the live-event webcaster has to be able to work with you, the facilities people at the event site, the phone company, and perhaps even other live-event webcasters supplying bandwidth and distribution servers.

The bigger the staff and fiscal resources of the live-event webcasting firm, the better the chances that they will have the equipment and people to put on your event, even in the event that something unplanned occurs. If you hire a producer to coordinate the webcast, ask about the resources of their alliance partners.

Typically, live-event webcasters will support two or three streaming formats, including Real Networks' RealVideo and Microsoft's NetShow.

The Rental Alternative

If you don't have extensive webcast requirements, a large capital expense budget, or the necessary personnel to set up and maintain your own broadcast Website, you may want to consider renting instead of buying. In this case, you have a choice of hiring a consulting firm to handle all of the webcast details or any single piece of the process—producing the content, preparing it for the Internet, obtaining any necessary licenses, or providing the site and required bandwidth on the Internet.

Letting an outside firm handle all of the details necessary for a live-event webcast is the easiest choice. Experienced producers cost $2000 a day with additional costs for planning and logistics. Some firms bundle all fees together, including ISP and bandwidth costs.

You may choose to provide one or more services yourself to keep expenses down, including acting as your own production manager, providing high-speed Internet connectivity between the encoding machine, and actually broadcasting the event with your own server.

Produce the Event

Live-event webcasting production requires managing the audio and video from the live event, handing off the audio and video to a machine for encoding, setting up and monitoring the telephone connections (analog dial-up or high-speed leased lines) for connecting to the Internet, and managing the distribution servers.

If time is short (45 days or less until the event) and this is going to be your first live-event webcast, you should seriously consider handing off the webcast production tasks to a professional firm.

Chances are very good that you'll end up with a better quality production and save yourself any number of stress-related ailments during the process. Delegating production to a professional firm will also give you an opportunity to observe the many steps involved in producing an event and to learn some of the tricks of the trade for webcasting.

In the following case study, Mark Weitz, president of New Orleans Web, the first company to present live, mobile webcasts on the Internet, offers some practical advice for webcasting live events based on his experiences.

CASE STUDY   NEW ORLEANS LIVE-EVENT WEBCASTING

Mark and Judy Weitz designed their webcast site specifically to stream live special events to a global audience. They began streaming Mardi Gras events live on the Net in 1996 and have gathered a wealth of experience in the past year, moving on to other special events and travel information for tourists considering a visit to New Orleans and the surrounding area. (See Figure 4.3.)

Millions travel to New Orleans for Mardi Gras every year, and many want to explore the city before or after the event via the Internet. As Weitz points out, "You can appreciate how busy our site gets months in advance of the actual dates. More and more people use the Net to check out where they are going, make reservations, and find out what's available. Our site features New Orleans attractions, places to go, hotels, restaurants, and (of course) Mardi Gras events."

"Our first event was a collaboration of resources. We traded our accommodations and behind-the-scenes, backstage access for video production services and Internet technical support. Mardi Gras LIVE 96 was

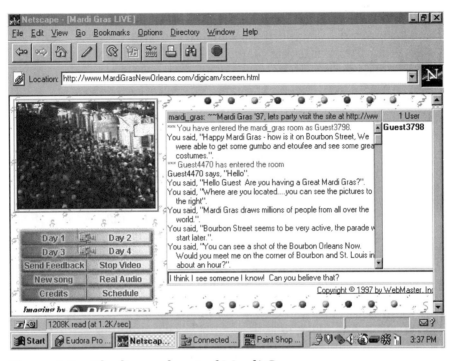

Figure 4.3 The live webcast of Mardi Gras.

an Internet first. It was supposed to be one of the longest single multicast events broadcast over the Mbone. Ten hours of live, real-time video and audio. We were using ISDN and T1 connections for Xing Streamworks and CuSeeMe technologies. We had three broadcast-quality cameras and a production van complete with a ten-person crew. The ISP supported the event with Internet connection abilities and coordination with live feed from the production van. Sun and Compaq donated workstations and servers for the ISP's use. With the Mardi Gras LIVE 97 event, we introduced DigiCam, a brand new technology that didn't require plug-ins and allowed us live video shots without streaming software."

Weitz offers a primer for webcasting a live event, based on his experiences in the past two years. The list of do's and don'ts emphasizes the complexity of webcasting live events.

General

1. Be sure to obtain contracts for every phase and every transaction of the event. Obtain exclusivity contracts with the event owners to help you maintain your control of the event.

2. Clearly define who will own the audio and video rights, including pre- and postproduction material, and establish when possession will take place. Decide how the site and event will be represented after the live webcast. Who will be responsible for archiving?

3. Determine, as early as possible in the process, what permits will be necessary and begin the procedures to obtain them.

4. Make arrangements for housing, transportation, meals, and so on for your crew.

5. Check to see if the maintenance staff of the building(s) where the event is going to take place needs to be involved in the setup, teardown, or event production. Is there a need to consult with maintenance and/or electrical personnel about your setup and production plans? Will your equipment and/or personnel interfere with any other staging or seating arrangements? What other production/film/sound crews will be there? Where do you intersect with them?

6. Create a timetable with all the details listed to be checked off as completed. Prepare a detailed plan for everyone who is involved in the produc-

tion, specifying who is responsible for each task and spelling out, minute-by-minute, when each phase will take place. Be sure to notify everyone involved of their specific responsibilities and of the overall plan. (Ask yourself what each person is supposed to be doing and what do they need to do it, from the time that they get up until they quit each day. This exercise can prove enlightening.)

7. Check all necessary work orders to ensure that they have been properly filled out and delivered.

8. Arrange for staff/crew production meetings prior to event time.

9. Determine, prior to the event, who will be responsible for teardown tasks and packing equipment and/or returning it to its proper location or owner.

10. Write down what inspired you to start on this journey and what you want to accomplish by doing it. This task sometimes helps to focus priorities and expectations.

Plug-Ins

1. Make it easy for your viewers to see your event. If possible, use software that doesn't require a plug-in or complicated download instructions, and make dry runs with the software to ensure that it works the way you want it to.

2. Don't avoid newer technologies just because they aren't standard. Many new products and/or technologies offer significant advances over existing products or services and there are relatively few standard technologies on the Net. Just learn as much as you can about the product or technology that you're using and be sure to test ahead of the actual event!

3. Select software that allows you to keep your site's name prominent in the window or that doesn't use up all of the valuable screen real estate.

4. Create realistic expectations by posting notes on the site prior to the event to notify prospective visitors of the date and time of the event and to explain what is going to take place, what kind of browser and/or modem speed is acceptable (or desirable), and how to use the plug-ins, if necessary.

ISP/Technical

1. Be sure that your ISP is familiar with your plans and can work with you in presenting the live event. Remember that the ISP is crucial to the success of live-event webcasting and must be familiar with the technology and your objectives for the live event. Be sure to invite an ISP representative to your planning and production meetings and to keep the ISP informed of any changes in your plan as the event draws near.

2. Obtain agreements from the ISP prior to the event to clearly spell out your service expectations. Ask the ISP to explain its services and procedures for presenting the live event and to provide at least an overview of its Internet connection, including the need for telephone lines and power sources at the event site. (You don't need a great deal of technical explanation, but you do need to know that the ISP has appropriate technical knowledge and facilities to meet your expectations for the live-event webcast. The ISP should be willing to disclose details about their connection and carrier service and, if necessary, consult with the carrier representative.)

3. If you will be operating from more than one location, determine (in advance) if your software requires 2B+D ISDN to operate properly. Is one T1 likely to be sufficient for your webcast? Is the telephone company willing to run lines to your event or will they just do a drop? How many weeks in advance do they need to get the line in?

4. Determine if the ISP will have technical support available on-site and at the office during the event. Ascertain what backups, if any, are available. For example, does the ISP have extra servers available for the event? (If your event involves potentially thousands of visitors, a few extra servers are probably not sufficient; some live-event webcasts require more than ten servers to adequately handle the load.)

Linking/Promoting

1. Be sure that you prepare all of the proper disclaimers for the event to, for example, state that you are not responsible for anything that goes wrong, and that any and all sites linking to your site request permission to link and offer proper accreditation prior to the event.

2. Be sure to understand the implications of a commercial on-line service company linking to your site. A commercial on-line service can generate a massive amount of hits which can easily overwhelm an ISP's servers for a live event. (Remember, linking to a commercial on-line service is a double-edged sword, with lots of advantages and disadvantages. Our only advice here is to be sure that you understand all of the positives and negatives and be sure to keep your ISP involved and informed. If possible, deal with a commer-

cial service that you know and get everything in writing beforehand.)

Postproduction

1. Summarize the event. Determine what went right and what could be improved? (This information can be invaluable for staging the next event.)

Weitz stresses that any webcaster should have basic familiarity with all of these tasks, even if you hire an expert to produce and manage your live-event webcast. Only by knowing all that is involved can you realistically assess the expert's knowledge and ability to perform the tasks involved in live-event webcasting and ensure that all bases are covered.

Providing the Connectivity

Providing your own connectivity for your own webcast can mean installing and connecting POTS (plain old telephone system) lines to the webcaster for a simple streaming media webcast. You may save money by installing a high-speed leased line Internet connection on your own, if you have the expertise on your staff.

Many convention centers and stadiums are beginning to provide preinstalled and pretested Internet connectivity, but you'll need to test these high-speed facilities well in advance of the event. If you already have connectivity in the building through your organization or business, it may also provide an alternative to dedicated connectivity.

On the other hand, providing your own connectivity has drawbacks. Any number of technical glitches can interrupt the smooth flow of data from the webcasting encoder to the distribution server. You are responsible for worrying about the number of router hops and packet loss between the live event location and the distribution server if you are working with a leased line connection. Connectivity provided by the facility or building you are in may not be up to the task of delivering uninterrupted data to the actual distribution server. Saving a few dollars up front by ordering and installing the Internet connection yourself may not be the best thing if the Internet connection cannot cleanly connect and transmit to the distribution server or splitter.

Broadcasting the Event

As a general rule, unless you practice skills—any type of skills, be it horseback riding, water skiing, shooting, sound system production, video editing, or live-event webcasting—on a regular basis, you aren't going to do it as efficiently and as effectively as a professional individual or group that performs the same set of skills every day, day in, day out to earn a living.

Most certainly, you may be able to handle your own audio equipment to broadcast and record speeches, and lots of households have purchased $499 consumer camcorders to make home videos for the future embarrassment of their relatives and children. However, unless you or your organization's in-house resources handle

Be Penny Wise

Always record live-event webcasts in audio and/or video form for archival purposes. Preferably both. There is a great temptation to skip over this fundamental activity when creating an audio/video file on a computer while a live-event webcast is running. The original source of the audio or video may be arriving at your computer to be encoded and sent to the live webcast. You should record the audio and video before it reaches the computer to maintain the best archival quality. Another point to remember is that the better the audio or video source, the better the audio or video quality that will appear on the webcast. It is essential to start with good audio or video to produce a good webcast.

audio and video on a regular basis, you'll probably get better results by having a professional firm come in and handle the details. For any sort of live events, you'll only get one take and you want to get the best quality you can out of your audio/video equipment before the final product goes out onto the Internet and on videotape.

The more important the event, the more certain you want to have audio/visual professionals. For smaller in-house productions, events outside of the company, media-drawing events, and/or events which will have more than a few hundred people in attendance, they should be handled by professionals, either an external firm or with skilled in-house personnel dedicated to audio/visual support.

Video becomes more problematic, with any number of bandwidth and networking issues that creep in to cause problems. Due to time considerations or resource constraints, you may be better off hiring an outside firm to handle the tasks of encoding video and running the servers necessary to distribute the event.

For audiences of more than 100 people located around the world, there is very little choice involved: The broadcast is more likely to be successful if you contract out to a specialized webcasting firm that has the bandwidth and servers in place to support such an audience, especially if the bulk of the audience is spread across multiple Internet service providers and/or across the country. Contracting means you don't have to develop and support a specialized audio/visual technical unit in your organization, nor do you have to worry about a live webcast overloading the available bandwidth you have established to the Internet (and disrupting services companywide).

Implementing a Push Site

The requirements for pushing content vary widely, depending on the type of content (straight text, text and graphics, multimedia, or software), the delivery medium (an intra/extranet or the Internet), the application itself, and the size of the audience. As we mentioned earlier, both Netscape's Netcaster and Microsoft's Channel Definition Format (CDF) support a limited approach to push. As we write this, Netscape does not support Microsoft's CDF proposal, favoring instead the use of the open HTML, Java, and JavaScript standards. These push wars, which will ultimately be decided by the W3C committee, are causing considerable confusion for push webcasters in the meantime. As we mentioned earlier, a number of organizations are hedging their bets by participating in multiple channels that support both format standards. For example, both The Wall Street Journal Interactive Edition and Ziff-Davis offer PointCast, IE 4.0, and BackWeb channels. (See Figure 4.4.)

One of your first—and possibly your most important—decisions in implementing a push Website is determining which formats and browsers to support. Fortunately, establishing a Website capable of basic push is relatively simple once you've gotten past that deci-

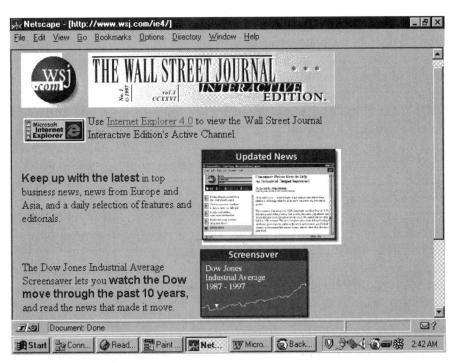

Figure 4.4   Wall Street Journal Interactive Edition.

sion, and this requires only minimal training for most IT personnel. Microsoft and Netscape both provide tutorials and code examples for basic push systems on their respective Websites. Also, both companies sponsor developer conferences to train IT personnel and introduce them to the many Website development tools that are available through third-party vendors. Finally, if you're considering using ActiveX controls on your Website to make it more dynamic or to increase its interactivity, you should be aware that this may increase the developer learning curve and, therefore, increase the implementation cost for a basic push solution.

Netscape Netcaster

Netcaster is a standard component of Netscape Communicator that lets users subscribe to channels, then pushes dynamic Web content to them for on-line or off-line browsing. (Off-line browsing lets users access any Website from their hard disk after pertinent information from the Website is downloaded to the disk.) Netcaster allows any Website to be downloaded in the background on a scheduled basis. With Netcaster, content providers can own desktop real estate. This means that IT managers can now use this space, which has historically been owned and controlled by the operating system and Windows or Mac applications, to push to their users just the information they want, manage bandwidth by controlling update intervals, lock down the channels that users are subscribed to, and centrally administer other Netcaster preferences throughout the enterprise. (See Figure 4.5.)

Netcaster can be integrated with Marimba's Castanet technology to provide a more robust push solution. Castanet offers channel developers additional options for automated delivery and updating of software applications. It provides an alternative, dedicated push server to offer increased automation, user feedback, efficient polling, and a distributed server architecture.

Microsoft Channel Definition Format (CDF)

CDF turns Microsoft's Internet Explorer 4.0 into a container for webcasted information. It permits Web publishers to offer regular

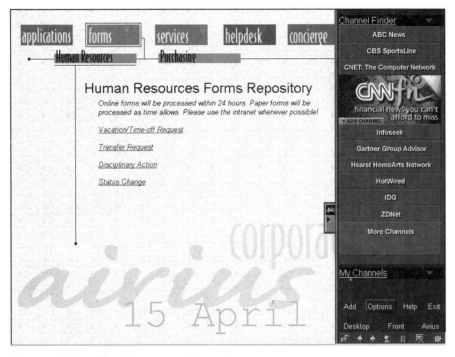

Figure 4.5   The Netscape Netcaster.

updates of collections of information or channels for automatic delivery to PCs or other information appliances. As with Netcaster, the user need only subscribe to a channel one time to receive scheduled deliveries of information without any further actions.

CDF activates a form of site crawling that retrieves an HTML page, stores the page locally on a PC, finds the links in the HTML page, and then repeats the process, stopping when the browser runs out of links or when the user-specified link configuration is achieved. After it runs out of links, the Web crawler retrieves the actual content for each link and places it in a non-HTML document for off-line browsing. (See Figure 4.6.) CDF lets the site provide an approach for grouping information in a logical fashion and for scheduling the frequency of updates.

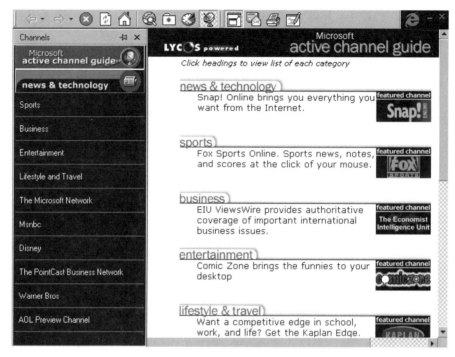

Figure 4.6   Microsoft IE 4.0 crawling capability.

Like Netcaster, CDF is intended as an open format that permits any Website provider to develop content and any server to run on CDF Websites. Unlike Netscape, however, CDF is an application of the Extensible Markup Language (XML) and requires the content provider to learn some new extensions to HTML.

Once you've determined the format standard, there are a number of other considerations for implementing a push Website. Figure 4.7 summarizes the capabilities that you should consider for any mid- or high-level push system for an intra/extranet or the Internet.

In addition to considering the features and capabilities listed in Figure 4.7, you'll need to determine what other products and technologies your Website may need to interact with. Many push products are designed to operate in conjunction with related technologies. For example, some push products (for specific products

Required features/capabilities (regardless of delivery medium or application):

- Intelligent delivery
- Ability to deliver any kind of content, including graphics, audio and video clips (e.g., WAV, AVI, QuickTime or Quick-Time VR) and plug-ins
- Choice of notification and display options (e.g., flashes, tickers, screen savers, wallpapers, applications, client, pagers)
- Integration with any backend (e.g., SQL or legacy databases)
- Ability to target a variety of hardware and software platforms
- Full scheduling control over content delivery
- Differential updates and versioning control
- User notification and content delivery anywhere, even within the user's active application
- Real-time delivery option
- Ability for geographically dispersed companies to easily manage content delivery
- LAN politeness via scheduled updates and control over bandwidth utilization
- Security
- Fully scalable without consuming large amounts of resources
- Backward compatibility with old versions of Microsoft's and Netscape's browsers

Additional required capabilities for intranet push systems:

- Departmental publishing capabilities
- Ability to create a customized client

Figure 4.7 Push system guidelines.

- Tools for easy client configuration after the clients are deployed
- Tool for automatic content generation
- Agent technology for customizing any Website into a feed channel
- Access to high-value external news sources

Additional required capabilities for extranet push systems:

- Compression and decompression of files being sent
- Polite background downloads of large files over 28.8 Kbps modems
- Ability to target different hardware and software platforms

Additional capabilities required for software distribution applications:

- Direct activation of channels through the Start menu
- Painless initial downloads
- Polite background downloads of large files over 28.8 Kbps modems
- Support for Java, and executables written in any language
- Differential and byte level updates
- Ability to set preferences for disk space allocation
- Trusted channels installing of software

Additional capabilities required for electronic commerce applications:

- Support for collaborative filtering and agents
- Control over timing of when content is played to match launch dates

Figure 4.7   *(Continued).*

- ◆ Complete branding and creative control
- ◆ Polite background downloads of large files over 28.8 Kbps modems
- ◆ Ability to maintain user's privacy if desired
- ◆ Ability to track interactions on-line and off-line with various portions of the content
- ◆ Ability to maintain database file confidentiality
- ◆ Control of your business model

Figure 4.7 *(Continued).*

and vendors please see Appendix A) allow users to take advantage of collaborative filtering agents such as Firefly and Net Perceptions to automatically select appropriate content to be sent to them. In addition, you'll need to ensure that the product you select for your Website incorporates adequate security facilities such as:

- ◆ Facilities to prevent spoofing, typically using a challenge/ response principal to ensure that no one can imitate a channel and send unauthorized content
- ◆ Encrypted passwords to prevent unauthorized server access
- ◆ Facilities to prevent denial-of-service attacks and stop flooding by hackers

Selecting a Push System Vendor

Because the push market is already consolidating, vendors and companies are changing rapidly—appearing and disappearing like waves on the shore. When you begin to investigate push solutions and narrow the field of products and vendors for your particular push solution, you'll need to look carefully at both the underlying product technology and the financial stability of the vendor, as well as the vendor's track record in developing and supporting new products and bringing them to market successfully. At this point, you'll probably want to look carefully at the five major contenders in the push market and their respective products: Netscape, Microsoft, BackWeb, Marimba, and Tibco. But, as we've said before, things change very quickly in webcasting so you don't necessarily want to limit your selection to these vendors or their products.

In addition, you should be aware that PointCast, a pioneer in push systems, is also very well regarded in the content area but, as we mentioned in Chapter 1, as the market changes, many push companies offer new services and products in one of three areas: (1) distribution, (2) content, or (3) interactivity. Distribution is the technical push of the data. Content is the filtered news or information, audio, and video. Interactivity includes real-time database exchanges and other responsive systems. Certain vendors specialize in one of these three areas and some provide all the services to customers. You may want to consider using PointCast's services to complement the capabilities of the other companies or products to, for example, supply news content for your intranet push channel.

BackWeb

The BackWeb Channel Server is based on a client/server platform that supports a full range of content, protocol, and display options, making it suitable for a variety of intranet and Internet applications including software distribution and electronic commerce. Back-Web can deliver any kind of content including executables, Java Applets, HTML data, Netscape plug-ins, Director files, and Power-Point presentations, as well as content from legacy systems and existing databases such as Oracle and DB2.

BackWeb supports a range of communication protocols as well as HTTP, BWTP (BackWeb's UDP-based protocol), and Tibco's IP Multicast. It also features a polite agent technology that supports incremental, interruptible downloads and provides differential updating capability and automatic compression on downloads. This capability allows BackWeb to deliver very large files to users with 28.8 Kbps modems.

BackWeb offers a complete set of tools, including the Client Administration Kit for developing custom clients, the Publishing Wizard to enable departmental publishing, the Proxy Server for bandwidth control, and the Channel Server Console for distributed management of channels. BackWeb's links operate with any popular browser, including older versions of Internet Explorer (2.0 and 3.0) and Netscape (1.0 and 2.0).

The BackWeb client is available for Windows NT, Windows 95, Windows 3.1, and the Apple Macintosh platform. The BackWeb server is available for Windows NT, Sun Solaris, and Silicon Graphics IRIX.

Marimba

Marimba Castanet automatically distributes and maintains software applications and other types of content within a company or across the Internet. It can support any type of channel, including internal corporate applications or multimedia consumer channels, and can deploy, manage, and update both Java-based and native-code software applications and files. The server, known as the Castanet Transmitter and the client, known as the Castanet Tuner, work in conjunction with one another to keep software and content continually up to date. An intermediate server, the Castanet Repeater, is designed to handle intranet applications that are dispersed across a wide geographic area and to resolve the administrative and timing issues that are associated with divergent time zones. Both of the Castanet servers (Transmitter and Repeater) operate under Windows NT, Windows 95, or Sun Solaris 2.5. The Castanet Tuner, which receives and manages channel subscriptions requested by subscribers, is available for Windows NT, Windows 95, Apple Macintosh (PowerPC), and Sun Solaris 2.5.

Because Castanet is written entirely in Java, all of its elements are available on the wide variety of machines that support the Java virtual machine (JVM), but since Castanet applications are also written in Java, content providers need to develop expertise in creating content using Java. Marimba does offer a development tool called Bongo, that facilitates the creation of Castanet channels. Acting as a visual interface builder for Java, Bongo includes a large selection of prewritten visual controls that allow users to drag and drop widgets to create visual interfaces.

Tibco

Tibco relies on a self-describing data object architecture and IP multicasting to provide real-time data delivery. The product is widely used in stock market trading applications that require instantaneous transmittal of information. Tibco's Rendezvous software treats each transmission as an object with specific attributes that determine its source and destination.

What's It Going to Cost to Establish a Website and Begin Webcasting?

The costs involved in establishing a simple Website configuration for streaming or push webcasting are quite reasonable, especially if you happen to have the basic hardware available (and many organizations do) and a staff that is familiar with webcasting technology. The costs are reasonable if you consider the potential audience reach of the Internet or the added efficiencies afforded by pushing information over intranets or extranets.

CASE STUDY   THE SYNC: LIVE-EVENT WEBCASTING ON A SHOESTRING

The Sync is a live-event video webcast company located in College Park, Maryland. Founded in 1997, they recently entered the market relying on a small, experienced staff and a shoestring budget to broadcast a variety of political events from around Washington, D.C. They have presented live events including Capi-

Figure 4.8   The Sync: A typical live-event webcast.

tol Hill hearings and association meetings. (See Figure 4.8.)

Table 4.1 summarizes the basic equipment that the Sync uses to broadcast live video events and its estimated purchase price.

Instead of buying a dedicated connection to the Internet or renting server time, the Sync chose to put its 200 MHz Pentium Web and distribution server in a colocation facility that provides power, rack space, and an Ethernet connection for high-speed Internet connectivity. Putting the server in the colocation facility saves several hundred dollars a month over the purchase of a dedicated leased line into the Internet

TABLE 4.1   Broadcasting Equipment

Audio/Visual Equipment	Cost
Canon ES 5000 8mm Camcorder	$1500
Panasonic VCR recorder	$300
Assorted microphones	$250
Assorted cabling and interface jacks	$100

Encoding Equipment	
MPower 266-MHz Pentium II workstation w/64MB RAM & 3GB hard disk	$2495
Winnov VO ISA Video Board	$99
Media 100QX PCI video processing board	$2000
PCI Ethernet card	$199
Real Video Encoder	(Included w/60 user Real Video server license)

Internet Connectivity Equipment	
Off-the-shelf 28.8K modem	$199
Generic 8-port Ethernet hub	$200

and provides a measure of stability as well; the physical business offices of the Sync are likely to move several times over the next several years as the company expands.

When the equipment isn't being used to broadcast live events, the VCR is plugged in, a tape inserted, and the live encoding machine becomes a video on-demand encoding machine. In addition, several other PCs are used to view the live webcast video for quality control; one PC on the local area network is used as a mailbox and chat window to take questions from viewers.

Live Facilities: The Cyberstudio
The equipment and budget list for the Sync represents the barest minimum necessary for live audio and video cybercasts. With a little more money and space,

a more advanced cyberstudio that can host live shows and interactive videoconferencing is easily within the budget range of most organizations. The cyberstudio is designed to be a dedicated facility that can produce a better audio or video event because of the additional equipment involved, both in terms of technical and production quality.

The shopping list in Table 4.2 represents the construction of an actual facility established in the fall

TABLE 4.2   Sample Shopping List

Audio/Visual Equipment	Cost
Two Panasonic AG-EZ1 3-chip digital video cameras	$6000 ($3K each)
Two tripods	$200 ($100 each)
Panasonic AG-5700 Super-VHS recorder	$1500
Vidionics MX-1 video mixer	$750
Two generic 12-inch color TVs	$600 ($300 each)
One set Lowell BP lights	$700
Four (4) surplus overhead stage lights	$200 ($50 each)
Mackie 1402-VLZ audio mixer	$500
Four Alesis sound compressors	$1000 ($250 each)
Three (3) Samson FM wireless microphones	$1050 ($350 each)
Two Marantz tape recorders	$600
Genter 1200 Hybrid Telephone	$1200
Assorted microphones	$250
Assorted cabling and interface jacks	$100
Assorted videotapes (VHS, S-VHS, DV)	$1200
Backdrops and furnishings	
Rented furniture and plants	$150 per month
Materials to construct backdrop (plywood, nails, cloth, and so on)	Less than $200
Duct tape and gaffer tape	$100

Note: Other costs may include installation, connectors, and wiring.

of 1996 and assumes buying everything from scratch. If you already have a television studio or broadcast facility of some sort, you may already have most of the audio/video equipment (and better quality at that!) which is necessary for broadcasting a live show. Some items listed below have been changed from the original equipment procurement to reflect newer hardware and lower pricing.

The two single biggest reoccurring expenses other than a high-speed Internet connection are the space that needs to be set aside for studio facilities and a dedicated staff person to operate the audio and video gear. In a pinch, a normal techie can be trained to handle the video and sound gear, but a better quality production requires the expertise of a visual arts or film major, producer, videographer, or lighting and audio technician.

The Sync chose the Panasonic AG-EZ1 digital video cameras because they provide near-Betacam quality video—a step above the off-the-shelf camcorders priced in the $400 to $1000 range and much more affordable than $25,000 professional units that television stations use. Both cameras feed into the Vidionics MX-1 video mixer to allow various scene combinations and effects, such as cuts, fades, and close-ups, as well as the insertion of opening credits and other clips generated on a computer (more on that later). The finished video is then fed into the back of one or more encoding machines, as well as the Panasonic S-VHS recorder.

As any film or video professional can tell you, lighting is an important part of any performance, especially if videotaping is involved. A set of fixed lights were attached to the ceiling, and the Lowell BP lights were used for getting rid of shadows.

Getting clean audio was the most vexing and challenging problem for the cyberstudio. While wireless microphones were initially used and fed directly into the Mackie audio mixer, pops and cracking from microphones picking up clothing movement and bouncing up and down tended to creep in. The Alesis sound compressors acted as filters to catch most of the unwanted background noise from microphone movement. A pair of boom-mounted and hard-wired microphones were added later to further improve the sound quality.

For audio-only webcasts at remote locations, audio was phoned in using the Genter hybrid telephone to pull audio directly from an analog phone call and feed it to the sound mixer. Several Capitol Hill hearings were broadcast using nothing more on the live event end than a phone call with the event audio. This may work in some cases, but the better the quality of the audio, the better the audio quality on the Internet.

Finally, rather than pay several thousand dollars for constructing a high-quality curtain set similar to those found in television studios and theaters, the A/V specialist brought in his own tools, purchased fabric from a remnant store, and nailed up his own backdrop within an afternoon.

Connectivity

The Sync selected a T1 frame relay connection to Bell Atlantic as the most cost-effective way to deliver one or more encoded video streams to distribution servers and splitters. Even with several encoded video types sent to the server, there is still sufficient bandwidth available to support two-way videoconferencing during a live show.

The POTS lines serve several purposes: viewers can call in to a live show and talk to the hosts directly, adding some spontaneity and occasionally humor, and remote audio can be brought back to the studio through the use of hybrid telephone equipment for conversion into digital form. In addition, there is a potential for combining multiple telephone lines to significantly expand bandwidth. Devices such as the US Robotics LAN Linker would allow remote broadcast of video directly back to the distribution server without the headaches of ISDN or leased line installation.

Table 4.3 summarizes the one-time and ongoing costs associated with connectivity.

Although costs for server equipment are significant (as shown in Table 4.4) given the Sync's shoestring budget, the company managed to conserve expenses in this area by re-using a Sun Sparcstation 5 that was left over from an earlier project and put to good use as a video server. And, while the 100-user RealVideo professional license may seem like overkill considering the bandwidth involved, the professional license has the added functionality of allowing the server to feed another splitter.

The Sync added an NT-based workstation to its configuration to allow for live-event webcasting in Microsoft NetShow format. Microsoft NetShow is freely available for download from www.microsoft.com and

TABLE 4.3 Connectivity Costs

Connectivity	Cost
Cisco 2501 router	$1500
Digital Link T1 CSU/DSU	$800
Generic 8-port Ethernet hub	$200
2 POTS phone lines	$38 per month
Frame relay T1 Internet connection	
Bell Atlantic	$475 per month
Internet connection	$1500 per month

TABLE 4.4 Server Equipment Costs

Distribution Servers	Cost
Sun Sparcstation 5 w/64MB RAM, 3.8GB disk, and Solaris 2.0	$3500
100-user Progressive Network RealVideo Server Professional License	$5000
Dell 266-MHz Pentium II workstation w/64MB RAM & 3GB hard disk	$2495
Windows NT 4.0 server license	$999
Microsoft NetShow	No charge
PCI Ethernet card	$199

is included with the Windows 4.0 server license. Microsoft and other Internet broadcast technology companies may charge in the future. Enhancements in the future may include pay-per-view, archives, databases, tracking, and better audio and video control. Actually, this may be a blessing in disguise because it may herald some improvement in the product and associated support. NetShow is quite difficult to configure (especially in comparison with the comparable product from RealVideo) and Microsoft currently provides only minimal technical support.

Expanding the Cyberstudio

The type of cyberstudio configuration described in the Sync case study represents a cost-effective compromise between spending very little money to establish a Website for live or on-demand audio/video webcasting and laying out several hundred thousand dollars to build a full-blown television broadcast studio similar to the ones operated by the major networks and cable companies. If your organization already has a broadcast studio facility, converting it into a webcasting facility is largely a matter of adding computers and a high-speed Internet connection.

Converting or adding the capability for audio/video webcasting to existing broadcast facilities is a convenient way to stretch dollars. But before you begin converting your existing facilities, you need to be sure that you really need a TV-quality broadcast studio and equipment for your webcasting application. If you plan to distribute video through means other than the Internet, such as cable TV or digital satellite, you've probably already made a commitment to produce high-quality video, so webcasting represents another means of delivering your program content to a larger audience. Even if you do decide to invest in sophisticated video production equipment and lighting facilities, you should look at microstudio concepts such as the latest facilities run by CNN and Bloomberg TV. A *microstudio* is a television quality broadcast facility that is highly automated to keep personnel staffing down. At the same time, the degree of computerization allows for faster editing and turnaround of video.

Distribution Costs

Once you've produced and digitized an audio/video webcast, you need to distribute it. For relatively small audiences (less than 50 people), a single NT or UNIX-based server with the appropriate software and a high-speed Internet connection is probably sufficient. Costs for distributing live and on-demand audio/video webcasts are generally comparable, but (as we mentioned earlier) bandwidth requirements are likely to differ since the viewing audience for an on-demand webcast is spread out over a period of time.

Distributing an audio/video webcast to a larger audience (more than 50 people) obviously requires more than a single server given the bandwidth and networking resources needed, including dedicated services specifically designed to handle large numbers of listeners/viewers without clogging up the Internet. AudioNet, itv.net, and the RealNetwork (a joint venture of MCI and Real Networks) all have specialized distribution networks designed to handle large audiences.

Costs to buy time on one of these distribution networks is based on a number of factors, including the amount of time that you buy, the number of simultaneous viewers, and the total number of events you want to run on the network. The more events you buy, the lower the cost per event. For example, the RealNetwork requires a commitment of $10,000 worth of event time over a six-month period. To broadcast one event per month for 500 people simultaneously will cost $1499. Five events per month will cost $5499, or an average of roughly $1100 per event. If you are broadcasting 20 events per month, the cost drops to about $815 per event.

Production Costs

Production costs are extremely variable, depending on the methods of accounting involved, the skills needed to complete the project, and the costs of those skills. A small shop or project may be able to borrow time from other departments or divisions without creating too much of a fuss, but this may not be possible for a bigger project, or in an organization with strict departmental cost-accounting policies. In general, you should expect some or all of the following personnel expenses with related equipment costs to creep into the production budget:

- Audio/video professionals
- Graphics artists
- HTML/Java programmers/Webmasters
- Producer

As we noted earlier, any live-event webcast that is going to be seen by many people and/or that is going to represent a company or organization should look and sound like a professional effort. Producing this type of event typically requires the expertise and equipment of an experienced professional firm to cable, balance, mix, and filter the event, as well as artists to create appropriate graphics and programmers to develop the necessary HTML links and implement custom controls for playing the audio/video content. There are numerous consulting firms that can help you with the artistic and/or technical aspects of webcast production. Hourly rates for professional webcasting firms can range anywhere from $150 to $300, depending on your geographic location and the firm's prior experience. Appendix A lists some of the firms that can help you to produce a webcast event, but this list is by no means complete or current, given the dynamic nature of the webcasting market. Check with your ISP and/or equipment vendors for other suggestions or ask business colleagues in your area to recommend webcasting consulting firms.

A live-event webcast should be more than a hit-and-run project, especially if you want to educate people about a particular issue or ensure that they visit your Website on a regular basis. Although you may be able to develop the necessary icons or images for a one-time live webcast without professional assistance, an ongoing venture in webcasting typically requires putting someone on staff to handle the graphics or contracting with a freelance artist. Similarly, the more elaborate your Website, the more likely you'll need either an HTML programmer or a dedicated Webmaster. Although basic live-event webcasts are accessible through standard HTML links, there are many custom-design tricks that can enhance audio/video webcasting. For example, Progressive Network's Web page showcase of three Spike Lee films took advantage of the programmable features built into RealVideo to build a virtual theater setting unique to the RealVideo player.

Hosting Costs

Where you choose to host information about a live-event or on-demand webcast largely depends upon your organization's resources and budget. Smaller organizations that expect to have small audiences for their webcasts may choose to use a single machine at the end of their own T1 Internet connection as both the server and host. After all, the bottleneck for the media server application is with clean Internet bandwidth rather than any demands on the CPU or bandwidth of the server. A Windows NT or UNIX Internet server is generally capable of running multiple applications without problems.

Larger organizations are likely to keep the Web pages they need on one machine with links to a separate media server that may be operated in-house or externally by a third party. This arrangement avoids overloading the Web machine and helps to eliminate some security issues, particularly if the Web pages contain sensitive information. It provides a tracking or audit trail that is useful for determining the webcast audience. Each visitor clicks on the URL that points to the media server, and each hit is logged and tallied up at the end of the live event or at the end of the week/month/year. An external server is not always possible, however. The firewalls that many organizations install between the corporate LAN/WAN and the Internet to prevent attacks against proprietary or confidential information, may not permit streaming media to cross between the corporate network and the Internet.

Some organizations choose to use a Website service run by companies such as MCI Internet, Genuity, or AGIS to host their webcasts. These services store the Website information in Web farms that are external to the company's network. This type of arrangement offers enhanced security and management facilities and offers the convenience of putting Web server information on a network with very high-speed Internet access and may even include limited on-demand webcasting. Most Web hosting services are beginning to provide the option of broadcasting to 100+ people for live-event webcasts. Externally managed Web hosting services along with a complementary webcasting capability keep the high-volume bandwidth and network engineering requirements outside of the corporate LAN/WAN.

Push System Costs

The costs for implementing push webcasting solutions vary widely—from free to several thousand dollars—depending on the sophistication of the Website, the delivery medium, and the particular push application. Microsoft's CDF is, for example, included as a free component of Internet Explorer 4.0. Netscape's Netcaster is a component of Communicator, which costs less than $100 in any computer retail store. You will need to run your push system off a

---

Beware the Too Many Cooks Syndrome

Some organizations have used a group approach to develop live-event webcasts. Presumably, this is an effort to save money or divide the many technical and administrative responsibilities involved in live-event webcasting. One group or individual contributes expertise in Internet connectivity, another contributes software, and a third group agrees to handle the encoding. Sounds like a good idea, but the problem is *there is no one in charge.* No single person or department is fully responsible; no one wears the "Buck Stops Here" sign.

Regardless of how many people or groups are involved in developing a webcast, someone has to be in charge and to make sure that all of the participants are fully responsible for their respective pieces. If someone drops the ball during any phase of the webcast development process, it shouldn't result in a noticeable gap in the webcast or a group of people standing around pointing their fingers at one another.

So, who should have the ultimate responsibility for putting it all together and making sure that the webcast happens as scheduled? A good manager. A good communicator. Someone

---

Microsoft or Netscape server, which you may already have to publish your Website. Otherwise, you will need to budget for these servers. Costs for mid-range push solutions, even those with extended push capabilities and relatively sophisticated notification and security features such as the products from Wayfarer, Intermind, and Astound, begin at about $5000. High-end, sophisticated push system products such as those from BackWeb and Marimba start at about $11,000 and scale up rapidly to hundreds of thousands of dollars for a full-blown, large-enterprise push solution.

Despite the variation in costs for push products, however, it is important to remember that the real costs involved in implementing and administering a push webcasting solution are not in the

who is good at administering details and motivating people. The individual doesn't need an in-depth knowledge of all of the underlying technologies, but he or she does need to understand all of the steps involved in webcasting. He or she also needs to be able to foster a "one boss, one team" attitude among the webcasting crew and to be capable of recognizing whether the individuals (or groups) on the team are effectively carrying out their responsibilities.

Too many cooks may spoil the soup, and they can create disaster in a webcasting project, particularly a live-event webcast from which there is only one chance to perform the event. New webcasting companies may offer your company free or discounted services. Many times these services are from inexperienced companies who are seeking to work with you for the exposure. You may want to utilize a project management or consulting firm that provides events producers to evaluate services and plan your event. These companies look for the most reasonable but reliable service and use different firms as needed by your event specifications. Some companies that provide these services are www.thesync.com, www.intervox .com, and www.mediacast.com.

tools but in the personnel expense associated with developing and managing the content that is pushed over the channel. Again, you will need a range of IT skills including programmers, technicians, and communications experts, as well as content developers that can organize complex information for desktop delivery. If you expect your audience—even a captive intranet audience— to read and remember the information that you're pushing to it, you will need to make that information attractive and interesting. Remember, just because the information appears on the user's computer screen doesn't mean that the user necessarily pays attention to the content of the message. In fact, as push systems become more commonplace on the Internet and corporate intranets, users are likely to become more and more complacent about the information they receive. Much like the old adage "you can lead a horse to water . . . ," you can push information to your audience, but you can't necessarily make them read or remember it. For that, you'll need content providers who can write and organize compelling text and artists who can provide useful, eye-catching graphics. Acquiring and managing these skills will ultimately cost far more than the tools required to implement a push Website.

The experiences of a large mutual fund company illustrate the difficulty of capturing audience attention—even on an intranet.

Figure 4.9   Sample page of information pushed to executives via intranet.

CASE STUDY — INTRANET EIS (EXECUTIVE INFORMATION SYSTEMS) PUSH SOLUTION

One of the country's largest mutual fund companies is using push technology to deliver information updates to 200 of its top executives. The push solution replaces an earlier attempt to keep executives up to speed by posting information on the corporate intranet. Initially, the MIS department culled departmental reports and financial news updates and posted relevant information on the intranet. The company soon discovered that this approach was only marginally effective; it took a conscious effort by busy executives to go look for the information.

The company considered using one of the basic push technologies from Microsoft or Netscape but decided that having the Web browser open in Windows at all times would be too invasive. Instead, it elected to install a more sophisticated push solution that could deliver information in a more compelling manner without requiring any action or effort by the executives.

The MIS department identified a set of six basic criteria for the push solution:

- Ease of use
- High performance, low wait times
- Aesthetic presentation of information
- Mobile/remote/stand-alone access
- Ability to assemble information scattered throughout the company (with various degrees of quality/completeness, assorted technologies)
- Maximal impact in minimal time

The company then investigated the push products and technologies offered by BackWeb, Marimba, Point-Cast, and Wayfarer. They selected BackWeb because it gave MIS the greatest degree of control over content delivery. Once the selection process was complete, it took only one day to implement a push channel with basic delivery functions. The company has since expanded the channel to interface with a number of existing databases (for example, fund performance and sales activities) and to incorporate a number of auto-mated delivery features.

Maintaining the Website

Of course, developing the Website is only the first step in your webcasting adventure. Once the site is up and running and you've begun to actually webcast—whether it's live events, on-demand, or push—you need to maintain your site. Given the constant state of change in the webcasting market and associated technologies, maintaining the site is likely to be at least as big a challenge as developing it. Because webcasting is still a very new technology with relatively few worthwhile market studies and even fewer experienced practitioners, it is difficult to obtain solid information on which to base your management decisions to, for example, determine the success of the webcasting project, or justify your ongoing expenses, or plan for any future expansion. In webcasting, as with any new and evolving technology, everyone is learning together. Chapter 7 focuses on the management issues involved in maintaining a webcast Website, but it is important to remember that the management issues (like everything else involved in web-casting) are very dependent on the specific type of webcasting that you're doing, as well as your application, your budget, and your (and your staff's) expertise in the underlying technologies.

Initially, you'll need to determine your personnel requirements for developing and maintaining the site and, if you're doing on-demand or push webcasting, you'll need to establish some sort of a routine for updating the information on your site. (Although updating is not an issue with live-event webcasting per se, you will almost certainly want to preserve the event tapes and make them available in an on-demand library, which will require some effort to maintain.) Finally, if you're doing live-event or on-demand webcasting, you're going to have to make sure that your target audience knows about your site and is motivated to visit it.

Personnel

The number of people necessary to operate a webcasting Website is directly proportional to the size of the project. We offer the following recommendations only as guidelines, not hard and fast rules.

Live Event Webcast with a Small Audience

A part-time crew of two or three people is probably sufficient for a small live-event webcasting project. You'll need one analog technology person to handle the audio and video setup and monitoring chores, including the microphones, sound mixing boards, video cameras, video mixers, lighting, and all other A/V devices. The second person should be responsible for everything digital, including the encoding machine and its operation, and setting up and managing the Internet connection and the video server software on the media server. If necessary, you can divide the digital responsibilities between two people, with one handling the encoding and the Internet connection, while the other manages the server side and the streaming media coming off the server. Both (or all) individuals should understand that quality control is part of their responsibilities; any number of problems can creep up between recording audio and video, encoding, sending it to the server via the Internet connection, and distributing it across the Internet.

Even if you're going to use a professional A/V team to handle recording and mixing the audio and/or video stream, you'll need at least two people to encode the video and get it to the Internet and a distribution server. Given the number of tasks that have to be completed and processes that have to be monitored, a crew of two is the absolute minimum for a small, live-event webcast, even if the event is taking place in a prepared and tested cyberstudio with dedicated Internet connectivity.

Live Event Webcast with a Large Audience

The number of people who need to be involved in a live-event webcast targeted toward an audience of 100+ doesn't increase proportionally with the size of the audience, but each member of the webcasting team needs to be a specialist. In general, a total of four or five people can handle a live-event webcast for any size audience if the production chores are farmed out to a professional crew and the in-house staff is only responsible for plugging the audio and video cables into their respective ports on the PCs. (You may, however, want to assign additional personnel to film the event behind the scenes to retain a copy in your own historical archives or as learning experience for future events.)

Two people may be required for the encoding and local network connectivity responsibilities. The event producer will in most cases want to webcast large events in more than one streaming media format, so you'll need multiple PCs for encoding the audio and video streams. The team members should be familiar with the PC equipment and the various streaming media software encoding programs, as well as the communications and distribution facilities. TCP/IP knowledge is a necessity.

One person can probably take responsibility for Internet connectivity, including installing and testing the high-speed leased lines prior to the event. This individual will also need to be familiar with configuring and managing the on-site router and have a good working relationship with the local telephone company. (If the leased line doesn't work, someone needs to be able to describe what's wrong and convince the telephone company to make the necessary repairs or changes.)

Another team member needs to be dedicated to managing the distribution server and splitter(s). This person needs to understand the media server software, the computer and its operating system, and any and all machines that are fed by splitters. This may involve responsibility for as many as 15 to 20 machines distributed on a nationwide network or the need to coordinate delivery of the streaming media to an MCI or itv.net distribution network. Once again, TCP/IP and system management skills are a must, along with a generous dose of diplomacy, especially if the event is being distributed through another network or networks.

The final member of the team is the manager/producer who is responsible for bringing all of the pieces together. This person coordinates activities with event planners, A/V technicians, and the webcasting technical crew. As we mentioned earlier, this person needs to have good communication and interpersonal skills and a firm conceptual grasp of the webcasting processes.

In an emergency or for a live-event webcast that uses only one streaming media format, you can probably pare the team size down to three people: an encoding/communications technician, a server person, and a team manager/coordinator. In this case, however, the encoding/communications person needs to be very highly skilled with PCs, router, and communications technologies, and the team manager needs to be able to back up the encoding person.

On-Demand Webcasting Site—Any Size

Typically, Internet connectivity is already established and the hosting and media servers are both up and running for an on-demand Webcast site. Unlike live-event webcasting, on-demand webcasting relies on existing audio or video that have already been translated into a digital format. Any necessary editing and/or adjustments to the sound track can be made before the digitized video is translated into an Internet-compatible format for storage and playback.

Staffing for an on-demand webcasting site is slightly different than for live-event webcasting, but two or three people are adequate for anything other than a site that processes and edits many hours of audio or video per week. One person can serve as the video encoder/editor while the other is responsible for the media server software and Website updating (that is, whenever new files are added). In most cases, the Web hosting machine and the media server are one and the same, so one person can handle both functions, as well as basic HTML and Web page updating. A third (optional) person can act as an activities coordinator to establish priorities for translating fresh videotapes into digital form and to review and acquire videotapes for use on the site.

Of course, if you're working on a very large scale or time-critical on-demand webcasting project, you're likely to need additional people to help with the encoding and editing and incorporating an audio or video search engine, database, or electronic program guide to display a directory for your users. You may also need another activities coordinator, depending on the volume of video that needs to be migrated from tape to digital form and the time frame in which the video has to go on-line. On-demand projects vary widely in the latter respect; 100 hours of videotape can become 10 hours of encoded video on-demand each week for ten weeks or 100 hours of video on-demand in a single week. For obvious reasons, the latter case requires more personnel as well as more computer hardware and software for encoding.

CHAPTER FIVE

DEVELOPING CONTENT

We all understand the world through sight, sound, feel, smell, and taste, and the more of these senses that we use, the richer are our experiences. Mass media has evolved to incorporate more of our senses with books, radio, and then television. Now, networked computers offer interactive multimedia.

All of these media still thrive because each has utility under different circumstances. Activity dictates which media you choose, such as reading a book in the bathtub or listening to the radio while driving your car. There are times, however, when you are prepared to sit down and offer your full attention to your computer. When you choose to enter into this interactive state, the Website that fills more of your senses will be the one that you find the most interesting.

Webcasting can enliven your existing content as well as provide the opportunity to develop new kinds of programming. Look at the benefits that webcasting offers, and then armed with a strategy, make your content choices, produce them with quality, package them for delivery, and schedule them for your audience's convenience.

Developing a Content Strategy

As we stressed in Chapter 2, webcasting is a business, and to be successful in any business venture, you need to have a specific strategy based on a concrete understanding of your target market.

In the case of webcasting, you need to know who your audience is and how large it is (that is, how many of them you intend to reach). To do this, you must anticipate the target audience's response to webcasting and understand the results that you need to achieve to consider your efforts a success.

To evaluate your audience for an intranet, explore the types of communication within each department of your company. Then look at the intercompany communication as well as the feed of information into the company from the outside.

For webcasting on the Internet you will be guided by your business model. You may be providing entertainment to increase the number and quality of visits to attract advertisers. Your site may be augmenting your marketing efforts in traditional print or broadcast media with detailed information or supporting existing customers. Many people are now creating sites for transactional purposes and delivering product on-line. In reality, your Website will probably be attempting to accomplish more than one of these objectives.

Once you have evaluated the types of communication needs that your audience has, decide what parts of your existing content could be more effective if presented by streaming or push. Then ask yourself what new content you can supply to your audience that takes advantage of the benefits of webcasting. Finally, look to see where you can get this content, or if needed, how you can produce it yourself.

After determining your content options, analyze the best webcasting technology to deliver that content. If it is live audio and video programming, you want to explore the opportunities inherent in streaming and on-demand technologies. If it is niche information that has a loyal audience of subscribers, then you may want to create a push channel.

In many cases, a combination of push and streaming technologies works well together. Push alerts can tell your users when a live webcast will take place and can automatically download the software that they will need to see the show.

Webcasting offers tremendous potential to increase communication, save money for your company, and provide the type of entertaining content that will drive users to your site to sell advertising or to market your product.

Selecting the Content

There are a variety of sources for webcast content. You can, for example:

- Repurpose existing content, such as converting your training videos to on-demand streamed files
- Buy it from sources such as Web content syndicators
- Have users generate it by allowing them to upload their own content (within guidelines)
- Create it from scratch

You will need to make your choices based upon your webcasting strategy and your budget.

Repurposing Existing Content

If you have an existing audience, you are already providing them content in some way. The nature of this existing content will determine whether you use live or on-demand streaming or push.

One of the best uses of live streaming content is when it can be broken up into individual units such as songs, videos, or television shows and past live events. A good use of live streaming is when these units exist in a continuous package, such as with a radio signal or with an event such as a guest speaker for your company, or a concert where the live factor adds to the appeal. A good use of push technology is the delivery of single units of specific interest to loyal subscribers. Delivering new versions of McAfee's antivirus software is an example of this. If you plan to repurpose content for on-demand streaming, you must either have existing audio or video or be prepared to produce it. For an intranet this might be a series of instructional videos from your company library. Live streaming would be used to webcast a guest speaker at a scheduled time. Push technology would be used to automatically download the calendar of meetings and events for that day and week.

If you are repurposing live-streamed content, you are probably either a broadcaster or are working with live events. There are three ways to provide repurposed live-streamed content: You can stream it yourself, rent server streams from an ISP, or form a partnership with a streamed content aggregator.

Dallas-based AudioNet, illustrated in Figure 5.1, is an example of an on-demand and live-streamed content aggregator.

CASE STUDY   AUDIONET

"My mission is to turn the Internet into a true broadcast medium," explained Mark Cuban, president and cofounder of AudioNet.

AudioNet (www.audionet.com) delivers more live and on-demand broadcasts with more viewers and listeners than any other company in the world. It originates about 75 percent of the commercial domestic webcasts. AudioNet webcasts a vast selection of live and on-demand content to Internet users around the world. Visitors can listen to live continuous broadcasts of more than 175 radio and television stations, play-by-play of thousands of college and professional sporting events, live music (including concerts and club performances), on-demand music from the CD Jukebox with more than 1,000 full-length CDs, live and on-demand shows, Internet-only webcasts, and live and on-demand corporate and special events.

The company has produced many large-scale events, including Super Bowls XXX and XXXI, the 1996 Major League Baseball World Series, the NHL Stanley Cup

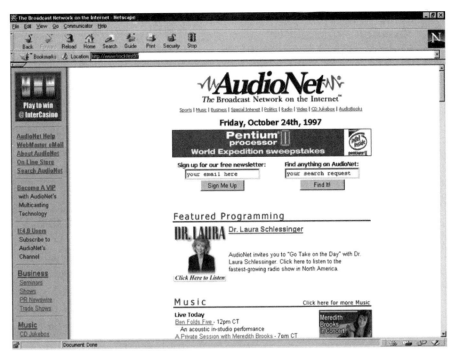

Figure 5.1 The AudioNet home page.

Finals, the NCAA Final Four basketball tournament, Intel CEO Andrew Grove's European Tour, C-SPAN daily broadcasts, presidential inauguration, and State of the Union message.

AudioNet webcasts or rebroadcasts via the Internet the largest number of live radio and television station signals. Its network includes America's top talk, sports, and music-oriented stations and networks. They offer every musical format through our growing network of radio stations from across the United States and Canada, including rock from WKLS in Atlanta, country from KZLA in Los Angeles, urban contemporary from KXOK in St. Louis, alternative from KNRK in Portland, jazz from WWOZ in New Orleans, and many more. AudioNet has delivered some of the largest live concerts on the Internet, including alternative chart-toppers Bush (courtesy of N2K productions), The Artist Formerly Known as Prince from Paisley Park Studio, and the Yes concert from Tower Records in Los Angeles.

AudioNet features a variety of shows, covering music, computers, sports, politics, and other special interest categories. For example, "Tech Talk" discusses high-tech trends while "Women in Music" features top female musicians. Many of their shows, like Ann-Online, are created specifically for the Internet. Popular talk shows with hosts like Janice Malone and Eliot Stein feature commentary from a variety of interesting guests each week. Fans who miss a live show can access archived broadcasts any time and listen on-demand.

AudioNet also offers Internet and intranet broadcasting services to corporations and organizations of all types. The company's technology enables the cost-effective, live broadcast of special events, such as annual shareholder meetings, quarterly earnings calls, conference calls, speeches, press conferences, product introductions, conventions, trade shows, political debates, and award ceremonies.

Buying Sources of Content

Buying sources of content for your webcast may mean licensing or purchasing, such as when you become part of an affiliated network that supplies streamed content.

We discuss some of the legal ramifications of licensing or purchasing content in Chapter 8, but you should be aware that either arrangement typically involves some type of payment, length, and specific type of re-use of their content. If, for example, you join an affiliate network, you will need to either pay cash or trade advertising time or ad banners. JamTV (www.jamtv.com) has an affiliate program that supplies live webcasts to its radio station affiliates in exchange for promotion.

The content fees common in traditional broadcasting translate onto the Internet. Playing music, for example, requires you to have to pay a licensing fee to the American Society of Composers, Authors and Publishers (ASCAP at www.ascap.com) and/or Broadcast Music, Inc. (BMI at http://bmi.com/licensing/web.html). Reuters has begun providing news in streamed audio. You can listen to the latest news clips from Reuters at www.grit.net. TheDJ Website (www.theDJ .com), seen here in Figure 5.2, is a new type of Internet radio station that streams more than 50 continuous, uninterrupted channels of

Figure 5.2　TheDJ Website home page.

music over the Web. TheDJ gets its content from record labels and, much like a traditional radio station, must pay the appropriate licenses and fees.

CASE STUDY   TheDJ

According to Jim Van Huysse, director of Communications and Content at TheDJ, "on-demand music is a bit dangerous. The Digital Performance Rights in Sound Recordings Act of 1995 limits its use; interactive broadcasters must obtain permission from artists and labels to broadcast music."

TheDJ, which is hoping to become the most popular source of music on the Internet, has an interactive site (TheDJi) for which it has obtained permission. The site is licensed by both BMI and ASCAP. Van Huysse says that the company is endeavoring to amass a music library that can provide a single source for people to learn about, listen to, and purchase music quickly and easily on the Net. "We are dedicated to providing a music-broadcasting vehicle with a degree of interaction and content depth far surpassing current radio formats."

TheDJ Network has created TheDJ Music Partner Program, which allows it to expand content on both its mainstream and Indie music channels while providing an effective distribution mechanism for record labels. The site currently represents more than 90 Indie labels and is partnering with Trans Cosmos of Japan to develop a Japanese version of the software for the specific purpose of showcasing global music content.

To broadcast the music, TheDJ uses Real Networks' RealAudio software which streams FM radio quality audio directly to the listener so it can only be played back in real time, not downloaded or copied.

TheDJ requires a label's permission to play music interactively for both its domestic and international versions. Recording companies retain the right to remove their music from any TheDJ site for any reason. In addition, the company provides proprietary software that includes functions such as customizable presets, a "Rate This Song" feature, and a "Buy This CD!" link, 10 preset channels, and a scan (try before you buy) feature.

End-User Created Content

In the past decade, video cameras have become so pervasive that it sometimes seems as if everything is being captured on film. Major television networks, recognizing the opportunities in this, turned these videos into the basis for content on shows such as *America's Funniest Home Videos* and *Real TV*. Newspapers have a longer history of using photographs from their readers due to the public abundance of still cameras. Now it's common to see amateur video footage on television news. Some of this content is so compelling and strong that the exposure it receives is greater than anything that a studio could have produced. An example of this is the video of police beating Rodney King.

The Internet brought a new era of communication by giving the general public the power to easily and inexpensively self-publish. Webcasting is the newest empowerment, enabling most anyone to produce their own audio and video shows.

You can take advantage of the same opportunity as the television networks by either tapping into the great public archive of audio/video content to produce shows for webcasts or by becoming a content aggregator where other individuals or companies provide the content and the production and you provide branding or webcasting technology.

GeoCities (www.geocities.com) has become one of the most highly visited sites on all of the Web by implementing the basics of this idea. GeoCities users can create their own Websites for free within an on-line neighborhood of their specific interests. Most of the site traffic comes from the content creators themselves.

Similarly, Microsoft's M3P program (www.m3p.msn.com/newlang .htm) solicits multimedia productions for MSN, and AudioNet's AudioNet Personal Broadcast Network program lets aspiring musicians, talk show hosts, and other future stars create and deliver their own weekly Internet radio shows and broadcast them live.

Create New Content

If you do not have existing content that can be modified for webcasting or if you are creating something new specifically to take advantage of live, on-demand, or push technologies, you'll probably need to produce content from scratch. Creating new content for a company intranet may, for example, involve filming a live news broadcast for employees, as the Boeing Company does. This type of project would have been cost-prohibitive prior to availability of webcasting. Another possible use would be to record an applicant for a job and place the video clip on-demand for several people to evaluate. In both cases the audio or video clip could also be pushed to the evaluators.

Creating new content for Internet webcasting can also be as easy as setting up a live camera. It may also be as involved as in creating a product demo on a marketing site, creating your own film, or a radio talk show.

GRIT Internet Broadcasting (www.grit.com), seen here in Figure 5.3, was one of the first Internet-only broadcasters. GRIT creates and produces original talk shows for live and on-demand.

CASE STUDY   GRIT INTERNET BROADCASTING

GRIT Internet Broadcasting webcasts an information talk format to a worldwide audience, billing itself as "The Talk of the Internet." The format is intentionally

Figure 5.3   GRIT Internet broadcasting home page.

nonintrusive so that people can listen in and still continue to work at their computers.

According to Rob Gould, president of GRIT, the content has one central theme: everything we do leads people to Websites. GRIT's content is all-talk Web reviews that advise listeners which Websites to visit. Each GRIT show has its own on-demand page with links to the sites that are reviewed during that show. Each page has information about the specific show, as well as a link to download the necessary software. The company also produces international broadcasts from all over the world for corporate clients like Chase Manhattan Bank and the National Federation of the Blind.

According to Gould, when GRIT creates a production, it takes a site, current event, or famous guest and blocks out some time, then broadcasts the session live in its state-of-the-art sound studio. The company has a complete mixing board, commercials, and three microphones with two incoming lines for phone guests. Sometimes the company takes smaller equipment and crew on the road for remote broadcasts, then streams the material out through their network of servers over the Internet in Microsoft NetShow and/or Real Networks' RealAudio format. The company also takes some of its most popular programs and makes them available on-demand so that people can listen at their leisure.

Choosing to create your own content is likely to be the most challenging and costly source of webcast programming. It is the most important, however, as it will be the content that is uniquely suited to webcasting. This is what will drive your intranet and Internet efforts as well as what will allow webcasting to fulfill its potential as the world's newest medium.

Scheduling Your Content

Although you initially need to decide when to make on-demand content available, the benefit of on-demand is just that, it is *on-demand*. As we mentioned in Chapter 1, on-demand webcasting is much like a VCR that doesn't require advance planning or programming. Your audience can play on-demand content whenever it wants, and rewind, fast forward, and pause during the playback. In many ways, on-demand webcasting is the optimal way of delivering content; your audience has it whenever they want it. Live events and push alerts are time-sensitive and require more strategy.

Scheduling Live Streaming

Most live-event webcasts (for example, concerts or conferences) are currently produced for a live audience or another medium such as television. Webcasts of these events subscribe to an existing schedule. When concerts and events are planned specifically for a webcast you will be able to choose the optimal time for your audience.

For a one-time event, the knowledge of your audience determines how you schedule your live webcast. Scheduling for a small and known intranet audience is much easier than for a general audience on the Internet. The worst-case scenario on the Internet is having a first-time webcast with no existing audience. The best is an audience so loyal that they have subscribed to your webcast channel so that you can let them know in advance, either through posting on the Website or with push technology, precisely when the event is going to take place.

For a general Internet webcast, you will most likely need to use traditional marketing tactics to let users know when to tune in. Once again, if you know your audience well enough to have an existing traditional communication channel such as a radio or TV station or magazine, you have a distinct advantage.

When is the best time of the day to webcast? According to Mark Cuban, president and cofounder of AudioNet: "For business, daytime is best because office workers have no other type of information or entertainment. For entertainment, the evening is best. A new phenomena is that everyone checks their e-mail when they come home at night. So if you can give them some entertainment while they check and read, you win."

Depending on your budget and the amount of content available to you, the best strategy for scheduling live webcasts is to have a consistent schedule. Regularly scheduled programming allows a user to anticipate when they need to get on-line to see their show. Radio and television have already learned this lesson.

CNET (www.cnet.com) is a television and Internet company that webcasts live three times a day with CNET Radio. The company also does some live-event webcasting such as conferences, panel discussions, keynotes, or exclusive interviews and, along with Intel, has created a Webisode Website: Mediadome. (A Webisode is a Website that focuses on a particular subject, such as top musical artists, major motion pictures, or comic book heros.) Each Webisode offers a variety of interactive elements that allows users to become participants rather than just observers. CNET offers on-demand content for each Webisode, scheduling an on-demand offering every two weeks.

GRIT Internet Broadcasting webcasts original content on a more regular schedule: 24 hours a day, 7 days a week. Each day, it broadcasts live from 12:00 to 1:00 P.M. (ET) leading off with "What's New, What's Hot" at 12:00 and following up with a feature show, then national and international news and the latest technology news from Reuters.

Content Schedule Guides

We all know how to use the television guides that are printed in our local newspapers or in specialty magazines like *TV Guide* to find out what is appearing on broadcast television. And cable television has channels that scroll a schedule. The Internet has similar guides that we can refer to on-line, but these guides also incorporate links to take us directly to the webcast we're interested in. The guides are often delivered on the Websites of existing webcasting technology companies such as Real Networks' Timecast (www.timecast.com), as shown in Figure 5.4, or content aggregators like AudioNet. The guides categorize content in a number of ways, including live versus on-demand, by type such as film or radio, or by audio or video. Some allow you to search by topic, while others provide entertaining interfaces such as an audio jukebox.

Webcast sites that originate the programming rely on having a schedule as a main part of the site. Live webcasts receive more urgent promotion than on-demand and are the focus of the home page at the time of the webcast. As mentioned in Chapter 1, electronic program guides (EPG) are being developed for use over many networks and Internet devices. Standards for EPG use are being proposed by the ITU.

Figure 5.4 Real Networks' Timecast guide.

Automatic On-Demand Archiving

With the enormous amounts of on-demand content that can be produced, some technology helps schedule on-demand content automatically. TheDJ, for example, uses proprietary technology called TheDJ Media Server that employs Virtual DJs to schedule content on their channels. They decide what songs are to be included on channels and program playlists every night for the following day. The Virtual DJs are pseudointelligent in the sense that they do not program the songs from the same artist in a given period. These programs also take listener "Rate This Song" data into account when they generate the playlists.

Other programs can automatically transfer live-streamed content to on-demand content. One such application is Real Networks' Real-

Server. The RealServer can be configured to automatically archive live broadcasts into a single on-demand file; an on-demand file based on elapsed time, such as every 30 minutes; or an on-demand file based on size, such as every 5 MB. The archive files can then be stored in a target directory. To remedy the enormous storage requirements of an automated archiving process, RealServer software can be programmed to automatically overwrite existing events with the same name. To create an archive of events, you merely assign unique file names to each version of the event. This does, of course, require a huge quantity of disk space.

Free Range Media (www.freerange.com) provides a content management tool called AudioVCR, which archives, rearranges, and manages audio content from a simple GUI. It eliminates the step of creating digital sound files. Instead, you can create files directly from live-streamed content. This opens the possibility for advertising opportunities by letting you attach advertising leaders to every program file you create. Because the leaders are attached to the files, rather than being part of the program recording, you can change advertisements at will.

AudioVCR software also allows you to manage from anywhere. You can take your laptop and a microphone to a live event and record. You then upload the program file to your Web server, tell AudioVCR where the file is, and schedule it into your programming.

Scheduling Push Alerts

When you schedule your push alerts depends upon whether your alerts are for regularly scheduled content or to announce timely information such as an upcoming live webcast. Because it is intrusive, push is a powerful form of webcasting. It can also be extremely annoying to users. So, if a user has entrusted you by signing up for a channel, you have a responsibility to act as a *guest* when delivering information.

As we mentioned earlier, electronic mail is the oldest form of push technology. CNET, with a wide variety of newsletter dispatches, currently has the largest number of mailing list subscribers:

the most successful being the company's CNET.COM's Digital Dispatch, which is delivered to more than 850,000 subscribers once a week. CNET's NEWS.COM dispatch is delivered daily.

Another example, JamTV (www.jamtv.com) uses e-mail regularly in conjunction with BackWeb Infoflashes to reach their viewers directly with concert and other music information.

Dynamically Updating Push Channels

Seattle's Intermind (www.intermind.com) offers a software program called Dynamic Publisher that webcasters use to update channels on the fly when there are specific changes in databases, Website content, or output from search engines. This program is particularly effective in data-intensive environments where new information is constantly being generated and must be delivered in a timely manner, such as a travel service Website that wants to provide its subscribers with updates that are relevant only to their prespecified destination and recreational preferences. Because travel packages change constantly, the publisher can use this software to automatically feed the information to the channels they have created.

The best advice is to schedule your content with your audience in mind. There may be events that are not within your control and which will create greater demands upon your marketing, but try to provide regularly scheduled programming that is in accord with your audience's preferences.

Content Design Considerations

Your audience, their hardware, software, and the speed of their connection will determine how you design your webcast programming. Webcasting to the broad general audience on the Internet is obviously far more difficult than targeting personnel on a corporate intranet.

Users on the Internet can have virtually any type of webcast client software and be capable of any variety of connection speeds. The most challenging situation is a one-time or first-time Internet webcast where you don't know your audience and there is little time to specify software for download. You need to assume that your audience is using a 28.8 Kbps modem and one of the popular client software packages. To reach the largest possible audience under this circumstance, you probably want to provide the webcast in several formats.

The longer you know your webcasting audience, the more you learn about their technology and content preferences. If you have a core of loyal followers, you can create a standard for the technology and scheduling of your webcasts. As the relationship with your audience becomes stronger, your flexibility increases.

Of course, the best webcast situation is over an intranet. You not only know your audience and bandwidth, but you also have control over the webcasting environment. You can dictate variables such as the use of a specific type of webcasting software.

General Webcasting Page Design

When creating your webcasting pages be a designer or information architect, not a fine artist. A fine artist creates to fulfill a personal desire or to express a personal feeling. A designer defines and solves problems to achieve a specific goal. Allow the user to immediately understand what the webcast is and how to navigate. Keep text that surrounds the audio/video short and lively. If you absolutely need to add more text, do it with hyperlinks within your paragraphs.

Consistency will reinforce your identity on every page. Don't force viewers to relearn each page as they come to it, either in different pages or in different visits. Try to keep your navigational elements in the same place as you go from page to page.

You undermine the purpose of streaming when the Web page that houses it downloads at an unbearably slow speed. Stay away from large, fancy graphics if you are reaching an audience with 28.8 Kbps modems. Keep the graphics easy to understand and simple to use.

To account for variances in connection speed, some Websites provide dual versions, one for 28.8 Kbps modems and below and another for 56 Kbps modems and above. You should provide this courtesy with your webcasts by allowing audio and video produced for different connectivity speeds. Providing several forms of media on a webcast allows all users to experience the event in at least some way. Provide the tools that your users will need by offering links to download the software from the pages that have live and on-demand content.

Designing for a Live Webcast

Designing around a continuous live stream of packaged content is challenging because of the variety of changing content found in a live stream. Radio and television sites that offer live streaming provide content that augments the shows and music that is being played in the stream. Some companies such as Intervox Communications (www.intervox.com) provide Now Playing Technology software, where a live audio and video stream initiates a change of live text, graphics, and ad content on the Website that matches your webcast audio or video.

Make the upcoming webcast the star on the page. Other content on the page should complement this primary focus. People want to see a hierarchy of elements. If images are all the same size, there is no distinction of order. Guide the viewer's eye through the different elements surrounding the audio or video.

Designing for a live event broadcast divides your efforts into before, during, and after sections. Prior to the event, your site serves as a marketing tool to prepare the audience for the show. You want to make sure that they know when it is and that they have the software they will need to listen or view the event. You want them to remember to come back at the right time, so you need to make the preshow content entertaining to encourage the users to invest their time and to feel as if they are already part of the event.

During the event, surround the stream with options in both content and technology. You may want to use speaker biographies, statistical data, or general background information to accompany business or educational events on an intranet webcast, for example. Live events webcast over the Internet may incorporate chat facilities, text of live interviews, roving commentary, and/or backstage coverage.

But remember, content that augments a live audio broadcast should be complementary without being intrusive. The audience should be able to continue to read and browse while they are tuned into the live stream. Similarly, the content that surrounds a live video webcast should help the audience to understand what they will be watching since there is less attention available for other media once the show actually begins.

N2K (www.n2k.com) is an example of an Internet webcaster that surrounds its webcasts with rich content. Based in New York City, N2K is a leading on-line music entertainment company. It operates a network of music-oriented Websites that include Music Boulevard, Jazzcentralstation.com (shown in Figure 5.5), classicalinsites

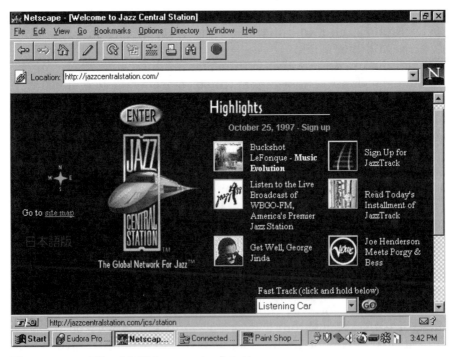

Figure 5.5   The N2K Jazzcentralstation page.

.com, and rocktropolis.com. N2K surrounds its webcasts with original stories, interviews, gossip, tour information, features, CD reviews, and chat facilities and offers its audience the opportunity to purchase the music they are hearing.

CASE STUDY   N 2 K

David Pakman, the senior director of Business Development at N2K reminds us that the two largest demand generators in music today—radio and live performance—end by foiling a customer's attempt to *buy* what they just heard. It is difficult to find a store, go to it, find the record, and buy it. On-line performances, on the other hand, allow the user to listen, sample, and purchase—all in one sitting. N2K always has the artist's releases available for purchase during its webcasts. Other webcasters that are interested in capitalizing on the audience's demand to buy can enroll on N2K's Remote Access Music (RAM) program (at www.musicblvd.com/ram) and offer musical titles for sale on their respective sites with N2K fulfilling customer orders (and, of course, collecting a commission for handling each sale).

N2K's investment in content is massive. The company has exclusive relationships with hundreds of content partners including magazines, artists, labels, journalists, radio stations, and so on. The goal of becoming a supersite within each musical genre requires a significant amount of content, both historical and current. To that end, each N2K site includes a team of editors and feature writers to create custom content. For example, Allstar Magazine, which is the news section of Rocktropolis, creates five original stories each day, in addition to interviews, gossip, tour information, features, and CD reviews.

The director of programming lays out programming objectives across all of the N2K sites. Each site has a site director, who must take these programming objectives and turn them into themes and specifics. Each team creates content and a format within these themes. All of the sites are database-driven, which allows the publishing process to be flexible. Stories and features can be written anywhere around the world and uploaded into the company database, then instantly placed in the appropriate site without further design or layout. N2K continuously polls its users and monitors their feedback to determine the most popular sections and features of each site, then tweaks the programming based on that information.

Each N2K site follows a similar format: all have chat, BBS, interviews with accompanying media elements (art, photos, audio, video, etc.), streaming programming, titles for sale, and so forth. Programming decisions are made by content and user desire rather than by technology features. The goal of the sites, for example, is to create communities by musical genre. The goal is not to provide chat for users, although chat is an important feature in helping to build a community of followers. The difference is subtle, yet fundamental. When an interview with Mötley Crüe is a feature on Rocktropolis, a video clip will be with the interview if the video content accompanying it is great. Formats (QuickTime, MPEG, etc.) are chosen to reach the widest variety of users in the highest quality possible. N2K stresses the fact that it is a content company, not a technology company.

Designing for On-Demand

You should design your on-demand streaming as an archive where shows can be accessed easily through a directory or search. Some sites like GRIT Internet Broadcasting provide a page that has specific information about the content of each of their live Internet shows, as well as a link to download the necessary software to hear the show. These links take the user to the Website of the technology company that GRIT has chosen to work with.

Webcast aggregators like Real Network's Timecast and AudioNet have massive amounts of on-demand content. They rely on pages that are accessed like a regular Website, in directory trees. They also rely on internal search engines.

Unlike designing for live webcasts, content surrounding the on-demand stream can take more of a leadership role. On-demand audio may exist to complement other types of media such as chat.

Some sites like CNET's Mediadome, shown in Figure 5.6, choose to use on-demand content as its primary webcast offering.

CASE STUDY   CNET

CNET takes advantage of the narrowcasting capabilities of webcasting to expand the audio/video delivery capabilities of broadcast and cable television. According to Kevin Edwards, senior multimedia producer, "Many of our TV segments must be cut down to five minutes or so, but if we have an exclusive interview or performance, we can put the whole thing up in streaming audio/video format." The company's presentation of a segment on David Bowie's fiftieth birthday party offers an example of its flexibility. The TV show was 30 minutes long (including commercials), and the TV.COM segment was about four minutes long, but CNET provided more than two hours of

Figure 5.6   CNET's Mediadome home page.

exclusive interviews, rare performances, and clips on-line all indexed by song or subject.

CNET offers weekly on-demand webcasts of its TV shows: TV.COM, The Web, and The New Edge. In addition, the company teams up with CNET Radio for three live webcasts each day. Most of its live webcasts result from the company obtaining the rights to web-cast a concert with one of the performers featured in a Mediadome Webisode. Edwards stresses the impor-tance of developing compelling content. "If one of our webcasts is going to be audio-only, we try as much as possible to give the audience compelling content to accompany the audio. We try not to just duplicate the audio with text but offer additional content in the text to let people mentally multitask. If it's audio on-demand, it's usually just the opposite, the audio is additional information to accompany the text. If it's audio/video, we try to provide the details necessary for people to get an understanding of what they're getting into by starting the stream. Once they start the stream, they are less likely to browse while a video stream is going."

The company uses a variety of products and technologies to satisfy its audience's wide range of interests and capabilities, including Mbed, Shockwave, RealAudio, RealVideo, StreamWorks, Vivo, Microsoft NetShow, and Vxtreme.

Designing for Push

Push technology also involves a set of content design criteria, whether the content is targeted toward the captive audience on an intranet or the general audience of the Internet. It is important to remember that when a user subscribes to your push channel, he or she has chosen you above other possible information sources on the Web and is entrusting you to provide consistently accurate and current information. Keep this relationship in mind when you are designing content and allow the users to make the decisions on what they want. Provide them with options based on the point of their inquiry and offer them lots of room to make decisions based on their needs. Because push is intrusive, the design of your channel needs to be polite in both how it alerts the user and the amount of information that it delivers.

For example, nearly everyone objects to blatant e-mail advertising or uninvited junk e-mail that downloads a file onto your computer. This misuse of push technology, which leaves users feeling as if they have been violated, makes it more difficult to accept the legitimate, polite forms of push that can actually add value.

Some push software automatically alerts users when new information has been added to a Website. If this type of facility is used in the right situation (i.e., when the information is timely and relevant), it can be invaluable. An alert should be as benign as a phone ring, door knock, service bell, or any of the other alerts that we use in everyday life. Don't use alerts unless you have a legitimate application and, if you do use an alert, don't show up screaming to be let in, just knock. One push vendor, BackWeb, is very savvy in the etiquette of push design.

CASE STUDY   BACKWEB

Deborah Lacy of BackWeb Technologies emphasizes that "the point of using push for an intranet is to make life easier, whether to enhance the flow of information so users make better decisions or to distribute software updates to reduce the cost of PC ownership. There have been plenty of great programs that, because they couldn't be implemented or executed, have been left in the dustbins of the corporate world. The implementation of push in the enterprise is governed by the same rules."

She offers the following guidelines for creating material for a BackWeb-style push channel:

1. The material needs to have all user interface components present in the graphics. Unlike a Web browser, which contains many of the controls used to navigate, push technology users are completely dependent on the controls added by the developer. Have you ever wound up on a

Web page that has no links? Think what it would be like if you didn't have the browser there, with its back button to help you out.

2. The controls that are added by the developer need to be standardized, so they are both easily recognizable and accessible by users. Although it's been said many times before, the Internet is a global medium, so many users will not recognize even one-word descriptions of a button's function. Having recognizable controls adds to the user's comfort and enhances his or her experience. For clients, using push is like inviting someone into their home. Developers need to remember that they are guests and follow the conventions already laid down by user interface experts so that their visit is remembered fondly and they are likely to be invited back.

3. While many push vendors say there are no size limits, there *are* size limits. An oft-espoused virtue of push is "no more waiting." While this is true to a great extent, there still is no way around the time it takes to physically push bits across the Internet. There are many issues such as:

   ◆ Is the material you are delivering time-sensitive?

   ◆ Do your users only access the Web briefly or have a slow connection?

   ◆ Are your users jealous of their disk space and/or system resources?

   ◆ Are others (such as other channels) competing for your bandwidth?

When developing for a push channel, all of these considerations and more come into play. Yes, the user does not have to wait for information to come down, but a far greater consideration is how the size of your data affects the delivery of your message.

4. The content, when it gets there, better be compelling! Many people begin their foray into push publishing with the goal of driving more traffic to their Website. Push publishing *is* about generating more traffic, but it's much more—it's also about building a relationship. Everybody has met someone about whom they could say, he's very nice, but he's *boring.* Such is the way with push. Sending a presentation that forces users directly to the Web is a tragic misuse of the medium, akin to setting up a complete home theater and then using it to watch reruns of *ADAM-12.* Push allows you to develop levels of presentation that are otherwise impossible, drawing users further into your message and captivating them. Once users are interested in your presentation and want more, they'll be clamoring for your Website. Push is a tool for providing a broader, richer experience for which users don't have to wait. Forcing them directly to a browser is anticlimactic.

Creating the Alert

The alert creates the user's first impression of your channel and is likely to be the one most remembered by users. Do you want to be remembered as the genteel guest who enlivened the evening's conversation, or the dog who wasn't housebroken? A few tips:

1. Keep it small; it's a teaser, to draw the user inside.
2. Don't use sound; the annoyance factor is far more costly than any benefit it may bring.
3. Stay to the edges; if the user likes what he or she sees, he or she is more likely to invite you to the middle of the screen.

The alert is the knock on the door to see if you're welcome. Once people click on the alert, they've invited you in and, chances are, you know what they want (be it raucous and extreme or discreet and refined). Remember, many of the users you target will be in office environments, and there's nothing like an unwelcome noise—and the embarrassment that goes with it—to have someone remove your channel from their system.

Internet versus Intranet

Although issues such as branding, look and feel, and consistency are paramount in both environments, these three elements reign supreme in an intranet. When you create content for the enterprise environment, the material must be:

1. Readily recognizable in terms of source and content
2. Easy to use to promote efficiency
3. As close to identical in functionality as possible so that users can extract the knowledge they need, practically in their sleep

The dynamics of webcasting have clearly created new demands on Website design. Live and on-demand streaming and push each have individual qualities that require separate considerations to highlight the benefits of each.

Producing the Content for Webcasting

When you produce content for webcasting, you are generally trading off quality for usability. Your audience, subject matter, and bandwidth will determine the quality that you can retain in your productions.

You can usually create better technical content for a company intranet than the Internet because of the higher bandwidth available on the intranet and less demanding types of information (i.e., text and simple graphics). You will also have more control over the capturing environment. Subjects for training videos, speeches, and meetings can be coached for the best results and the physical area can be altered. Backdrops can be made as simple as possible, proper lighting and microphone placement can be obtained. Subjects will know not to use extreme inflections in speech and to keep still on camera.

Unless you are doing a studio-based production like an Internet talk show, the subject matter for entertainment over the Internet has a lower chance of being within your control. There will be more motion in audio and video. Live events such as concerts are filled with music, colored lights, and moving band members.

Both audio and visual content can be broken down into components. Audio is composed of samples and resolution. Video can be broken down into frames as well as resolution and colors. If your user's eyes and ears receive these components at a certain rate they perceive them as being realistic. The challenge in providing audio and visual over phone lines is to keep file sizes functional through manipulation of these components, yet retain their quality. Providing on-line video is difficult because of its great demands on bandwidth. However, small clips and streaming make it possible to webcast moving images.

When producing audio and visual content, the single most important factor is the quality of the original capture. You should record and shoot at the highest quality level available to ensure that you have the best samples before beginning the editing process. Keep in mind that this content you are gathering can also be repurposed for other uses such as CDs, tapes, and videos.

Producing audio and visual streaming content for your webcast involves two steps: (1) content capture and (2) editing. Creating a push channel allows you to imbed various multimedia for your alert interface and requires special software depending upon the technology you plan to use.

Audio

As we mentioned in Chapter 4, audio webcasting is significantly easier than video webcasting because without the visual content there is much less demand on memory for production and streaming. Thus, there are many more webcasting sites using audio streaming than there are using video streaming.

Capture

Begin the capture phase of audio content development with the best recording setup possible given your budget and personnel constraints, if any. If possible, record in a studio. If you can't record in a studio, try to make the recording environment conducive to good sound reproduction. Use a professional microphone in acoustically positive surroundings. If you are recording several subjects, use a separate microphone for each. And be sure to test record and set microphone levels before the event.

If possible, record at CD quality (i.e., a sampling rate of 44.1 KHz and a resolution of 16 bits). At a minimum, record at 22,050 Hz. And record in stereo because you can always go from there to mono if necessary—but not the other way around. Be sure to make the input level as high as possible (without distortion) when you are recording and keep in mind that one minute of stereo CD quality sound recording takes up 10 MG of storage space on your hard drive. So, be sure you have lots of hard drive space available!

Once you've finished recording the sound, you'll need to feed the audio source into your computer. If you are recording directly into your computer, keep the microphone away from the computer because it can be noisy.

Editing

When you are preparing sound files that will not be streamed, you'll need to downsample them to reduce their download time. As a reference, downloading one minute of 44.1-MHz, 16-bit CD quality sound will take approximately 11 hours over a 14.4 Kbps modem, 5 hours over a 28.8 Kbps, 2.5 hours over a 56 Kbps modem, and 38 minutes over a dedicated T1 facility.

How much you downsample depends upon your content matter. It is generally advisable to downsample voice more than music. Music can retain its quality if reduced to half of that of a CD to 22,050 MHz and 8 bits. Voice is still fine at one-quarter of CD quality at 11,025MHz and 8 bits.

There are a variety of formats available for saving your audio files. AU is generally good for voice, and WAV or AIFF are preferable for saving higher-quality audio such as music. WAV files can be read by all Windows and most Macintosh sound programs and by the Windows and Macintosh versions of Navigator and Explorer.

To edit for the best type of file for on-demand streaming you will alter your sound file in a variety of ways to allow quality encoding. Use compression to turn down the loudest parts of your audio to enable the entire file to be louder, use expansion or noise gating to turn off the quietest unwanted parts, and use equalizing to turn up the most important parts of your audio. The last thing you do is to normalize your audio, which is a function of your recording software that automatically makes the sound file as loud as possible without distortion.

Save the files into sound file formats such as WAV, AIFF, and AU as an uncompressed file.

You are now ready to use a streaming encoder or multimedia authoring tool to filter and compress the file. Some editing tools work with streaming encoders to allow you to produce the final file from one application. The tools and instruction for encoding your files vary depending on the technology you choose.

Video

Adding visual attributes to a webcast may be as simple as using still photographs or as involved as streaming video. Due to higher bandwidth connections, intranets are more conducive to streamed video delivery than is the Internet, which generally reaches a user with a 28.8 Kbps modem. This is changing, however, with higher line speeds and better compression technologies.

Capture

You can use either a conventional film camera or a digital camera to shoot still photos for a slide show-like webcast. But conventional images require photo processing and scanning to put them into digital format. If you use a digital camera (and have the appropriate software), you can download the files directly into your computer. After you've loaded the images into your computer (by whatever method), you can sequence and/or stream them with audio to produce a reasonable facsimile of realistic motion video.

When capturing video, once again you should start with the best possible source material. If possible, avoid using regular indoor lighting since low-level lighting is likely to produce odd colors and video noise, otherwise known as snow. Try to use professional quality lighting equipment, use solid color and no patterns for backgrounds, and avoid unnecessary motion such as panning or zooming. The various video formats yield different qualities when digitized. The best formats in order of quality are: Beta (which is what professionals use), Laserdisc, Super-VHS, then VHS. Film may also be converted to digital for streaming.

The more powerful your PC, the better you'll be able to work with video. Use the guidelines for audio as the minimum. Save your files in the proper format in 24-bit color depth. Do not compress your files.

Editing for Nonstreamed On-Demand

The memory demands for video are much larger than for audio. The frame rate for video and television quality is 30 fps. Once digitized, one frame at standard resolution produces 780,000 bits of uncompressed data. A CD-ROM can store only 30 seconds of uncompressed video.

Apple's QuickTime format is generally a good choice for a video format. It currently has the largest market share and is compatible with both Windows and Apple Macintosh. It is also quite conducive to editing. Other video format options include Microsoft AVI and Active Movie as well as MPEG Video.

You will need to compromise your video in a number of ways to make it functional. The size of the screen for playback will not be a full screen, or even as big as a CD-ROM image. The frame rate will not be even close to 30 fps and even the CD frame rate of 10 to 15 fps will not work for on-line purposes. If necessary, you can reduce the bandwidth demands by making the movie gray scale instead of color and reducing the quality of audio. Once you've finished editing, you can compress your video.

MediaCast (www.mediacast.com), the first company to specialize in live Internet broadcast solutions, produced the Primus webcast in May 1996, shown in Figure 5.7.

CASE STUDY   MEDIACAST'S PRIMUS WEBCAST

John Luini, of MediaCast, recalls the steps required for the Primus webcast. "Once we decided to take on the task of bringing a band like Primus to the Net with a live show, we began to realize the tremendous amount of preproduction coordination that was necessary with the label company, the venue, and the band's management. In addition, there was constant interaction with the band and touring management."

The Promotion

Does a falling tree in a forest make a sound if no one is there to hear it? Producing a webcast is not very useful if no one is there to experience it. To begin promoting its webcast, MediaCast used its own events newsletter and, to build local awareness of the event, established a relationship with local San Francisco Bay radio station Live 105 for on-air promotion. But most importantly, it wanted to reach the huge audience of Primus fans on the Internet! To this end, the company worked closely with the band while it was on tour around the country to bring Tales From The Road to the event Website. MediaCast digitized and uploaded content received from the road for two weeks prior to the live webcast. It

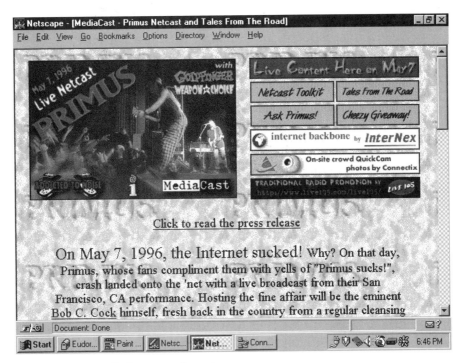

Figure 5.7 A Primus webcast.

also worked closely with the band's official Website (www.primussucks.com) and formed an alliance with the record label and management to sponsor a promotional giveaway contest, allowing fans to answer questions about the band and win CDs, shirts, and posters.

The Network Architecture

Internet connectivity to the venue was secured in the form of three ISDNs that dialed up into the MediaCast network partner for the event (Internex). Streaming media and content from MediaCast's Living Web Page was uploaded and sent through the ISDN lines into a colocated server network for redistribution to the Internet audience. According to Luini, this arrangement required bringing only as much bandwidth into the venue as necessary to send a single copy of all content out to the redistribution servers. "It doesn't make sense to spend tens of thousands of dollars installing a T3 line into a venue for a single show!" And, because of physical limitations, the company also had a plain old telephone (POTS) dial-up line for use in the live chat backstage.

The Delivery Technology

At the time of this event, live streaming was still in its early stages, so in order to reach as wide an audience as possible, MediaCast used a wide variety of technologies to deliver the show. To reach everyone—from 14.4 Kbps dial-up users to those with T1 access—the company used Mbone, CU-SeeMe, and RealAudio for real-time video and audio streaming. Live chat was used backstage before the show, and a variety of proprietary systems were used to automate the uploading of digital photographs and editorial coverage into the Living Web Pages. Other on-demand-based content was encoded using QTVR (for a virtual 360-degree panorama of the venue), QuickTime (for preshow emcee introductions and live video clips), and MPEG audio.

The On-Location Layout

One of the keys to a successful live webcast is being able to gather all of the required content without getting in the way of the normal live production that is occurring at the same time. MediaCast brought in its own video (BETA-SP) and audio (live to DAT board and ambient room mix) crews and arranged for the necessary space for them with the sound board in the main hall. The audio and video feeds were sent out to a command central operation in the lobby area. The physical setup allowed for all editorial, photography, and roving video crews to easily stop by to upload new content throughout the show, while also providing a roped-off environment for the technicians involved to work.

After the Event

Luini recalls that after the live-event webcast ended, they didn't just turn out the lights and go home. "The first thing we needed to do after the event was to make sure the Website reflected that the live streaming had ended so that browsers would be aware of the content that had been captured and uploaded throughout the show." In the days following the event, the MediaCast staff continued to process the audio, video, and editorial content to continue further expansion of the site and provide on-demand archives of the performance.

Tools for Creating and Enhancing Content

The following paragraphs describe some of the applications that can help you to create or edit webcasting content. Some perform dual functions.

Audio and Video Editing

Kohesion by in:sync

www.kohesion.com/

Kohesion is a video editing tool for the Internet and CD-ROMs. It creates video hotspot and time-event hyperlinks for Websites. It captures, edits, and outputs from one package. It edits video and audio in real time, adds special effects, creates composite images, and outputs directly to the Web.

Sound Forge 4.0 by Sonic Foundry, Inc.

www.sfoundry.com/pages/forge.htm

Sonic Foundry incorporates full file support for RealMedia and NetShow. Both Sound Forge 4.0 and Sound Forge XP 4.0 allow Internet and intranet content developers a straightforward conversion and editing environment for creating and moving media to the Web. (Windows)

V-Active for RealVideo by Ephyx Technologies

www.ephyx.com/

V-Active is a powerful HyperVideo authoring tool that lets the author automatically define moving hotspots (ImageMaps) on QuickTime and AVI video clips and link them with ImageMap links, such as seeking positions in the same video and URL addresses.

Sample Wrench by Dissidents

www.dissidents.com/products.htm

Sample Wrench is a sound sample editor with numerous effects such as EQ, reverb, time compression, pitch shifting, echo, flange, transfer functions, AM, FM, and more. Save sounds in several formats, or send to/from MIDI/SMDI samplers. Includes a comprehensive Visual BASIC compatible script language for custom DSP, batch processing, and bulk transfers. (Windows 95)

Peak by Bias

www.bias-inc.com/

Peak is a remarkably powerful and easy-to-use digital audio editor/processor for the Macintosh supporting encoding of Real Audio 3.0/2.0 files, batch file processing, scrubbing, graphic non-destructive editing with unlimited undo, extensive marker/loop control with marker transcription during record, and it supports AIFF, .WAV, SDII, and QuickTime files. Peak is native for Power Macintosh and also runs on 68k Macs and supports plug-ins for preprocessing including WAVES AudioTrack to create the highest quality encodings.

Cool Edit 96 by Syntrillium

www.syntrillium.com/cool96.htm

Cool Edit is Syntrillium's popular audio editor for Windows. Edit, convert, and enhance audio files in more than two dozen formats. Effects include 3D echo, reverb, noise reduction, compressor/limiter/noise gate, filter, delay, distortion, flanging, pitch and tempo adjustment, noise and tone generation, cue/playlists, and much more. Includes user-definable Presets and Batch/Scripting features.

SpeedRazor Mach 3.5 by in:sync

in:sync's SpeedRazor Mach 3.5 provides the editing and compositing for video. Works for TV or corporate in-house training, compositing special effects–rich ads and animations, doing straight cuts for long form documentaries, making music videos or multimedia games, or video for the Internet.

SmartSound for Multimedia by Sonic Desktop Software

www.sonicdesktop.com/formm.html

SmartSound for Multimedia creates professional-quality music soundtracks for use with any application which can play sound. Use it to create music for Websites, CD-ROMs, presentations, videos, and more. (Macintosh and Windows)

Converting Multimedia Presentation to the Web

PointPlus by Net-Scene

www.net-scene.com/

PointPlus enables users of Microsoft PowerPoint to publish their presentations on the Web as compressed files. These presentations are viewed on-line and immediately via the Point-Plus Plug-in Viewer within the Web browser window.

ASAP Webshow by SPC

www.spco.com/PRODUCTS/WSMAIN.HTM

The ASAP WebShow creates presentations on the Web. With ASAP WordPower presentation and report software, you can create presentations for the Internet. ASAP has the ability to synchronize sound clips to individual slides.

Astound by Astound Inc.

www.astound.com/

Astound allows multimedia presentation on the Internet. Presentations include animation and interactivity. Astound now has a serverless webcasting product.

The AudioPoint System by Competitive Edge Software

www.cesoftware.com/

The AudioPoint System allows you to put a PowerPoint presentation and then put a synchronized slide/streamed audio show on your Website. The Web show also gives the audience many viewing options.

Summary

Choosing to webcast the type of content that your audience finds truly useful and that is most effective in either live, on-demand, or push form is essential, even before the production begins. When you choose to capture audio and visual content, the best quality recording you can come up with within your budget will determine the finished product that your user experiences. Until greater bandwidth is available, there are a growing number of tools to help you produce the best quality content for your needs.

Tony Liano, vice president of Sales and Marketing for Verity, Inc., provides the following insight into the future of webcasting content: "The future of webcasting must be considered from two viewpoints—the user and the technologist. From the user point of view, webcasting will give rise to a new relationship between end users, like you and me, and information, or content. This new relationship will be a fusion of the relationship we have with traditional broadcasting and personal relationships, friends, and family. Webcasting will preserve the proactiveness of traditional broadcasting, but will be dramatically different because content will not be limited by time and space. Content will not be orchestrated by prime time or daytime, but your time. However, unlike broadcasting, webcasting will not be one-to-many, but one-to-one. There will be less content created based on averages (e.g., Seinfeld) and more content based on differences (e.g., Italian Cooking). Like your personal relationships, webcasting will know when it's the best time to reach you and will recommend new content you are likely to be interested in. And, of course, it is expected that webcasting will give rise to the promise of interactivity. From a technologist's point of view, webcasting will require that information and content be managed as a dynamic asset, not static. There are many technologies that are hoping to deliver this capability right now, but the jury is still out on who will win."

It is important to remember that the Internet and intranets are composed of two worlds: technology and content. You have chosen to use the most advanced technology available, live and on-demand streaming and push. Your challenge now is to provide the most applicable content from the sources you have available and to present this content in the most user-friendly and lively way to your audience. The future of your on-line endeavors and of the Internet and intranets truly relies on the success of your effort.

CHAPTER SIX

Marketing and Promotion

What if you had a party and forgot to send out the invitations? All of your planning and hard work could go to waste if no one knew about the party. The same is true of webcasting! The most enticing webcast can go for naught if you haven't planned ahead to identify a target audience, then promoted the event so that the audience knows when, where, and how to tune in to it. We can't overemphasize the importance of creating a thorough marketing plan that spells out the details and timing for connecting your webcast with your target audience. A good marketing plan should not only reflect your goals for webcasting as a business, but should also help you to research comparable programs, evaluate specific marketing strategies, and plan for the most efficient use of your personnel and advertising dollars.

Marketing is not a one-way street that simply involves sending out press releases or e-mail notices. It is a learning process in which you combine your research and awareness of the target audience with a technique for evaluating the success of your webcasting project so as to continually refine your efforts to achieve your goals.

This chapter will lead you through the processes involved in reviewing your business, analyzing the obstacles, setting overall objectives, targeting your audience, setting marketing objectives, budgeting your promotional activities, choosing your marketing tools, and measuring your success.

Generating the Marketing Plan

Begin your marketing plan by reviewing the objectives for your business. Webcasting itself may be your core business or an extension of an existing one. Your company may have more than one focus; it may focus on selling products or services or providing customer service. Look at how webcasting may be able to help you increase efficiency or effectiveness in achieving company goals and be aware of any ways in which it could become a hindrance.

Also look carefully at your existing and prospective customer base, as well as your employees and the Internet users that compose your general target audience. Then, try to determine what types of hardware and software they use and their Internet literacy level. Overall, you need to assess their interest in and likely acceptance of webcasting. In other words, how well will the audience accept webcasting?

Remember, your webcasting project should have clear, well-defined goals. As we emphasized in Chapter 2, if you're webcasting merely because your competitors are doing it or because you like new technology, you're not likely to reap the many benefits that webcasting offers. And you can spend a lot of time and money in the process. Clearly define your goals and your target audience at the beginning of the project and be sure that the goals are realistic and measurable.

Recognizing Hurdles and Opportunities

Your webcasting project may be targeted at overcoming existing business obstacles (i.e., increasing efficiency or effectiveness) or taking advantage of new opportunities that exist in your current business environment (i.e., increase revenues). Or, you may hope to accomplish both goals with webcasting. You may, for example, be able to improve communications within your organization by webcasting your employee newsletter and new product training information. Because webcasting offers fast, universal delivery via the corporate intranet, you can decrease the costs associated with printing and delivering the information to employees at the same time that you improve both the timeliness and quality of the information by incorporating audio and video content. You may also be able to repurpose some of the new product introductory material for webcasting on the Internet, building awareness of your company and products and possibly creating a new source of revenue.

To set realistic goals for your webcasting project, you need to be fully aware of the underlying technologies and ongoing changes and to understand how—and how successfully—your competitors are using webcasting. If your research indicates that none of your competitors are using webcasting, you might want to think twice about your own project: Do your competitors know something that you don't? Are they merely unaware or uninformed about the technology, or simply unwilling to spend the time or money necessary to launch a webcasting project? Or, are you ahead of the curve on the technology? Can webcasting benefit your company now, or would it be more practical to hold off for awhile, monitoring the technology and periodically reappraising its feasibility for your company?

We recommend asking the following ten questions to determine if and how your company can benefit from the use of streaming or push technologies:

1. Will webcasting help us to introduce new products and services?
2. Will webcasting reduce our costs?
3. Will webcasting generate leads?
4. Will webcasting generate direct revenue?
5. Will webcasting contribute to market expansion?
6. Will webcasting create or help to maintain brand loyalty?
7. Will webcasting help to decrease the sales cycle?
8. Will webcasting help us to communicate more effectively with customers?

9. Will webcasting help to improve business-to-business communication?

10. Will webcasting help to improve internal communications?

Unfortunately, we can't give you a simple key to the correct responses. There are no easy answers, but asking these questions, and others specific to your company and industry, should ensure that you thoroughly explore the feasibility of webcasting and arrive at definable goals for your project. And there are some challenges that are inherent to webcasting itself that you'll need to factor into your marketing plan.

In general, webcasting involves the following challenges:

◆ Users must have the appropriate hardware and software to receive webcasts and, in general, be more savvy than typical Internet users.

◆ You need specialized hardware and software to webcast and are likely to reach fewer people via streaming webcasting than with traditional broadcast technologies.

◆ Streaming video is restricted by bandwidth limitations.

◆ The quality of the audio and video delivered over the Internet is below that of radio and television broadcasting, depending on your user's connection and computer.

◆ Because webcasting represents a new technology, you may need to retrain your content providers to take advantage of its strengths and, at the same time, educate your target audience to overlook some of its weaknesses.

◆ Finding experienced webcast vendors and/or proven products is difficult because the field is still so new. And there is little consistency among products and services, making it difficult to predict the outcome of webcasting projects.

Of course, webcasting also offers a set of comparable opportunities. For example, it offers the opportunity to roll many traditional marketing methods into a single, interactive tool. You can repurpose such traditional marketing tools as direct mail or television, radio, and print advertising for delivery on the Web. Essentially anything that you produce for on-air delivery can be viewed on the Internet or an intranet. In addition, webcasting offers you the opportunity to tailor various advertising messages for a specific audience. And, by using information about your audience's choice of webcast materials, you can predict their future needs for information and products. For example, National Semiconductor Corporation monitors its customers use of the company's PointCast channel to determine areas of key interest, then uses this intelligence to determine its own product development and manufacturing priorities.

Defining Objectives

After you determine that webcasting is appropriate for your organization and establish some general goals for the project, you're ready to define specific, measurable objectives.

If, for example, you're going to use webcasting on the corporate intranet to develop a more knowledgeable staff or improve communications within the organization, you need to determine how many employees you're likely to reach and how often. You can express your webcasting objectives in terms of numbers and/or percentages. One objective of your intranet webcasting project might be, for example, to provide new product information to 90 percent of all employees within one week of a scheduled product release or provide 100 percent of employees with corporate benefits information within 48 hours of any change in benefits.

Similarly, if increasing revenues is one of the goals of your webcast project, you need to realistically determine how webcasting can accomplish that goal and how much revenue the project can be expected to generate in the first year, the first three years, and the first five years (or whatever timetable is practical for your particular company and industry). In this case, your objective might be to increase sales revenues by 5 percent during the first year (from $1,200,000 to $1,260,000), by 8 percent in the second year (from \$1,200,600 to \$1,301,400), and by 12 percent in the fifth year (from \$1,301,400 to \$1,457,568). And, of course, you need to match those objectives against your estimated costs for launching the project. Although you may not have to cost justify the webcasting project in strict dollar terms, you certainly need to understand what it's going to cost the company in terms of dollars and personnel resources, and you will need to predict what tangible and intangible benefits the company is likely to reap from the project.

If, for example, you can realistically expect only a minimal gain in revenue over the course of the first two years and you know that it will cost the company about \$500,000 to obtain the necessary hardware and software for the project, you'd better be able to define some measurable objectives for the nonrevenue benefits of the project. You might, for example, focus on decreasing the costs associated with employee training while also improving the quality of the training materials, or increase awareness of your company or products within your target audience. But, you need to provide the specifics: name names (Which departments are likely to benefit from improvements in training techniques? Whose budget will reflect decreased costs for printing and delivering training materials?) and provide realistic numbers or percentages (decrease training costs by 10 percent during the first year or reach approximately 1 million potential buyers on the Internet during the first two years of the project).

Even a relatively knowledgeable corporate audience may, however, require some reeducation to introduce them to webcasting and some active promotion to convince them to use webcasting to deliver content to the captive intranet audience. Your marketing plan should include some specifics for convincing various departments within your organization to use webcasting. Don't assume that the training and/or human resource departments will take advantage of webcasting capabilities just because they're available. You need a plan for educating the other members of your organization about webcasting and for helping them to develop plans for using webcasting to supplement or replace existing methods of communication. Webcasting over an intranet can provide a lot of benefits and cost savings but only if all of the relevant departments know about the technology, know how to use the technology, and are willing to use the technology. Otherwise, it's just an empty promise!

Setting the goals and objectives is only one step in creating the marketing plan, though. You also have to be able to measure the results during the course of the project to determine if you're on target or if you need to either change some elements of the project or redefine your objectives.

Identifying the Target Audience

It is very important to determine who the target audience is for your streaming media or push webcast so that you can plan accordingly. What proportion of your general audience is likely to be a target for webcasting? If your company already focuses on people who are familiar with the Internet and who have access to the appropriate devices for receiving webcasts, you're likely to reach a high proportion of them with webcasting. It is, however, important to understand who your audience is (e.g., educated white males over age 35), how that audience is currently using the Internet (e.g., primarily e-mail or research), and what type of equipment they're using. If you already have a Website or have done some webcasting and were wise enough to collect information from the members of your Internet audience, you can probably use that database to derive the details of your target audience. If not, you'll have to rely on market statistics about the Internet audience and their receiving devices.

Targeting Employees and Clients over an Intranet

Developing a marketing and promotional plan for an intranet webcast is significantly easier than planning a webcast project for an Internet audience. You are likely to be familiar with the demographics of your target audience—whether that audience is composed solely of employees or also includes clients, suppliers, and customers—and with the details of the communications infrastructure and receiving devices. Because the audience is a closed group, you can determine specifically who has access to your webcast and who actually tunes in to receive information. (Unfortunately, you can't determine who pays attention and who doesn't, but nothing is perfect!)

Having a high level of control over the intranet audience enables you to target specific messages to individuals or groups within the general intranet audience. This capability is particularly important for ensuring that appropriate information is distributed to the corresponding individuals or groups without violating security precautions. You don't, for example, want to deliver a streaming webcast designed to teach technical support people how to debug a new product to your potential customers. Many companies develop a grid that resembles a television schedule to segment information categories and target delivery groups (see Figure 6.1).

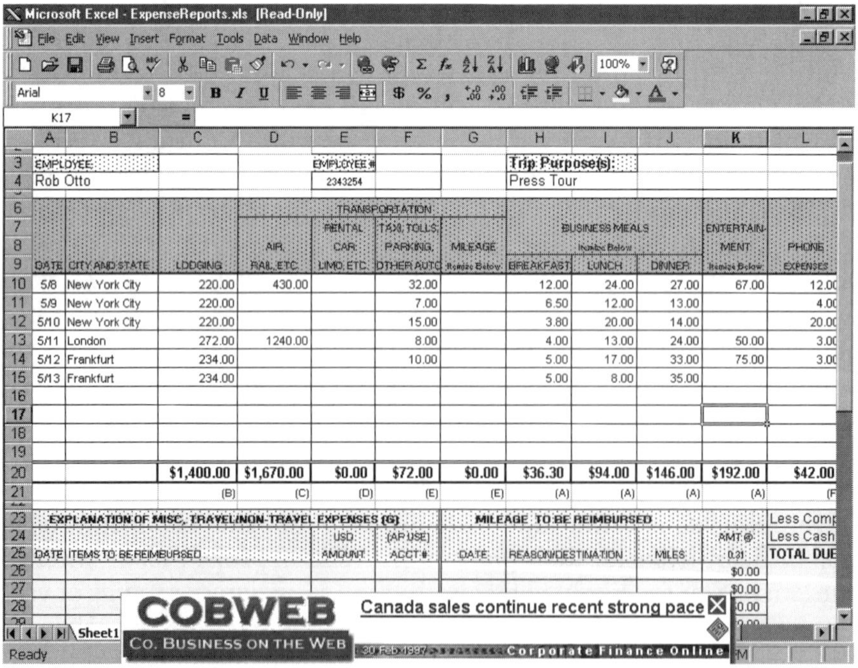

Figure 6.1 Sample grid: information categories and target delivery groups.

Although it isn't necessary to include the details of information segmentation in your marketing plan, it is necessary to define your target audience by delivery groups (i.e., sales personnel, support staff, sales prospects, previous buyers, active buyers, and influential personnel such as consultants or the media) and information types (i.e., confidential, corporate-only, technical support, or sales training).

In some cases, promoting a webcast to a target audience presents some unique challenges, such as GRIT.NET's broadcast of the National Federation for the Blind's annual conference in 1997. See Figure 6.2 for a screen shot from that conference.

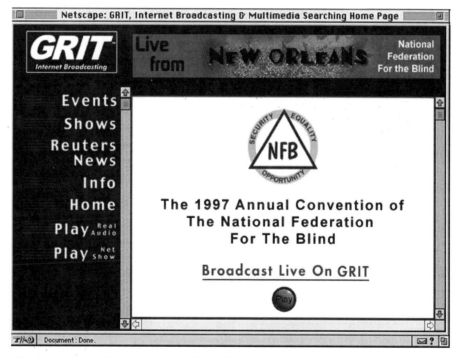

Figure 6.2 The GRIT.NET broadcast of the National Federation for the Blind's annual conference.

CASE STUDY   NATIONAL FEDERATION FOR THE BLIND

How does a national organization communicate with thousands of members when only a limited number are able to travel to the annual convention? The National Federation for the Blind resolved this challenge by providing a live Internet audio broadcast from its annual convention.

More than 3,000 people from around the nation converged on New Orleans in June 1997 for the group's annual convention. But the federation relied on audio webcasting to reach the vast majority of its 50,000+ members, contracting with GRIT.NET to provide live audio coverage of the convention and to broadcast the coverage from the GRIT.NET Website.

By webcasting the event, the federation overcame the limitations of traditional broadcasting. Rather than reaching only a local community, webcasting enabled people around the world to attend the annual event. Listeners everywhere heard speeches and comments from notables in the federation and the blind education community, as well as the presentation of scholarships and awards. The annual banquet, which is traditionally the highlight of the annual convention, was broadcast live over the Internet. Before arriving in New Orleans, GRIT.NET staff members created radio-style 30- and 60-second announcements that played daily on the Website to promote the event. They also sent e-mail notices about the event to the administrators of the numerous blind listserves (mailing lists) asking them to post information about the event for people who would not be traveling to the convention. GRIT.NET supplemented these promotional efforts with banners on their Website and information in their newsletter. They also created a special Web page that people could access to find additional information about the broadcast, download the necessary software (for free), and link into the stream on the night of the banquet. Because the broadcast was targeted at people with varying levels of visual impairment, the Web page was designed to be accessible to the browsers and specialized software programs that blind people use.Blind people browse using a screen reader or WebSpeak to let them know what is on a Website.

And, because GRIT.NET makes its shows available on-demand for people to listen anytime, convention attendees or on-line participants could return to the site to relive their convention experiences. With GRIT. NET's help, the National Federation for the Blind was able to dramatically increase the reach and overall value of its annual convention.

Targeting the Internet Audience

There are only two basic sources of information about an Internet audience: the information that you've gathered through your own research or prior webcasting efforts, or information published by research organizations such as The Yankee Group or Jupiter Communications. Of the two, your own research is infinitely more valuable since you're likely to collect the type of statistics that relate directly to your business interests and audience. But, if you're just starting out with a webcasting project, you'll probably have to rely on information that someone else has gathered. That's not all bad, because you can refine the general information as you gain experience with your own webcast audience. In general, you'll want to know the following characteristics about your audience:

- Age
- Sex

- Marital status
- Children
- Income
- Education
- Profession
- Geographic location
- Personality characteristics (psychographics)
- Past purchase behavior

It is important to remember, however, that not all characteristics are equally important in developing your marketing and promotional plan. The degree of importance of the various characteristics will depend on the specifics of your webcast effort. Your marketing plan should include a target profile for your audience. If, for example, you are offering live and on-demand webcasts that are intended to educate people about nutrition and food preparation, your target audience is probably female, aged between 20 and 50, with at least a high school education. Therefore, the characteristics that you're most concerned with are gender, age, and education. Conversely, if you're attempting to market expensive new automobiles, your target audience may be male, over 30 years old, with an annual income of at least $75,000. In this case, the most critical audience characteristics are likely to be age, income, profession, past purchase behavior, and possibly, geographic location. You may, of course, refine or change your target profile after you begin webcasting, using actual audience demographics to reshape your message. You might, for example, find that women over age 50 are very interested in purchasing that expensive new automobile because it offers a number of safety features that are unavailable on less costly models. In this case, you could develop a message targeted at the female, age 50+ market that emphasizes the reliability and safety features of the car.

If you don't have access to specific research about your target audience, or you are reaching a first time audience, it may help to take a look at some generalized demographics of Internet users. According to the Spring 1997 Internet Demographic Study by Nielsen Media Services, of the 220 million people over the age of 16 in the United States and Canada:

- ◆ 23 percent are using the Internet
- ◆ 17 percent are on the Web
- ◆ 73 percent of Web users search for information about products and services
- ◆ 5.6 million people (or about 15 percent) have purchased products or services on-line in the past 12 months

It is interesting to note that Nielsen's Spring 1997 survey indicates a clear narrowing of the gender gap on the Internet. According to the survey, approximately 58 percent of Internet users are male, a decrease from the fall 1995 study that indicated 66 percent of Internet users were male. The most recent survey also indicates that although males are more likely than females to search for product information on-line, females are more likely to make purchases. So, if selling products or services on-line is one of the goals of your webcasting project, you'll probably want to target both male and female users in the Internet audience. Your message may differ for the two groups, however, providing factual details for the male audience and directions for purchasing or warranty information for the females.

The Target Audience for Streaming.   If your webcasting project focuses on streaming audio and/or video live or on-demand, your target audience is likely to consist of frequent Internet users who have already tuned in to a streaming webcast. The following characteristics describe the Internet audience that has attended a streaming webcast:

- ◆ 70 percent are male; 30 percent are female
- ◆ They range in age from 16 to 50 years

- They are college educated
- Most earn more than $40,000 per year
- Most (75 percent) use 28.8 Kbps modems to connect to the Internet; 20 percent use 14.4 Kbps modems, and 5 percent still connect at speeds of 64 to 128 Kbps
- They connect to the Internet from one to three hours per night, one to three nights per week
- They use relatively new computers, purchased within the past four years
- They spend approximately $240 per year on their Internet connection

Of course, these characteristics are changing rapidly. Webcasting is still a very new technology, embraced primarily by the early adopters that tend to be well educated and comfortable with computer and communications technologies. Now that major computer companies like Microsoft and Netscape are taking an active role, webcasting is likely to move out of the domain of the early adopters into the mainstream. We are now seeing click and play audio and video webcast through new television sets and/or relatively low-cost portable Internet devices. Each device and development will substantially change both the characteristics of the target audience and the streaming programs that are delivered to it.

The Target Audience for Push.   Like streaming webcasts, push applications are still primarily in the domain of the early adopters. Because of their commercial appeal, however, they're moving rapidly into the mainstream. Quite a few companies are already using push technology on corporate intranets and, to a lesser degree, on the Internet. According to The Yankee Group, push technology represents the next step for direct e-mail on the Internet. Using webcasting technology to push direct mail–type information over the Internet offers some distinct advantages over traditional direct mail, most notably the ability to distribute information to a huge potential audience at minimal cost. But, like any direct mail campaign, the need to target the audience correctly is paramount to the success of the project. Obviously, the target market for a push webcast depends on the specific product or service that you're promoting. Pushing too much, too little, or inappropriate information to an Internet audience that has no interest in it will result only in wasted time and money for the marketer and frustration for the audience. Just because you can distribute information to thousands or even millions of people doesn't mean that you'll sell more product or service, or even that your company will gain greater market presence (except possibly in a negative context.)

After you've identified your target market and gained a reasonable understanding of the size of the potential market, you should go back and review the objectives that you defined for your webcasting project. Are the numbers and/or percentages that you specified realistic? Now is a good time to make adjustments if necessary. You can probably also add some details to your objectives at this point. Determine which (if any) behavior in your targets you need to change in order to reach your goals. Do you want them to learn something specific from your webcast? Do they need to tune in for a certain amount of time?

Budgeting Your Webcast Promotion

Although some organizations assign a percentage (e.g., 2 to 5 percent) of their overall webcasting budget to marketing and promotional activities, this is not always a satisfactory means for determining the promotional budget because it does not consider either the tangible and intangible objectives of the webcasting program or the wide range of costs involved in producing and delivering the webcast. Instead, we recommend that you begin by reviewing your objectives for the webcast effort. What are you trying to accomplish? In both the long and short terms? If you're trying to sell a product or service, what percentage of attendees must make a purchase to meet your revenue goals? How many impressions, invitations, or advertisements will you need in order to obtain the required percentage of purchasers? What are the competitive factors involved? Are your primary competitors using webcasting to capture market share or audience attention? Are there any time pressures involved? (That is, do you have to attract audience attention within a specific amount of time or before a particular event or date?)

Once you've reviewed the objectives and pressures on your webcasting project, consider your options for reaching your target audience and capturing the required number of attendees and purchases. Then develop a first pass media plan with cost estimates for each appearance of the various media. While it's not generally a good idea to use the overall webcasting budget as a determinant of your webcasting promotional budget, you do need to keep the two budgets in perspective and achieve a reasonable balance between them. If, for example, your first pass media plan represents 50 percent of your budget for promotional expenses, you need to go back to the plan and start paring media costs. Unfortunately, there are no strict guidelines for achieving the necessary balance between producing/delivering and promoting the webcast; your promotional budget should probably not represent more than 20 percent of your overall webcasting budget.

However you determine the actual numbers, your budget for promoting the webcast should be sufficient to:

1. Effectively reach your target audience and communicate sufficient information about your webcasting project to make it attractive for them to attend.
2. Influence the volume of sales necessary to achieve your objectives and/or revenue goals.
3. Take into account your need to build market presence and/or your competitors' use of webcasting to achieve the same goal.

Positioning the Webcast

Positioning your webcast involves creating an image in the minds of your target audience about your organization or about the information that you're delivering via the webcast. To position effectively, you need to understand your audience's interests, what other sources of information or entertainment they rely on, and their perception of those sources. Then, you need to be able to differentiate your webcast from the competitive sources, whether those are traditional sources such as books and magazines or television and radio broadcasting, or new media technologies accessible through the Internet.

The way in which you position your webcast will depend to a great extent on the goals for your webcasting project, your business model, and your target audience. If you're providing business news, for example, on a subscription basis, you may want to position your webcast as "the most comprehensive or timely source available" and emphasize that this information is delivered automatically to the users' desktops. If, however, you're webcasting live and on-demand jazz music and relying on advertising revenues, you want to attract as large an audience as possible by emphasizing the benefits of attending live concerts around the world, differentiating the live webcast from conventional radio or TV broadcasting by emphasizing the interactive capabilities and chat rooms that enable audience members to exchange comments with one another and share mutual enjoyment without having to leave the comfort and convenience of their homes. Or, you may want to emphasize the on-demand aspects of the webcast program and the audience's ability to tune in for a replay the next day, or whenever is convenient for their schedules.

While it is likely to be relatively easy to differentiate your webcast from traditional delivery media, positioning your webcast in relation to conventional Internet Websites or other webcasts is considerably more challenging. Competition for user attention is fierce on the Internet. Essentially, you need to emphasize the strengths of your webcast to your particular target audience. What is it about *your webcast* that makes it unique? If the webcast itself isn't unique, how is the content that you're delivering better than that available from Websites or other webcasts? What value do you add for your target market? Positioning a webcast for an intranet audience is a bit different than positioning for a general Internet audience, since an intranet (especially one composed primarily of employees) does not involve the same level of competition. But it does require that the members of your audience accept webcasting as a legitimate source of information, and you must still capture and hold the audience's attention. As we mentioned earlier, just because someone tunes in to a webcast doesn't necessarily mean that he or she is paying attention to the content. Positioning an intranet webcast largely involves making it easy for your audience to use and ensuring that the content is palatable to them. Again, the specifics of the position will depend on the nature of the information that you're webcasting. If you're pushing corporate news and benefits information to employees on a regular basis, there is likely to be little positioning required. If, however, you're using on-demand webcasts to provide employee training, you need to position the webcasts as a practical alternative to live training seminars, emphasizing that employees can move through the training course at their own pace and tune in when it's convenient for their schedule. And, of course, the webcast audio and video has to be attractive and compelling as well as informative. Positioning in this case may be to create a fun and simple image.

Marketing your webcast provides the opportunity of creating a cutting edge image of your product. Even the world of high fashion has proven to be responsive to the allure of high technology.

CASE STUDY   YVES ST. LAURENT LIVE

In the fashion industry, competition is great for media attention and for opportunities to expose new clothing lines. In July 1996, Yves St. Laurent broke new ground by using video on the Internet to showcase its haute couture collection (see Figure 6.3). The webcast not only heightened interest in the collection, but

Figure 6.3   The Yves St. Laurent haute couture collection webcast.

also allowed others from around the world to take part in the event as it was happening. Normally, many of these parties would have had to wait to see the latest fashions on a television show or even longer until the designs hit the boutiques. The live event was also used to promote the release of Fashion Live, a Web magazine that features exclusive presentations of the couturier's latest collections.

Gilbert Cattoire, president of the Voo Doo Agency in Paris, France, and one of the World Media producers who launched the Yves St. Laurent webcast, sees these marketing merits for the event: "It promoted the launch of a fashion magazine and started a long-term relationship with a fashion industry leader. Analysis of the event was used to develop a business model based on branding. This was used to finance future Internet publishing and webcasting activities. It allowed Yves St. Laurent to communicate at a new and innovative level, achieving exceptional media feedback, and increasing exposure for the company. It presented an image of being on top of the industry in terms of technology and innovation."

Promotion for the YSL webcast, which was almost exclusively on-line, started only two weeks before the event (for confidentiality reasons). The event producers created a specialized mailing list from information sources on the Internet related to fashion, supermodels, and webcasting technology. They then added the specialized mailing list to a general list of Websites that included all of the major universities and media. The on-line information was supplemented by a live YSL press conference that attracted key fashion editors.

The results of the webcast were outstanding. During the show, which lasted 55 minutes, the three servers dedicated to the distribution of the video stream registered 25,000 different IP addresses. The total number of visits, audited by a third party, amounted to an estimate of 500,000 in five days on the video pages alone. Two thirds of the users also took the time to visit many of the 250 additional pages on the YSL Website, increasing exposure to other promotions and fashion information. The event generated more than 70 articles in French and international newspapers and magazines, including the *Wall Street Journal,* and five news features on major European TV networks.

Promoting the Webcast

As we said at the beginning of the chapter, marketing a webcasting program requires two elements: (1) identifying the target audience and shaping the webcast to fit their needs or interests and (2) a means of notifying that audience about the webcast and convincing them to tune in. No matter how clearly you've defined your goals or identified your audience, the webcasting program cannot succeed if the target audience doesn't know about it or doesn't know when or how to access the webcast.

Developing the Message

Your message to an Internet audience is much like the invitation to a party. You need to tell your prospective guests about the webcast and let them know when and how to attend. And, of course, you want to convince them to come. Your marketing message depends on your target audience and the content of your webcast. If you're webcasting to an intranet audience, you probably don't have to do a lot of selling but you do need to provide the prospective audience with information about the webcast schedule and/or any details about the required technology. If, however, you're webcasting over the Internet, you're competing for audience attention with literally millions of Websites, as well as traditional delivery media. So, your promotional message has to sell the benefits of attending the webcast as well as provide relevant scheduling and technology information.

And, just like a party invitation, the marketing message should correspond—in both style and language—to the target audience for the webcast (see Figure 6.4). If, for example, you're promoting a live rock concert, your message can use a hip informal style with lots of flashy graphics and accompanying music. If, however, you're promoting a webcast that updates stock prices for the business market, your message should use a more serious, formal tone.

You may need to include an incentive of some type in your marketing message (i.e., a reason to attend) and/or a reply mechanism.

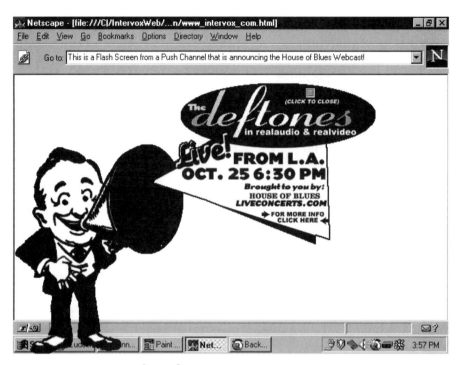

Figure 6.4   A sample webcast announcement.

The incentive can be something as simple as "the opportunity to receive timely information about investing in the stock market" to something more tangible, such as the chance to win a prize, for example, tickets to the next live rock concert or a free one-month subscription to the stock update service, or an unrelated gift such as discounts on merchandise or a business research report. While tangible incentives have proven very effective with some types of promotions, their success depends largely on the target audience and the type of prize that is offered. If you do elect to offer a tangible incentive, you must be sure to spell out the terms of the offer very clearly in your webcast promotional message. Specifically what actions are required on the part of the attendee? Do they just have to tune in to the webcast, or is there something they need to do (i.e., answer a questionnaire about themselves or their receiving device? or sign up to attend the concert webcast?). And, you may need to clearly state what you're offering: Will everyone who tunes in receive discounts on some type of merchandise, or only those that respond to the questionnaire, or respond in a particular manner? Will everyone be eligible to win free tickets or only those who meet specific criteria? Be careful, though, that in providing the details of the incentive offer you don't overwhelm the promotional information about your webcast. You don't want your audience to remember only a chance to win free tickets; you want them to remember when and how to attend your live webcast of an upcoming rock concert.

In general, the promotional message should also contain these elements:

1. Call to action—the headline of the promotion. What are you promoting and why should the audience care? This element should gain the attention of the audience and convince them to stay tuned for additional information.

2. Invitation—the where and when elements of the webcast. Be sure to reference the specific time zone when providing the when information.

3. Response vehicle—how can prospective attendees contact you to get further details about the webcast?

4. Instructions—what do attendees have to do to receive the webcast? What are the specific hardware and software requirements (if any) for receiving the webcast?

5. On-demand availability—where can the attendees view the archives or programs that were just webcast? What segments will be available?

Delivering the Message

Once you've determined the basic message for your webcast promotion, you need to decide how to most effectively deliver that message to your target audience. Any type of marketing and promotional plan includes a variety of tools. Although you may focus most of your webcast promotional efforts on on-line delivery media, you may not want to totally overlook traditional media such as television, radio, print, direct mail, or outdoor billboards.

Traditional Advertising Media

If your company is currently using traditional advertising media to promote your products or services, you may want to add information about your webcasting efforts to the existing advertising message. This can have a twofold effect: notifying members of your target audience about the webcasting effort and, at the same time, making your company appear high-tech and progressive.

If your company is not currently using any of the traditional media for advertising and you don't have prior experience in buying or placing advertising, you should probably consider working with an experienced advertising agency or marketing consultant to determine which (if any) medium is appropriate for your webcasting message and target audience and to help you deliver an effective message. The costs of traditional advertising media vary widely, but cost alone should not be the determining factor. You need to be sure that the media delivers your message effectively to your target audience. Table 6.1 summarizes some typical costs for traditional advertising media.

Timing and frequency are also crucial factors in advertising. If you have an unlimited budget, you can purchase a series of advertisements to notify your target audience, then continuously remind

TABLE 6.1   Typical Cost for Traditional Advertising Media

Advertising Media	Typical Cost
One-page ad in a major daily newspaper	$50,000
30-second TV commercial in a major market	$2,000
60-second radio spot for major market	$1,000
Direct mail piece for a list w/40,000 people	$2,000
One-page 4-color ad in major, national magazine	$100,000
30-day outdoor billboard ad	$30,000

them about your upcoming webcasting event or series of programs. If, however, your budget is limited (and most are), you'll need to plan the timing of the advertising very carefully, making sure that the ads appear (on whatever media you select) prior to the event or series initiation, but not too long before the actual date or the audience is likely to lose interest or forget. And timing is somewhat tricky because advertising deadlines vary widely among the media. Placing a print advertisement in the daily newspaper, for example, typically requires getting the camera-ready copy to the newspaper office two or three days before you want the ad to appear. If you're placing the same ad in a weekly newspaper, plan on delivering the camera-ready copy to the newspaper office one to two weeks before it is to appear, and, if you're placing the ad in a monthly magazine, you'll need to deliver camera-ready copy at least 30 days prior to the publication. Deadlines for television and radio broadcasts also vary significantly but are generally shorter than those required for traditional print media advertising.

The best advice is to plan ahead! Your webcast marketing and promotional plan should include a detailed media plan that specifies what type (if any) of advertising you're going to be doing and in what publications or on which stations. Then check the advertising copy deadlines for each of the target media and determine when you'll need to prepare the print or broadcast message for each publication or broadcast station. It is recommended that you seek advice from an experienced consultant, media planner, or advertising agency who specializes in new media.

Promotional Offers

Promotional offers are much like incentives; they are intended to encourage the audience to perform in a specific manner in response to the offer, for example, to purchase a product. Unlike incentives, promotional offers always involve something tangible. Any of the following items are commonly used in promotional offers:

◆ Coupons and gift certificates
◆ Retail discounts for specific stores or merchandise

- Premiums (awards), points programs, and benefits like frequent flyer programs
- Refunds for purchasing merchandise at a specific retailer
- Contest entries

Often, you can combine promotional offers with other types of traditional and new media advertising. You can, for example, include information about a promotional offer in a print advertisement, radio or television broadcast, direct mail piece, or a push webcast. If your organization markets a product, you might want to include information about your webcasting event or offer in the product packaging along with some type of promotional offer (i.e., include a coupon for additional discounts on your product). See Figure 6.5.

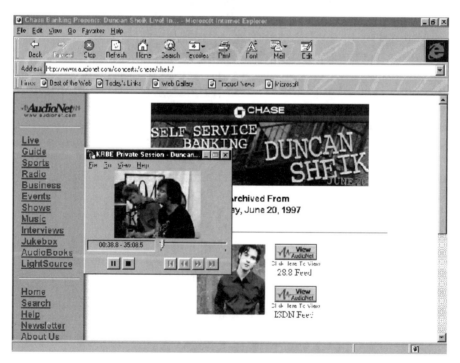

Figure 6.5 A promotional offer in webcasting promotion.

Public Relations

Public relations is often associated with acquiring free press or air time, but it is actually much more than that. A primary goal of public relations is to build awareness of your company or product and create a positive image in the mind of your target audience. Public relations can be as simple as sending thank you notes to individuals who have purchased your product or service or as sophisticated as distributing a multimedia press release about your organization to print and broadcast media around the world. Public relations activities should begin prior to the event and carry through after it's over to achieve maximum results. Activities include establishing contacts, creating mailing lists, writing news releases, producing invitations, and providing on-site contact at or during an event. While you can probably do many of these events yourself, you may want to consider hiring a professional to handle some of the specialized tasks like writing the releases or creating well-targeted mailing lists. Figure 6.6 shows a sample press release for a live webcast event.

Public relations activities should be coordinated with other forms of advertising and promotion to achieve maximum value. Just as it's important to plan the timing of your advertising efforts, it's equally important to plan your public relations activities so that they coordinate with and reinforce the other promotional efforts. You might, for example, want to initiate a public relations campaign for your webcast event or series prior to actually beginning the paid advertising. In this case, you'll need to notify the relevant media of your event at least one week before the advertising begins to appear. Or, you might want the public relations activities to begin at about the same time as your paid advertising. Again, this takes some careful planning and coordinated effort.

The most common mistake on live webcasting press releases is omitting the time zone. Remember, your live event can be heard around the world. You may want to include as a reference the time in GMT, Greenwich mean time as well as your local time zone, such as EST or eastern time zone. Other items that are commonly forgotten on news releases include the URL, date, contact name, e-mail address, *and* phone number.

From: Gary Worth, Real Networks
Subject: Hong Kong Handover

ABC, FOX, MSNBC, BBC, CBC, C-Span among 20 Broadcasters Worldwide to Deliver Daily Broadcast Coverage of the Hong Kong Transition in RealAudio and RealVideo.

SEATTLE, WA, June 30, 1997. Progressive Networks today announced that more than 20 major broadcasters worldwide are broadcasting Internet coverage of Hong Kong's return to the People's Republic of China in RealAudio and RealVideo. This announcement marks the first time a global event of this magnitude will be broadcast over the Internet. RealAudio and RealVideo coverage of the event will begin Monday, June 30 and run through Wednesday, July 2. Internet users can also access the Web broadcasts in several different languages directly from Progressive Networks' Timecast Website, www.timecast.com.

"I think the opening of China was one of the most important diplomatic initiatives of the last 30 years and I continue to believe that good relations with China are the key to peace, stability, and progress in Asia," said Henry Kissinger, former U.S. secretary of state under President Nixon. "For someone like me who wants to stay current about events such as this, these RealAudio and RealVideo broadcasts are invaluable. This is my first time on the Internet," said George Shultz, former U.S. secretary of state under President Reagan. "The Hong Kong handover is significant and the Web can certainly spread information and provide a forum for people to interact, which is a big plus in understanding issues of global importance."

Figure 6.6   A sample press release.

"We are very pleased to see that premier broadcasters world-wide are using RealAudio and RealVideo to broadcast the Hong Kong transition over the Internet," said Rob Glaser, chairman and CEO, Progressive Networks. "The fact that millions of Internet users today can surf the globe for local and national broadcasts of this event, accessing many different points of view in many languages, is an illustration of the power of this new mass medium."

For Press Only, Contact:
Jay Wampold, Progressive Networks,
Johanna Range, Progressive Networks,
Gary Worth—Associate Editor of Timecast

Figure 6.6 *(Continued).*

You may want to stage a press conference or related publicity event to further publicize your webcast launch. While a press conference or other event can be very useful for introducing members of the media to your organization or to the concept that you're promoting with your webcast, it typically adds another level of complexity to your planning process. In addition to promoting the webcast itself, you'll need to promote the press conference or event also, contacting the appropriate people to attend, lining up a program or speaker who is likely to be of interest to the media, and sending out the appropriate invitations. If you don't promote the press conference adequately, it's likely to be overlooked by the media and may do more harm than good for your overall webcast promotion. As a general rule of thumb, don't schedule a press conference unless you actually have something of interest to tell the press. Otherwise, you're likely to get a ho-hum response that may divert attention from your real news event: the webcast!

On-line Marketing and Public Relations

Regardless of your other marketing and public relations efforts, you're likely to find that the majority of your promotional efforts will focus on on-line techniques. In many respects, it is practical to focus your promotional efforts (and dollars) on a marketing medium that reaches the individuals who are capable of tuning in to webcast technology. But, it's important to remember that on-line marketing differs from traditional marketing in a number of ways. Where traditional marketing is generally intrusive, on-line marketing is interactive; it relies on a different type of interaction between you and the target audience than traditional marketing. For example, although the on-line environment is changing as Websites begin to require some type of payment from users in exchange for information, on-line marketing currently exists as a polite invitation to users—in the form of banners or flash messages—to explore further for more information. And, the current generation of on-line advertising is primarily limited to graphics and text as opposed to the sight and sound of television and radio broadcasting. Again though, this is changing as more and more companies delve into webcasting.

One of the greatest advantages of on-line marketing is the ease with which you can develop a database of users that visit your Website. Some Websites use a guestbook technique in which users actually sign onto the site and provide some basic information about themselves or their interests. This type of database is invaluable for targeting future webcasts and/or for refining your product advertising messages to fit the users' needs. The type and amount of information that you receive from users depends to a great extent on how much they trust you and what (if anything) they receive in return. Proceed slowly when you're attempting to gather information from users; ask only for user names and e-mail addresses in the beginning. As your relationship continues, you can ask for additional personal information. One common strategy is to offer general entry into a site but reserve exclusive access to some content for those users who respond to a questionnaire or otherwise provide further information on themselves or their interests. Some sites even create a loyalty club with special offers and discounts for users who regularly respond to questionnaires or provide other types of feedback. See Figure 6.7 for a sample questionnaire. Don't forget that building trust is a two-way street. Once you've developed a following of loyal users and understand their wants and needs, be sure to send them only the information that they've requested or, at least, indicated an interest in. You've developed a base for pushing advertising information, but you'll soon lose your base of loyal users if you take advantage of their trust by sending large quantities of information or information in which they have no interest.

On-line public relations is efficient, inexpensive, and—best of all—reaches the target audience who understands webcasting. You can use on-line public relations techniques to gain media attention for any type of webcast, especially if your webcast promotion is

Figure 6.7   A sample questionnaire to gather user demographics.

viewed as news. On-line public relations also offers the advantage of immediacy; when you post a news release on your Website (and possibly on related Websites as well), it is immediately available to your target audience. You can supplement the posted information by e-mailing press information to a select list of media, either attaching the body of information or notifying them of the major news points and referring to the complete information on your Website. This dual action approach lets you keep your marketing messages to a minimum and use the Website for more complete information. You do, of course, need to develop a database of media e-mail addresses, but this is relatively easy since many newspapers, magazines, and television and radio stations maintain their own Websites with personnel directories and e-mail addresses.

You can use conventional e-mail messages or e-mail forums to notify Internet users about your Website and/or upcoming webcasts. As we mentioned earlier, however, e-mail can be perceived as intrusive and annoying, so it's generally best to limit your use of e-mail to major news messages. E-mail forums or lists, which require users to subscribe, are often more effective for promoting webcast information since the users have already indicated an interest in receiving such information. (See Figure 6.8.) It's also a good idea to subscribe to e-mail forums that deal with content similar to that of your webcast or Website because you can use the forum to let other users know—in a nonintrusive manner—about your site or webcast and solicit feedback from them.

Web Search Engines and Webcasting Program Guides

Because search engines and program guides are the most common means for finding webcasts on the Internet, it is essential to list your webcast on as many search engines and/or program guides as possible.

While some search engines periodically sweep the Internet for Websites and automatically list their URLs, others require you to submit the Website address and category to them. There are a number of services (e.g., www.submitit.com) that allow you to submit your Website URL to several search engines at one time. Be sure to

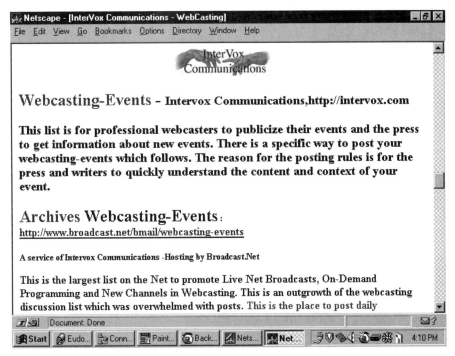

Figure 6.8 Sample e-mail forum/LISTSERVE.

submit as many relevant keywords as possible to adequately represent your webcast. To do this, you'll need to understand your audience and their perception of your webcast. If, for example, you are webcasting stock market updates, you'll need to list all of the keywords associated with the stock market and perhaps also add keywords relating to financial planning or retirement savings. It is also useful to know that some search engines prioritize their listings according to the number of appearances of a keyword. Consequently, you may want to list some keywords several times to gain a higher priority than sites with just one listing of the same keyword.

Internet program guides are much like television guides. Internet program guides are actually Websites that list webcasts by content category and type of technology. (See Figure 6.9.) Some program

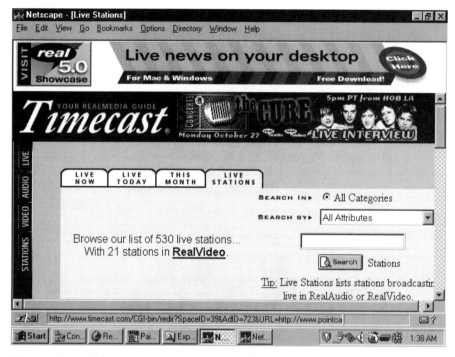

Figure 6.9   The www.timecast.com home page.

guides are published by companies promoting their own type of webcasting software while others are technology-independent content aggregators. Some of the most popular program guides—and ones that you should be sure to include in your webcast listing—are: www.timecast.com, www.realaudio.com, and www.audionet .com. Check the respective Websites for details on how to list your webcast. There are also e-mail lists that send notifications of events, and these can be found on www.broadcast.net and www .intervox.com.

Banner Advertising

Banner advertising can provide a very effective method for notifying Internet users about your Website and/or webcasts. You can place advertising banners on your own site and other (related)

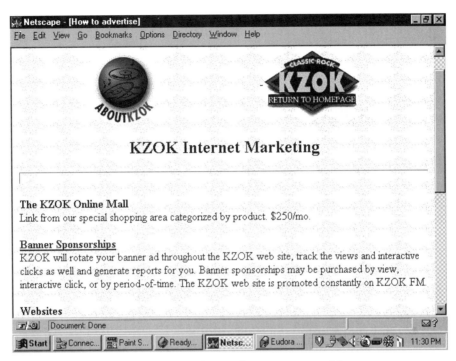

Figure 6.10   Example of Website that accepts ad banners.

Websites to drive traffic to your webcast. (See Figure 6.10.) The costs involved in placing ad banners range widely, from free to a fee per clickthrough which is defined as an actual transfer of the user to your site when they click on your banner. Some organizations are willing to barter banner advertising, placing banners for free on their sites in exchange for comparable placement on your site. You may also use a service like the Link Exchange (www.linkexchange .com) where you earn exposure on someone else's site by offering promotion on yours. Sites that accept advertising usually post the rate information on the site, along with the necessary contact information and any restrictions on advertising.

How you choose your on-line marketing mix depends upon the type of webcast that you're promoting and on your own experience. Kevin Edwards, the senior multimedia producer for CNET and senior producer for Mediadome, shares the following insights about his choice of marketing tools for promoting the live webcast of the press conference for the Rolling Stones tour.

CASE STUDY   CNET AND THE ROLLING STONES WEBCAST

"The Rolling Stones event went *very* well for us. According to Microsoft, it was their busiest day for NetShow client downloads ever. For us, it ranked below some of the other live webcasts we've done, but it was much higher than we expected given the fact that we didn't have the opportunity to promote it in any of our TV shows.

When we do a webcast, or Webisode, I typically look at how I can spread the word around on-line. For me it seems to make sense to break the options down into four categories:

- *Ads.* Ad banners, portals, and so forth are a great way to draw traffic if you can afford them, and if you have the time to create and place them. But ads are relatively expensive. We use URL tracking with all of our ads so we can determine their relative effectiveness.

- *Barter links.* For us, these are portal graphic links (like the "Get NetShow Now" button). Sometimes there's a fuzzy line between barter links and editorial links. Since Mediadome isn't an editorial site, we have some leeway as to what we can offer for barter links. We wouldn't place a barter link that had absolutely nothing to do with our content, but we might place a barter link that does something like point people to where they can get tickets to the physical content. The portals on our site do have a value that should be considered, and setting up the deal can take time and involve contract signing.

◆ *Editorial links.* It's somewhat time consuming to create the press releases, but once that's done, it's just a matter of distributing it to the media organizations and individuals that you think might be interested in covering the event. And, while this is also a time-consuming task, it's pretty mindless work that offers a potentially big return in promotional value.

◆ *Automated listings.* We post information on a variety of general-interest sites like EVENTS .COM, events.yahoo.com, intervox.com, webcasting-events, UBL, Usenet, as well as lists and sites that have a particular interest in our webcast content. In the case of the Rolling Stones event, we posted on all of the mailing lists for the band and sent e-mail to the owners of the fan sites. Again, this activity can be very time consuming, depending on the type of equipment and communications facilities you're using and how popular the content is on-line (it took a very long time for the Rolling Stones) but it's a great way to see what people are doing with their fan sites, and to understand what they're interested in. Communicating with the people whom you know are likely to watch the webcast also helps to put things into perspective."

Edwards goes on to emphasize the need to protect your webcast content. "Webcasting pirates *are* out there. Whenever we do a live webcast, we get a few people who try to pretend that it's their own. I check for this before launch, and if we're doing a barter link with someone, I ask in advance how they'll be linking to us. When you're working with a bandwidth or server vendor, they often don't realize what your objectives are, so it's important to discuss that up front. I've worked with vendors who thought they were doing us a favor by pirating our metafile instead of pointing to our site. They didn't realize that the ad banners on the top of our pages are our bread and butter."

Measuring Success

As we mentioned in the beginning of the chapter, webcast marketing should be a continuous loop of planning, executing, and evaluating. After the webcast event or a specified amount of time, you need to measure the success of your efforts. Your marketing objectives should include a unit of measure that represents your target for success. This measure may be a number or percent of employees (for an intranet webcast) or a quantity of pages viewed (for an Internet webcast) and may also include some definitions of frequency or duration (e.g., view the webcast site four times within a week or visit the webcast site for at least 30 minutes).

To evaluate the success of your marketing effort, you'll need to relate these measurements to prewebcast (and possibly postwebcast) behavior to determine the success of your webcast promotional activities. But, be aware that a simple rise or decline in webcast viewing does not necessarily indicate success (or failure) of your webcasting promotion. There may be—and in fact, probably are—many factors that affect webcast attendance. If you've been webcasting for some period of time, you may want to compare current attendance figures with attendance figures for the same time period last year, or last quarter, or last month, to determine if attendance is cyclical in nature. If attendance has decreased, you may want to determine what other events (webcast and otherwise) of interest to your target audience were occurring at the same time as your webcast. If your target audience was diverted to another webcast, you should probably determine what media the other organization used to promote that webcast.

If your webcast uses streaming or push technology, it should be designed to gather on-line user information to, for example, indicate surges of interest and/or the duration of user visits. You can use this information to fine-tune your future webcasts, capitalizing on the activities or information that causes a surge of view attendance and avoiding those activities or information that shorten the typical user visit. At some point in the not too distant future you'll be able to use intelligent, adaptive agents to instantly change the approach of your webcast as it is actually occurring to respond to user feedback.

The success of a webcasting effort can't, however, be measured strictly in terms of attendance or duration. You may also want to try to evaluate such intangible factors as how webcasting has affected the image of your organization in the minds of your target audience or increased their awareness of your product or service. To do this, you'll need to conduct research, most likely user surveys, at various points during your webcasting effort (i.e., before you begin webcasting, after your first webcast, after your tenth webcast, and so on). Remember, most changes in user perception or awareness are not likely to be evident until the webcasting effort is well under way. Unfortunately, the exception to this is negative perception; if you target the audience incorrectly or push information that is offensive in any way, the webcast attendees are very likely to form a negative impression of your webcasting effort and possibly of your organization and products as well. Overcoming a negative perception—even over a long period of time—is far more difficult than creating a positive impression in the first place. Be extremely careful about the type and quantity of information that you present on your webcast! You never have a second chance to create a first impression.

Your research should include more than user statistics. In addition to determining how many users attend your webcasts, you need to gather user feedback. Some organizations create attendee focus groups to determine why users attend or avoid their webcasts, and what they like and dislike about the webcasts. Focus groups can help you to find out if there are problems in locating the webcast or connecting to it, or if you have targeted your content correctly.

In addition to the number of webcast attendees, your ongoing webcast research should include information about the following:

1. User preferences on content and delivery, as well as any change in their interests
2. Users' software, hardware, and player types
3. Users' country of origin and language preferences
4. Duration of visits to the webcast Website
5. Demand on your servers (to evaluate the true costs and address potential service problems)
6. Statistics on user trends, including use of pay-per-view, pay-per-listen, and comparable payment schemes

In summary, it's important to remember that your webcast marketing plan can determine the ultimate success or failure of your entire webcasting project. Regardless of the quality of your content or presentation, your webcasting efforts may go to waste if you don't target the audience correctly and convince them to attend. Remember, "if you build it, they will come . . . ," but only if you develop a thorough marketing and promotional plan and execute it well.

CHAPTER SEVEN

MANAGING YOUR WEBSITE

Webcasting represents a fusion of multiple departments and disciplines. Technical issues are likely to require the services of PC and network technicians, as well as the involvement of server managers. When you add in audio and video specialists for live-event webcasting or for processing prerecorded material, the fun is just beginning.

Depending on its mission, however, the webcasting department may also need the input and guidance of the marketing department, salespeople to sell the webcasting services, and customer support personnel or event managers to work with the participants to webcast a live event or to convert a prerecorded happening into a webcast-compatible format.

Management Issues and Goals

A webcasting department needs to have clearly defined goals within the overall organization so as to understand the following: (1) what it is expected to do, (2) when to draw the line when corporate expectations exceed capabilities, and (3) what to do when the department is drawn into tasks that it is not suited for or which do not fall under its charter. Time, after all, *is* money, and a webcasting department that gets sidetracked into other duties, such as supporting corporate A/V needs, cannot adequately fulfill its own responsibilities.

The webcasting department must be able to define its customers, to understand who uses (or wants to use) the content that it's pushing, who is tuning in to watch and/or listen to the audio and video it's delivering, and just what the users expect from the department. In many cases, those expectations change, as do the audience needs and wants, between the time that the department is created and as it matures. The webcasting customers will probably like some of the things the department is delivering and begin asking for additional content. If, however, you're totally off base about the customers' needs, they're not likely to use the content that you're producing. In this case, your department will soon be out of business. On the other hand, if you are absolutely correct in your assessment of the customers' needs, you're likely to receive a shower of accolades and possibly a larger staff and budget for the webcasting department.

Not many organizations hit the bull's-eye dead-on in their first attempt at webcasting. Most have to go through an interactive process of building and gradually improving a department that can adequately serve their webcasting needs. This is partly because no one can design a perfect management structure that addresses all of the current and future issues the first time out, but it is also because tastes and information needs change as the world changes. The 15-minute video clip on the week at the home office may turn into the 30-minute video on new product releases. The push project that starts out as a highly targeted means to deliver weekly market reports may evolve into a daily intelligence brief discussing the pricing, techniques, and sales programs that your competitors are using. Can your sales force use this information at their desktops? Does your sales force need this information in raw form or in an interpreted summary? You won't know the answers to these questions until your customers—the sales force in this case—begin to use the information and provide you with feedback about what they like and don't like.

Don't take it personally if your customers don't like a particular part of your webcasting program. Instead, try to find out why they don't like it! Is there a problem with the way in which the information is presented? Or, is it the information itself? Is the information too detailed? Not detailed enough? Don't be afraid to ask questions, lots of detailed questions, especially at the start of your webcasting program. You're going to have to tweak aspects of the webcast, so you need to establish an administrative structure for gathering user input and implementing changes on a continual basis.

Prescreenings or focus groups with select customers before you actually roll out your webcasts to the entire audience are recommended. Prescreening is a proven technique which works for television, movies, and software design. It allows you to refine your message and information delivered within the webcast before the boss or the public sees the end product for the first time.

Having specific measurable reachable goals is a must for webcasting. The people who are committing time, money, and personnel for the venture will want to know what they are getting for their investment. You (even if you and they are the same person!) should be able to clearly define a set of measurable results and be able to stick to those results within reason. For example, the goal of a weekly video webcast may be to increase Web hits on a specific server by 10 to 15 percent within a month of starting the weekly webcasts. If, at week four of the webcasts, you're only hiking Web hits by 9 percent, you're moving in the right direction, albeit a little slower than expected. But, if you're only up by 2 percent and there are no other factors involved (e.g., the Web server was down for six hours in the middle of the week), it should be pretty clear that there's a problem with either the webcast itself or with your goals for the project. Your goals and expectations for the webcast project must be valid and measurable. If, for example, you're using webcasting as a sales tool, you may find that a weekly video webcast is not a particularly effective vehicle for directly closing sales, but may reinforce your brand. In this case, you need to reassess your use of webcasting as a sales tool and/or redesign the webcast to be more effective.

Whose Responsibility?

Because webcasting requires a variety of skills and involves participation by several departments within an organization, one of the first questions that inevitably arises is: Whose responsibility is webcasting? Which department should have responsibility for developing and maintaining the webcast site and/or the content for the site?

Webcasting can fall within the confines of an existing department or be organized into a separate, stand-alone department with its own assigned staff and budget or contracted to another company. The decision depends on the type of webcasting (push, on-demand, or streaming), your organization's objectives for webcasting, and the existing organizational structure. If earning revenue is the primary goal for the webcasting department, it may be practical to organize a separate webcasting department. If, however, webcasting is being used to complement or enhance another function such as marketing or public relations, the responsibility could be assigned to that department, with the necessary staff and budget drawn from that department's existing resources or an outside company. In any case, unless the webcasting department *is* the entire company (that is, established solely for the purpose of webcasting), even the most basic webcasting project requires assistance from and/or interaction with any or all of the following six departments. Indeed, if webcasting is not established as an independent department, it may well fall under the responsibility of one of these departments, sharing personnel and budget.

Public Relations

A public relations department may use webcasting to deliver product or company information (i.e., press releases, product announcements, company background, and so on) or events (live or on-demand) such as press conferences, interviews with executives, shareholder meetings, or employee training sessions. Conversely, the webcasting department can use the PR department to generate interest about its services. For example, live-event webcasts may be of interest to the press. Both Yahoo! and Real Networks have Web pages that are dedicated to live-event webcasts, while *USA Today* publishes a cybercast listing on the same page as the daily television listings. See Figure 7.1 for an example of a cybercast listing. A PR department should know (or can find out) the appropriate person within a news agency to whom you can send information and how they like to receive it.

Marketing

The marketing department is generally responsible for determining who the company's customers are and for developing plans to promote the company's products and/or services. Because these tasks are often closely allied with the goals of a webcasting department,

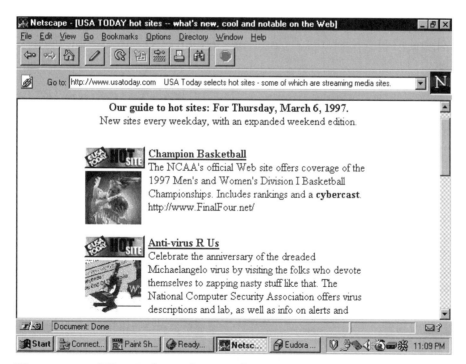

Figure 7.1 *USA Today* cybercast listing.

and because webcasting can be used to support direct and indirect marketing activities, responsibility for webcasting projects often falls to the marketing department. Webcasting can be used to deliver information to customers on new products and services, monthly promotions, and the like. Audio and video webcasting can be used for commercials, infomercials, and special events; a television commercial can easily be turned into a video on-demand clip. Many companies use webcasting to attract potential customers to their Websites, either putting on their own webcasts or sponsoring those from other companies. Using something unique and compelling as a lure often encourages people to visit Websites that they normally wouldn't or to behave in ways that they might not otherwise. The use of webcasting or datacasting is being used as a new "remote" Internet appliance. This new type of Internet broadcasting is significant as an indication of how webcasting may be used or combined with products to make them interactive. The partnership between Microsoft and PBS that created an interactive version of the Barney doll, capable of speaking and taking orders on television, is an example of this type of innovative marketing. (See Figure 7.2.)

The marketing department is also likely to play a major role in promoting webcasting activities to potential customers, regardless of the goals of these activities. People need to know what webcasts are available on the Internet and how to get to them. Although, as we discussed in Chapter 6, some Webmasters steadfastly believe that the Internet itself is the only appropriate medium for promoting webcasts (i.e., via Websites, Usenet newsgroups, or electronic mail), most marketing professionals recognize that the Internet is only one of several means to promote webcasting. Traditional promotional media including direct mail, company newsletters, space advertising, and television or radio announcements are other highly effective ways to notify a potential audience about a webcast and to provide them with the necessary URLs for tuning in.

Sales

Salespeople deal with customers on a daily basis and will (if surveyed appropriately) understand what the customers want (and

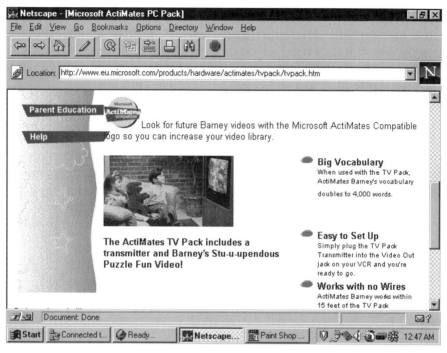

Figure 7.2 Barney doll speaks and takes orders from TV.

don't want) from a webcasting department, and what they like (and don't like) about the webcasting services. The webcasting department needs this information to develop services that meet the customers' needs and to fine-tune the existing ones. On the flip side, the webcasting team will have to educate the sales representatives about webcasting. It is, after all, a new type of service that involves numerous, constantly changing technologies. To sell the service effectively, the sales representatives will need to understand both its potential and its strengths and weaknesses. They will need basic information about the market, the major contenders, and the functions of the various webcasting services. While these activities are by strict definition marketing functions, the webcasting department will likely be asked to contribute knowledge and experiences.

Customer Support

Customer support personnel generally talk to customers after they've bought a company's product or service, often working out problems or support issues. The customer support department may embrace the webcasting department as an extension of existing support activities using electronic mail and traditional Websites. Push webcasting is often useful for informing customers about product updates, changes, service interruptions, and frequently asked questions (FAQ), delivering information directly to the customer's desktop within seconds. (See Figure 7.3.) Audio/video webcasting can be useful for delivering a combination of live-event briefings and archived on-demand clips. Leading-edge companies understand that a good customer support department can be an effective method for building and retaining a solid base of loyal customers, providing them with the necessary information to keep them happy with the products and the company and responding promptly when they have problems.

MIS

The MIS department or any department that attempts to maintain exclusive control can either be a webcasting department's best friend or its worst enemy. A territorial MIS department is likely to want to have control over the webcasting department. This arrangement is not totally unreasonable given the fact that the webcasting department often requires a significant portion of the organization's computing resources and technology budget—money that may be taken out of the MIS department if webcasting is established as an independent department. In addition, in most large corporations MIS usually controls the links to the Internet, is the gatekeeper of bandwidth and data security, and is responsible for building and operating the corporate network. A responsive MIS department can work with a webcasting department to make sure that the webcasting services are accessible to the people who need them and can help to ensure that those services are delivered in the most cost-effective manner possible without compromising security or overloading available bandwidth.

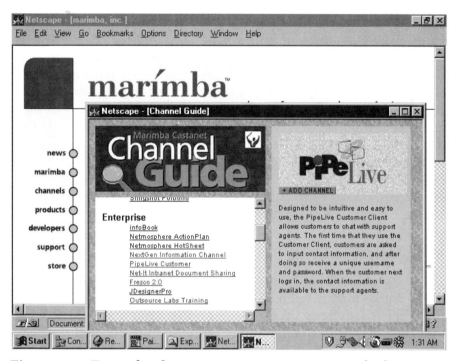

Figure 7.3   Example of customer support message pushed to users.

The bottom line is that, regardless of the organizational structure, webcasting and MIS have to work together. The MIS department has resources that the webcasting department needs, and the webcasting department has the potential to overload the enterprise network if it mismanages its webcast projects. Even if it's not a direct responsibility of the MIS department, webcasting is likely to be a very demanding customer of MIS services—one that requires a close association with frequent interaction.

Helpful tip: Many companies have decision support systems and executive information systems that reach executive management. It is recommended that you review communications through this system and provide a concise schedule of your webcasting activities directly to that system if it is not connected to the Intranet or LAN.

Accounting

In most business organizations, virtually anything that has to do with money has to go through the accounting department. The accountants will need to review budget and revenue projections at each stage during the webcasting planning and implementation process. And they will need to keep track of webcasting expenditures and develop procedures for authorizing payment, billing services, and tracking budgets. Regardless of how a webcasting department is organized, it needs to interact closely with the accounting department and such related functions as purchasing (to authorize new equipment and service purchases) and billing (if the company is billing customers for its webcasting services).

A Stand-alone Webcasting Department

A stand-alone webcasting department is key when the primary goal of the department is to make money for the company, that is, when it has clearly defined profit and loss responsibilities. Public relations, marketing, customer support, and MIS are not profit centers, but are, in the strictest sense, overhead costs. A stand-alone webcasting department can bill other departments for services rendered (and vice versa) without having to be bound by the conventions or budgetary restrictions of any one department.

If a webcasting department doesn't have profit and loss responsibilities, it is often difficult to gauge its success by other means because its success is tied into the capabilities of other departments. If webcasting is being used as a customer support tool, you need to establish mechanisms for measuring and comparing the use of webcast information with traditional customer support functions. For example, if the number of customer support telephone calls remains steady while the total number of customers increases by 3 to 5 percent per month, this may be completely or partially attributable to the webcasting activities. Or, it may just be a result of someone rewriting user manuals for the company's products in plain English rather than technobabble. If webcasting is being used as an indirect marketing tool to generate hits on the corporate Website, tools should be in place to track which hits on the Website are being generated by the webcasting activities themselves, rather than just random activity in the month because the corporation was written up in *Business Week* or *Red Herring.*

Start-up Considerations

Starting a webcasting department may be a difficult proposal to sell to management, especially if it is going to require the company to spend money without a clear return on investment. In fact, creating a new department is never an easy task, since the money to fund and operate it must come from somewhere. One or more existing departments and managers are very likely to resent the fact that you are starting from scratch, probably by getting funding that they would prefer to spend in their own departments.

Half the battle in starting a new department is in having a well-organized, well-written statement and a set of well-defined, obtainable goals. The better the goal definitions, the more likely it is that you can convince management that you know what you are talking about and that they will be willing to commit resources toward a webcasting department. Showing that you can clearly define your conditions for success, be they more hits on the corporate Website or putting the project into the black within the first year, is more likely to win supporters than "Hey, this is a really cool idea."

The idea of webcasting may be so new that they may not be willing to spend a whole lot of money on day one, preferring to start out slow in exchange for a demonstration of the concept. Once the concept has proved to be valid—especially if it generates a profit or a great PR bonanza—you can ask for a larger budget and more personnel.

Even if a webcasting department is being started in a relatively friendly corporate atmosphere, there will be a number of stresses as the other departments begin to learn about webcasting and to adapt it into their own plans. Because webcasting is a new technology, many people take a show-me stance, skeptical that either push or audio/video webcasting can contribute to their own goals and missions.

Communication, training, and proactive internal marketing are the keys to winning over these skeptics. Be very clear about what you are doing through the company's internal communications channels and what services you can offer to departments to help them accomplish their tasks. Use multiple forms of communications, including electronic mail and paper fliers, to let people know what you can do; paper, while old-fashioned, is still preferred in many circles, including high-level decision-making circles. And, do your homework. Are your competitors using webcasting? If so, how? Are they offering services through webcasting that you aren't? Do they appear to be making money or saving money? If they are, selling a webcasting department to management is likely to be a bit easier, especially if you can prove that their webcasting services are contributing to their bottom line—directly or indirectly.

Once senior management has given the go-ahead, all the other players that you have identified as internal customers—PR, marketing, MIS, sales, and customer support—need to become involved. You have to focus on getting the rank and file employees involved in the process during the early stages. If people believe in the project, they are more likely to come through with either time or moral support. Be prepared to do a lot of in-house marketing through electronic mail. Plan to conduct a couple of show-and-tell or open house sessions to educate people throughout the company about what the webcasting department is capable of doing.

A department launch to kick off the new department can serve both as an educational and internal marketing tool, especially if attended by corporate management (e.g., the CEO and vice presidents) to illustrate the company's backing of the new department. The department launch should definitely include an open house with demonstrations of the various webcasting technologies which will be used for information delivery, preferably with the participation of one or more other departments contributing their information and support.

Once operations start, document *everything,* including every live or on-demand webcast conducted, when it took place, the date it took place, and the importance of the activity. Effective logging will help demonstrate to skeptics what you are doing and (hopefully) how it contributes to the company. Similarly, any press mentions or articles should be logged, copies kept, and a request for reprints sent into the publisher. Press coverage keeps the company name in circulation in a way that dry press announcements do not and webcasting activities are still unique enough to break through the mundane barrier that foils typical weekly product announcements. A good trade reporter receives literally hundreds of announcements per week, 90 percent of which end up in the trash.

Personnel/Staffing Issues

If a webcasting department is intended to generate profit, a standalone organization is probably appropriate, reporting directly to a vice president or other corporate officer. If it is not burdened with profit and loss responsibilities, responsibility for webcasting can rest with any of the departments that we discussed earlier, although the marketing department is the most common choice.

The Webcasting Cast of Characters

We offer the following job descriptions (in subheadings) as guidelines for small- to medium-sized webcasting departments within organizations. Start-up departments in small companies or departments that constitute an entire company (i.e., a webcasting company) generally require people with diversified skills that can contribute to the project in a number of ways. Large-scale webcasting departments typically require larger staffs, greater budgets, and more managerial experience.

Department Manager

The manager or director of the webcasting department needs to have strong diplomatic skills. This is especially true in a large company where the webcasting activities are likely to affect the operations of other departments. At the same time, the manager needs to be able to supervise and direct the operations of a two- to five-person production department (more if the webcasting department is working on multiple projects at the same time).

Smaller operations, typically where the webcasting department *is* the company, will require a broader range of skills, especially when working with paying customers for on-demand or live-event audio/video broadcasts. Skills to look for might include sales, marketing, or customer service experience.

Whatever the webcasting department's size, the manager will also have to be the de facto cheerleader/promoter. As such, he or she will have to plan and lead the internal marketing campaign to keep the corporation informed about webcasting services and activities.

For a small audience audio/video webcasting site, management candidates should have the following:

- BA/BS degree in communications, computer arts, or business-related degree
- Two to three years of experience in computers or Internet technology
- One to two years of management experience, including budget work or financial planning

For a large audience audio/video webcasting site, add the following characteristics:

- Two or more years working in the Internet service provider field or in the broadcast industry (radio or TV)
- Supervisory responsibility of at least two or three people

Webcasting Sales/Marketing

Regardless of the size of the webcasting effort, a webcasting salesperson should have at least two to three years of experience either in a technical field, sales, or the broadcast industry. The salesperson does not have to have a detailed technical knowledge of how webcasting works, but should be able to describe the benefits of the particular webcasting products and services to the customer, as well as be able to close the sale (i.e., get the signature on an order). You also want a salesperson who recognizes the value of building long-term customer relationships as much as making the month's quota. Unhappy customers who have been promised something that doesn't exist often transfer their allegiance to another company.

A candidate for a marketing position in a webcasting department also needs to understand the basics: Who are the customers? And what's the best way to reach them? The best candidate for the position also needs to have some experience, preferably two to three years, with an Internet company so that he or she understands how the technology works and who the major competitors are. With rare exceptions, marketers who don't understand the Internet typically need from three to six months to come up to speed and understand the difference between a URL and streaming media—valuable time that may not be available. Remember, the basic conditions of the Internet (i.e., the way you are delivering information through webcasting) change every three to six months as a result of new innovations and technology advances. If it takes six months for your marketer to learn the basics of the Internet, you'll be lagging behind by the time that he or she begins to develop and promote webcasting projects, and the Internet will probably have changed significantly during that time.

Be prepared to spend money on hiring someone who already has experience marketing Internet products and services. Even if you are pitching push or audio/video services to a vertical market, it may be easier for an experienced Internet marketer to pick up the characteristics of the vertical market than to have to wait for an experienced vertical marketer to get up to speed on the specifics of the Net.

Webcast Audio/Video Specialists

A good audio/video specialist should have some artistic capability, an eye for quality, and a real interest in creating informative, innovative A/V clips. If a candidate for an audio/video specialist position doesn't have a love for your product or webcasting, you probably don't want to hire him or her. The A/V specialist is responsible for setting up and monitoring all of the audio and video equipment, including the microphones, the sound mixing boards, video cameras, video mixers, and lighting facilities. Because any number of problems can creep up between the recording and distribution phases, the A/V specialist has to be tuned in to the details at each stage in the process, constantly monitoring the quality to ensure its consistency throughout the webcast. At a minimum, we recommend that the A/V specialist have a degree in RTVF, video, or computer graphics from a four-year college (or a similar degree from a two-year college) and at least two years of webcasting-related work experience. He or she should also be familiar with all types of audio and video equipment and with nonlinear editing and software, such as Adobe Premier.

Webcasting Technicians

Two types of technicians are required for audio/video webcasting projects: an on-site technician and a server manager/distribution network coordinator.

As the name implies, an on-site technician goes onto the site for live events to set up high-speed telecommunications equipment and any necessary local area network gear for the encoding machines (desktop PCs, for the most part) to take the analog audio and video, encode it, and then transmit it to a splitter or distribution network. An experienced technician knows all the ins and outs of PC hardware, can install software, understands the configuration and quirks of encoding software, and knows how all the pieces fit together between the encoding machine and the distribution network. If something goes wrong between encoder and server, the on-site technician needs to be able to troubleshoot and resolve the problems. He or she has to be responsible and be on time, particularly for live-event webcasting projects, willing to work odd hours (no nine-to-fives need apply!), and be willing to travel whenever and wherever it's necessary. In general, the on-site technician needs to be a jack-of-all-trades, someone who has configured PCs and LANs and Internet connections and has the ability to understand and work with the big picture. Good people skills are important as well, since an on-site technician has to deal with the customer and all of the other parties involved in webcasting.

A server manager/distribution network coordinator is responsible for coordinating operations between the encoding machine and the server, and for ensuring that the server talks to the Internet and, if necessary, to the distribution networks (for larger-audience, live-event webcasting). This individual needs to understand the machines that will be running the appropriate software, be they UNIX or NT machines, and to have a solid understanding of network operations and the Internet. These qualifications are particularly important for large-scale, live-event webcasts that can adversely affect the company's Internet connection.

At a minimum, the server manager/distribution network coordinator should have a degree from a two-year college, two (or more) years of experience working in an Internet or TCP/IP environment, and some experience with desktop computers, Ethernet networks, and dial-up communications. In addition, any experience with the various webcasting software tools, ISDN or leased line services, and routers can be extremely beneficial, as can experience managing UNIX or NT server environments.

Content Developers

Like webcasting technicians, content developers come in two flavors: those who are skilled with the written word (i.e., writers) and those who are visually enabled (i.e., graphic artists). You are likely to need both types if you are doing either push or on-demand webcasting. Fortunately, content developers are generally easier to find than A/V specialists or webcasting technicians and, of the two types, people with good writing skills are generally easier to find than good graphic artists. But, both need to understand the differences between creating content for webcasting and creating it for other conventional delivery media. If the content developers don't already have experience creating content for an on-line or broadcast medium, they're likely to need at least some degree of retraining since a lot of the old rules don't apply to the newer media like webcasting. And both will also need an eye for detail and good organizational skills to sort through reams of information to present clear, concise content for webcasting.

When you're evaluating writers, look for on-line experience and be sure to review writing samples—both for conventional delivery media and on-line. Some technical background (or at least a solid understanding of computer and communications technology) is beneficial but not necessarily required. With a little training, nearly anyone can master HTML or learn to use any of the tools that are available for translating conventional text into HTML. In general, it's easier to teach a good, versatile writer any required technology or specialized terminology than it is to train a technician to organize and write material clearly.

Many of the same qualifications hold true for graphic artists; to be effective in developing webcasting content, graphic artists need experience with on-line delivery media and in using a range of computer software tools including, but not limited to, drawing and presentation programs and photo and video editing programs. Ideally, the individual will be as comfortable working in various video editing programs as he or she is working in Adobe Illustrator or Photoshop. Again, be sure to review the candidates' portfolios, paying careful attention to their experience with computer graphics and the on-line media. Also, each graphic artist has an individual style and or preference for presenting material; be sure that the style and preference suits your needs and those of your webcast audience.

Staffing Alternatives

Realistically, given budgetary constraints or internal political considerations, you may not be able to go out and hire the webcasting staff that you need. Or, you just may not be able to find appropriate candidates for the positions that you need to fill. Fortunately, there are some options available; you may be able to retrain some members of your existing staff to perform the webcasting chores or you may be able to rent or hire a company for the people that you need.

Training Existing Personnel

If you have qualified computer technicians available with some experience on the Internet, they can probably pick up most of the skills necessary to operate streaming media software for webcasting. Competent PC technicians can be cross-trained in the basics of TCP/IP connectivity and router operations in short order even if they haven't worked with the Internet before.

High-speed telecommunications skills, such as installing and properly configuring a leased line, definitely require some training and on-the-job experience. In most organizations, leased lines, once installed and tested, stay up and plugged in day after day, month after month. For a live-event webcast, a leased line has to be installed and working the day before the event and has to be taken down the day after the event. To compound matters, telephone companies may install lines, do some cursory testing, and then walk away without allowing the customer to install equipment and do full end-to-end testing of a circuit. Problems can exist in the phone company installation, the equipment, or at the Internet service provider; if you are trying to webcast a live event, you don't have the luxury of taking a week to find and resolve the problems.

The biggest drawback to training in-house personnel is time. It takes time to train people to become comfortable with new tasks, and training time will divert personnel hours that were expected to be applied to current projects. The ramp-up time may be relatively insignificant if you are getting a skilled employee who has worked on a variety of projects over the course of his or her career.

Another hurdle is the replacement of the skilled employee within the company. Assuming the person you are going to retrain and integrate into the webcasting department was contributing productive work for another department, you've suddenly created a hole for that department to fill. The head of that department is not likely to be too happy about the situation unless he or she wasn't satisfied with the employee that you poach for your department. In that case, you may solve the other department manager's problem at the same time you create one for your own department.

Outsourcing

Many webcasting projects, particularly live-event webcasts, are on a relatively short time line (i.e., 30 to 45 days or less). If you are gearing up for a one-time live-event webcast, or even a biannual webcast event, you aren't likely to have the time to recruit the best candidates for your webcasting staff, or even to retrain in-house personnel. You may seek professionals to complete your project on time. But you need to plan ahead and budget accordingly for professionals.

For specialized projects, such as quality video editing with lots of special effects or graphic arts design, farming out tasks on a selective basis may be more cost-effective than hiring specialized personnel. It may also make more sense depending on what the department's goals and mission are.

Outsourcing is useful when the webcasting project is of such magnitude or expected quality that everything must go right. For example, an in-house three-person audio/video webcasting department will probably need to hire a professional audio/video firm to handle the cameras and sound at a significant event, such as a stockholder's meeting that will be viewed and monitored by the national press and Wall Street analysts.

However, outsourcing isn't without disadvantages. On an annualized basis, the cost for outsourced labor may run higher than a staff member on payroll. If you plan on producing a number of webcasting projects over the course of a year, hiring has economic advantages.

Hiring New Personnel

Bringing new faces into a dedicated webcasting department is the best long-term solution if your company intends to webcast on a regular basis (i.e., push marketing or customer support information), provide a library of on-demand webcast programs, or produce a number of live-event webcasts. Hiring allows you to build a team of individuals who can (and must!) work together. But, as we mentioned earlier, webcasting personnel, especially experienced A/V specialists and technicians, are often difficult to find and expensive to retain. The combination of a healthy economy and a glut of high-tech jobs available around the world means that you'll either have to pay for someone with the appropriate amount of experience or (more likely) take someone less qualified and train them in the necessary skills.

Finding an experienced person who is conscientious, detail-oriented, and creative is, without argument, a challenging task, but one that is well worth the investment in time and effort. Appendix A provides a list of webcasting resources that can help you to develop a successful webcasting project or department. This list is only a starting point, however; you'll need to check the Internet for current listings and be sure to ask other organizations in your area or industry for their recommendations. In any case, remember that good webcasting personnel—whether they are full-time, permanent staff or hired guns—are not easy to find, nor are they likely to be cheap. We summarize some of the personnel expenses in the budgeting section of this chapter.

Tools to Help Build the Department

The three basic software tools you'll need when starting a webcasting department are a word processor, a spreadsheet, and a graphics presentation program. The word processing program is necessary to create a variety of documents, including:

- Department mission statement
- Measurable and documentable goals for the first six months of operations
- Business plan to achieve the goals listed in the first six months of operations
- Job descriptions for staff members
- Operating procedures for the new department
- Definitions of responsibility for how the webcasting department interacts with other departments

A spreadsheet is necessary to generate such information as:

♦ Revenue and sales projections, plus profit and loss statements if you are expected to spend money
♦ Documentation of money spent
♦ Employee manual that includes basic information as well
  as specific codes of conduct, events, and copy rules.

You need to have a ballpark idea of how much money the department will spend over the course of its first 30/60/90 days, each
quarter, and for the first year. Once operating, you also need to
know if you are burning through money faster or slower than your
projected estimates. If you are spending less money than projected
while obtaining the same or better results, you're definitely in better shape than overshooting the budget. If the department has profit
and loss responsibilities, another set of spreadsheets will have to be
created to support planning and monitoring for those responsibilities over the appropriate periods.

Finally, presentation software is necessary to condense the key
points about your webcasting effort into summary form to brief
everyone in the company about your goals for the department and
your plans for accomplishing them. Not everyone needs to plough
through your business plans and spreadsheets; everyone needs to
know something about the new department and how they can best
utilize it in their own plans.

Budgeting for the Webcasting Department

The figures that we present in this section are estimates based on
our own experience and general knowledge. Obviously, these figures will vary widely depending on where your organization is
located, the business and personnel costs in your geographic area,
and the type of webcasting that you're doing. It stands to reason
that if your company is located in the Washington, D.C. or New

York City area, with their high cost of living, your webcasting department is going to need a significantly larger budget to cover personnel and business expenses than if it is located in Memphis, Tennessee. If you are located in a major metropolitan area, a competitive hiring environment generally translates into higher salaries, and experienced personnel nearly always command higher salaries than new college graduates with lots of good ideas but little or no real-world work experience. Finally, the opportunity to work on interesting, challenging projects may have a positive affect on salary expectations. For example, if you're pushing new product training material over an intranet for a life insurance company, you may well need to pay higher salaries than the company down the street that specializes in live-event webcasts of rock concerts. (Conversely, the company down the street may have difficulty finding webcast technicians who are willing and able to travel all over the world and work long hours at a time with relatively little notice.)

Attracting good personnel is only the first step in building and maintaining a webcasting department. You also have to retain those staffers, especially after you've spent some time and money honing their various skills and adding to their experience. Be sure to plan for regular salary increases and possibly bonuses if the project is successful. Plan for continual training and conferences or workshops by consultants because of the rapid changes in this field. It is nearly always cheaper in the long run to retain good personnel than it is to have to frequently rehire and retrain staffers. It is also much better for staff morale and helps to maintain consistently high quality in your webcasting service. Experienced employees don't grow on trees; they are nurtured by smart companies that recognize their value and try to keep them satisfied. Remember: There are lots of companies out there trying to initiate webcasting departments; if you don't keep your experienced Webmasters happy and challenged, someone else is likely to steal them away!

Table 7.1 summarizes typical salary ranges for webcasting personnel.

TABLE 7.1   Webcasting Salary Ranges

	Base	Experienced
Audio/visual specialist	$35–37,500	$42–45,000
Encoding/on-site technician	$32–35,000	$37–42,000
Internet connectivity technician	$35–37,500	$43–47,500
Server operations	$35–37,500	$43–47,500
Team manager/producer	$42–45,000	$55–57,500
Sales/marketing	$28–40,000	$40–75,000+

Personnel Training/Retraining Expenses

Even if you manage to hire relatively experienced people, you may need to send them to school, either for vendor training on the particular webcasting software you're using or to update their technical skills (i.e., catch up on the latest developments in communications technology). Training courses by webcasting software vendors should also be viewed as a (human) networking opportunity to get to know sales representatives, technical support people, and developers. You may need a personal contact at some point in your webcasting activities, either by getting an extra software key for a large event before the PO is cut, a bug fix or workaround, or a feature to be included in the next server release. If your vendors know you as a person, not as some nameless firm, it makes them a lot more amenable when you need them the most.

Typical Costs for Outsourcing

Unfortunately, it is very difficult to predict outsourcing expenses. In reality, there are no typical costs for outsourcing projects since the costs depend on what tasks and what size tasks are outsourced. Processing audio or videotapes and hosting the digital files on a third-party server is, for example, far less expensive than hiring a firm to produce an entire live-event webcast—from filming the event through distributing it to the target audience. And, of course, the cost of outsourcing is in addition to all of the standard expenses for communication and ISP services. Regardless of whether you outsource a portion of a webcasting project or the entire project, be sure to plan ahead! Failure to plan, or delaying decision making *always* adds to the cost of outsourcing. Last-minute events require lots of rushing around to procure the necessary equipment and services and coordinate all of the details—taxing the patience of even the most experienced firms.

Totaling It All Up: The Costs of Managing a Webcasting Department

Personnel represents the largest single expense for any webcasting department, regardless of the type of webcasting involved, but as we mentioned earlier, these expenses vary widely depending on a number of factors. When you begin to create a budget for your webcast department, be sure to include one-time acquisition and recurring expenses for all of the following elements:

- Salary and benefits for the webcasting staff
- PC and server hardware
- Software tools
- Communication facilities (i.e., leased lines or higher-speed facilities)
- Internet connectivity services
- Marketing and promotional expenses

In addition, you may need to budget for the recurring expenses involved in ISP services, contracting with a video distribution network, leasing studio space, and/or equipment maintenance contracts. Of these, Internet connectivity and (if necessary) time on a video distribution network are likely to be the most significant. Internet connectivity can vary from a few thousand dollars per month for a T1 facility to tens of thousands of dollars per month for T3 speed. Purchasing time on an Internet video distribution network usually involves paying per viewer/stream and can range from $2.50 to $5.00 per viewer per event. Discounts are generally available for frequent purchases or for large-volume purchases.

Site Management Issues

If you have a popular webcasting site that attracts viewers through on-demand or live material, you also have the opportunity to generate revenue by selling advertising space or to swap advertising space with another firm for increased promotion to your Website. Cash or more exposure? It may be a difficult choice, since more viewers can translate to higher advertising rates down the road.

If you are selling advertising space on your webcasting site, you need to have a systems administrator manage the actual posting of banners, as well as a salesperson to sell the space and someone to bill customers once the ads have run. (Refer to Chapter 2 for details on the various options for charging for advertising.) You'll also need to establish some standards for accepting and displaying ads. There are some products and services that you may not want to advertise, and you may have some companies requesting exclusives for advertising space on your site.

Even if your webcasting venture is being evaluated solely by the amount of revenue that it generates for the company, you'll need to keep track of who tunes in to the webcasts, how often they visit, and if they return to the site. This is particularly true of live webcasting over the Internet, but even if you're webcasting to a captive audience on a corporate intranet, you'll need to know if your customers are taking advantage of the webcasts. All of this information contributes to your knowledge of the audience—ultimately, your customers—and your understanding of their likes and dislikes.

Web logs offer the simplest way to keep track of webcast visitors. They automatically record every click that a visitor makes to a particular Web page and every time that they click on a URL to access either an on-demand video clip or a live-event webcast. Even basic Web log analysis programs keep track of the total number of hits per Web page and URL across a period of time, and can sort them out by day, week, month, and year. As a manager, you need to look at summary reports on a weekly or monthly basis and be able to compare current performance with prior performance on a monthly, quarterly, or annual basis. You need to be able to understand why the number of visitors has suddenly increased over the past month (e.g., exposure from an article published in a recent issue of *Business Week*) and be prepared to increase capacity of Web and/or broadcast servers if necessary.

Most programs permit you to break down the number of hits from a particular domain (computer or ISP), so that you can use deductive reasoning about who is watching your on-line video. For example, anyone from a .EDU domain is typically viewing from a four-year college. Do you want people from colleges watching your webcast or do you want more .com (commercial) sites?

Finally, if you want to become exclusive, you can set up a password-protected site for a pay-per-view type of service and solicit detailed demographic information (age, income, sex, martial status, etc.) in exchange for access to better webcast information or broadcasts.

Updating/Refreshing Content

Websites can become stale if the information and its presentation isn't changed on a regular basis. Viewers become impatient and want compelling visuals on their screens, be it an audio clip or a Java applet of a dancer from a rock video. Stale Websites become unvisited Websites.

On the other hand, you may not have the time or resources to change the look and feel of your webcasting Website every day or every week. Decide upon one look for the hosting side of the Website and lay out a plan to make additions and changes on a scheduled basis.

Content—the audio and video on your Website, be it live-event audio/video or on-demand—should be the driver by which changes are made to your Website. If you want people to visit your Website on a regular basis, you should be prepared to put up new and interesting things on a weekly basis, even if you are running a smaller Website. For large-scale operations which expect many hundreds of live viewers or tens of thousands of on-demand visitors per day, content should be changed and added on an hourly or more frequent basis.

New video content can be as simple as a prerecorded 30-minute weekly briefing produced in-house or a more elaborate live show with interviews, chat, and viewer telephone call-in. Regularly scheduled live events should always be saved digitally and converted into on-demand files. Prerecorded shows should be turned into an on-demand archive. More on-demand content may mean people spend more time exploring the Website.

Video footage, either on analog tape or in digitized form, should *never* be erased. You may want to re-use the video or portions of it for high-speed digital satellite transmissions of webcasts.

CHAPTER EIGHT

LEGAL AND REGULATORY ISSUES IN WEBCASTING

Like every medium before it, webcasting presents a broad range of legal issues. Many of these issues will be familiar to webcasters who have experience in other media, although the unique characteristics of the Web and of webcasting may change the ways that the problems appear, and the ways in which we should resolve them. Some genuinely new legal problems also confront webcasters. Whether the questions are new or merely new twists on old questions, webcasters face far greater uncertainty than traditional media operations because the law has been unable to keep up with the extraordinary pace of technological change on the Web and in webcasting.

In this chapter, we'll show you how to protect the rights to your webcast content and how to use the content of others with minimal risk of liability. We'll also identify other potential pitfalls to avoid with respect to defamation, rights of privacy and publicity, and similar rights and discuss government attempts to regulate or censor Web content. This chapter discusses legal issues relating to privacy and security on the Web and outlines some of the types of agreements that you are either likely to encounter, or that we recommend that you use, as you engage in webcasting.

Protecting Your Webcast Content

Creating custom content for webcasting, as we pointed out in Chapter 5, is nearly always preferable to repurposing existing material, but it is also generally the most difficult because it requires an entirely new effort to make the message fit the media effectively. Even if you purchase or license existing content, you may well have to tailor it for your particular webcast, adding audio and/or video elements to take advantage of webcasting's unique capabilities or to capture (and hold) the attention of your target audience. It stands to reason that, once you've purchased or created webcast content, you want to protect it, preventing others from reusing it or piggybacking on your creativity by borrowing elements for their own webcasts.

Protecting Rights in Material You Create or Own

When you create graphics, text, artwork, photos, music, motion video, and other material for your webcast, you are creating property that you own. Even though the material you have created may be intangible, it contains your creative spark, and your rights as owner of the material may have great value. The United States, like virtually every country in the world, has enacted copyright laws to provide rights to the owners of certain kinds of works that qualify for copyright protection. The sidebar or shaded boxed text contains a brief outline of the basics of copyright law.

As the sidebar indicates, you do not have to apply for copyright protection, or observe any other legal formalities, in order to have copyright rights in a work you have created. Since 1978, U.S. copyright law has provided that copyright exists in a work as soon as the work has been created in a tangible form. This means, for example, that if you have an idea for a song and all that you have done is work out the lyrics in your mind, you do not yet have a copyright right in the song. As soon as you have scribbled the lyrics on a piece of scratch paper, however, you have created a new copyrighted work in which you own the copyright. Similarly, when you

The Basics of Copyright Law

Q: What is copyright law?

An attempt to encourage people to create original works of authorship, by giving authors or other owners certain exclusive rights for a limited period. It tries to balance between the rights of the creators and the users of material.

Q: What kind of material does it protect?

Works of authorship, including literature, music, art, drama, choreography, motion pictures and other audiovisual works (for example, movies and radio and TV shows), sound recordings, and software. It can also protect collective works and other compilations.

It doesn't protect facts, ideas, procedures, or discoveries, and it doesn't protect compilations or databases of fact that are not selected, coordinated, or arranged in an original way.

Q: What does it give the copyright owner?

The exclusive right to do or authorize the following:*

1. Make copies of the work
2. Make derivative works based on the work

Continued

* In addition to the five listed rights of the copyright owner, many countries (especially France and other continental European countries) recognize a moral right of the author. The two main components of the moral right are the right of paternity (i.e., the right to credit as the author) and the right of integrity (i.e., the right to stop mutilation of the work through significant changes, such as changing artwork, colorizing films, or using film editing techniques such as panning and scanning or letterboxing). The moral right is not yet generally recognized in the United States, except with respect to works of visual art, such as sculptures and artwork.

3. Distribute copies of the work

4. Perform the work publicly (including transmission over a computer network or the Internet)

5. Display the work publicly

Q: Are there any exceptions or exemptions?

Yes, lots of them. Some are very specific and apply in certain situations to broadcast stations, libraries, schools, phone companies, and so forth. The main, general exception is the fair use doctrine, discussed under the subheading "Fair Use."

Q: What do I have to do to have a copyright in a work I create?

Nothing. For the past 20 years, the copyright law has provided a copyright automatically to the author of a work as soon as the work has been created in a tangible form.

Q: Are there advantages to using a copyright notice and registering a copyright?

Yes, though both steps are optional. Copyright notice consists of the symbol ©, or the word *Copyright* or the abbreviation *Copr.,* the year of first publication, and the name of the copyright owner (e.g., © 1997 John Wiley & Sons). The notice makes others aware of your claim and avoids defense of innocent infringement.

You can register your work with the Copyright Office by using the applicable Copyright Office form (e.g., for textual or literary works, use Form TX) and submitting a copy or two of the work and a $20 filing fee. Registration is a prerequisite to filing suit for copyright infringement. In addition, if you have registered a work before the work is infringed, you receive valuable advantages in the litigation, such as the ability to recover statutory damages and to recover your attorney's fees and costs.

Continued

> **Q: What are the consequences of infringing on someone's copyright?**
> The infringer will be liable for damages and subject to injunction. The court may impound materials, such as computer equipment, that were used in the act of infringement. For infringing registered works, the infringer may be liable for statutory damages and the plaintiff's attorney's fees and costs. There are also criminal penalties.

create a Web page that resides on a server or exists in some other tangible form, you have automatically obtained the copyright in the material on that page, as long as it is the kind of material that is subject to copyright protection (see sidebar).

While the law gives authors or creators copyright protection in their works immediately and automatically, we recommend that you use a copyright notice on your Website, and that you consider registration of the more valuable components of your webcast material, for the reasons outlined in the sidebar. You can simply place a copyright notice in legible type at the bottom of your home page, and perhaps at the bottom of other pages as well, particularly if users are readily able to deep-link into your site without entering through your home page. In addition to the notice, you may want to add the phrase *All rights reserved,* which provides additional rights under international copyright treaties.

Copyright registration also is a relatively simple process. The U.S. Copyright Office or a copyright law attorney can help you determine which form to use. The forms are only two pages long and have been designed to be simple. The Copyright Office typically grants applications within a few months of filing, and the grant dates back to the date of filing. While there is little point in seeking registration for material that you will not use for long, or that is unlikely to be taken or used by others, you should not hesitate to register a work that you believe has commercial value or is likely to be an irresistible temptation to competitors. Once your staff has collaborated with a copyright lawyer on an application or two, there will be little or no need to involve a lawyer in the process of preparing and filing additional copyright registration applications. (The controversies surrounding the structure of domain names, which entities will have authority to grant domain name registration, and how trademark rights can be protected in the domain name context are beyond the scope of this chapter, which focuses on webcasting issues. For information on these controversies, see useful Websites at www.gtld-mou.org/ and www.inta.org/wpwhole.htm.)

Acquiring Ownership in Materials You Did Not Create

Once you create a copyrighted work, you can sell or assign ownership of the copyright in the work to someone else. Indeed, many artists, songwriters, authors, photographers, software developers, and others make a living (some better than others) this way. After this sale or assignment, the buyer has become the copyright owner and can exercise all of the exclusive rights.

The copyright law requires that agreements to sell or assign ownership in a copyright must be in writing and signed. Similarly, agreements that grant an exclusive license (for example, exclusive rights to broadcast a particular show in a particular local television or radio market, or exclusive rights to webcast a particular work) must also be in writing and signed. (Agreements that grant only nonexclusive licenses or rights need not be in writing, though using written agreements is a good practice, because it helps avoid disputes about the terms of the deal.)

In addition to assignment agreements, the law provides another method by which you can obtain ownership of works that you have not created: the works made for hire doctrine. Most webcasters are not individuals but companies. Companies, of course, only create materials or engage in any action through the efforts of their employees or others whom they have hired or commissioned to perform work.

Under the works made for hire doctrine, an employer owns the copyright in (and, in fact, is even considered the author of) any work prepared by an employee within the scope of his or her employment. Like employment law, copyright law uses a series of tests to determine whether someone you have hired to do work is an employee or has some other relationship with you, such as simply being a freelancer. For this reason, we suggest that you review the nature of your employment relationship with anyone who is preparing valuable copyrighted material for you, from software developers and Web page designers to writers, photographers, and artists. If you want to own the copyright in the material that they are creating without having to enter into formal, written agreements, you should structure your relationships with them so that they will be considered your employees.

The works made for hire doctrine also applies to work by freelancers, but in a different way. For freelancer or other commissioned works, the employer will be considered the author and owner only if the parties have entered into a signed, written agreement that states that the parties consider the work a work made for hire. Moreover, even this careful and formal approach applies only with respect to certain categories of works; for some types of works, even a signed, written agreement of the parties stating that the works are works made for hire will not automatically make them works made for hire. Of the nine categories of works by freelancers that can be turned into works made for hire, two categories have been the most useful for webcasters:

1. Works commissioned for use as contributions to collective works
2. Works commissioned as parts of motion pictures or other audiovisual works

Both of these categories are likely to cover some of the areas in which webcasters are hiring freelancers. Still, in view of the uncertainties of using work made for hire agreements with freelancers, we recommend what lawyers call the belt and suspenders approach in such an agreement. The agreement should contain work made for hire language but should also contain a provision that, if a court concludes that the agreement is not a valid work made for hire agreement, then the agreement is an assignment agreement, under which the freelancer assigns his or her rights to you. We have outlined the key provisions of a standard freelancer agreement in the "Agreement Checklists" section at the end of this chapter.

Policing Your Copyright Rights On-line

Copyright owners have struggled for centuries to find effective ways to police their rights and curtail piracy and infringement, and content providers on the Web face the greatest challenges of all. First, the culture of the Internet, though changing, still contains elements that are fundamentally hostile to copyright law and to any limitations on one's rights to use information. Second, the sheer size of the Web and the Internet, and the fact that they are growing without governance or enforced organization, make it less likely that you would stumble across an infringer. While you can, and should, engage in routine search engine searches to find others using your material, it is likely that if others are using your content without authorization, you will not know about it. We'll discuss some of the security measures that are being developed to deal with the problem of piracy later in this chapter.

Bear in mind that copyright infringement is a double-edged sword. You may, through the actions of a code writer, software developer, or other employee, inadvertently infringe on someone else's rights on the Web. We strongly recommend that you obtain insurance to protect you from liability for copyright infringement and related claims (such as trademark infringement, unfair competition, misappropriation, and violations of the rights of privacy or publicity). This insurance is available in policies that are typically called *errors and omissions* insurance or *media perils* insurance.

Using Content Owned by Others

Many webcasters are broadcasters, cable television programmers, or other companies that operate in media outside the Web. *Others* are companies or schools that obtain material from a wide variety of sources for a wide variety of purposes. One thing that most webcasters have in common is the urge to take material that they have obtained from outside sources and adapt (or repurpose) it for use in webcasting.

As we noted earlier, some material is not or cannot be protected by copyright law and is generally available for use without permission; in addition, some content is material in which the webcaster owns the copyright. With respect to the large universe of remaining copyrighted material, you will either need to find a specific, applicable exception or exemption in the copyright law, or obtain a license (that is, permission) to use the material in webcasting.

Licensing

Copyright licenses are simply grants of permission to use copyrighted material in one or more of the five ways that the copyright law has reserved exclusively for the copyright owner (as the sidebar notes, these are making or distributing copies, making derivative works, or publicly performing or displaying the work). Webcasting certainly involves the public performance right, because transmission of material to the public over a computer network constitutes a public performance of that material. The Copyright Office recently recommended that Congress should *not* create a compulsory license (that is, an automatic right, upon payment of statutorily prescribed fees) to cover Internet retransmissions of radio and television station broadcast signals. See *A Review of the Copyright Licensing Regimes Covering Retransmission of Broadcast Signals,* U.S. Copyright Office, released August 1, 1997, http://lcweb.loc.gov/copyright/more.html#rpt.

Webcasting often also implicates other rights as well. For example, if you have placed a copy of a song or a clip from a video on your server so that a user can click on them at their convenience, then you have made a copy, which involves the copying right. If you permit users to click and download material, you are making a distribution. And if you are altering material in any of a number of ways (such as changing the lyrics of a song or the medium of a work), then you are creating a derivative work. Each of these kinds of uses of third-party material typically requires a license.

Music Licensing

We begin with music licensing because music licenses are central to webcasting and because, unfortunately, music licensing is the most complicated and thorniest area of licensing for webcasters. You will need to know about music licensing if you are streaming music or providing it on-demand, or even if you are incorporating it into your Website in more than the most trivial of ways.

For music, there are two basic sets of rights held by two separate types of copyright holders. The composer of a song (or anyone who has acquired the composer's rights) has rights in the composition or musical work. Copyright law, however, also recognizes separate sound recording rights that are owned by the sound recording copyright holder, which typically is a record company. For many of the most common kinds of uses in webcasting, you will need permission from both sets of copyright holders.

Public Performance Licenses.   The first set of licenses that you will need for webcasting, or playing, music are public performance licenses. These are rights that are granted by the composer or owner of the rights in the musical work. While it is theoretically possible to obtain these rights from the individuals themselves (and might even be practical if you only need rights to a very few songs), most users obtain blanket public performance rights through licenses with the performing rights societies, including ASCAP, BMI, and SESAC. Between them, ASCAP and BMI (the two largest U.S. performing rights societies) control the public performance rights to nearly all of the popular music that you are likely to want to use.

For decades, ASCAP and BMI have operated as collective licensing organizations, providing blanket (and, in some cases, per program or more limited) licenses to users of music in their respective repertoires. They license users from broadcasters, broadcast and cable programming networks, and cable operators to dance studios, restaurants, and stores that play music. Both organizations have now made available licenses for Web use of music. ASCAP's experimental license is available at www.ascap.com/newmedia/licensing.html. BMI's Website license is at www.bmi.com/licensing/web.html. Each license currently requires a minimum annual payment per site of $500, with fees increasing as site revenue increases. Most music-intensive webcasting services are likely to use music from both repertoires, so they are likely to need both licenses.

Broadcasters that begin webcasting sometimes incorrectly assume that their existing ASCAP and BMI broadcast licenses will cover their webcasting activities. In fact, the broadcasting licenses do not, and broadcasters do need separate Web licenses to engage in webcasting. It is our understanding that services such as Audio-Net, which facilitate webcasting by broadcasters and others, can handle the necessary arrangements with ASCAP and BMI, but you should confirm this in your agreement with a streaming or other webcasting vendor.

Synchronization and Mechanical Licenses. In addition to the public performance licenses, you will need an additional license in the likely event that you are creating a copy of the musical work to reside on your server. This copying right also comes from the owner of the rights in the musical work, or its representative. In fact, most holders of these rights are music publishing companies, and The Harry Fox Agency, an arm of the National Music Publishers Association (NMPA), operates as a clearinghouse for many of these rights. This license operates under either of two names. If you are creating a copy of the music that will be played in timed relation with video material (as in a TV show, a movie, or video streaming, etc.), the license is called a synchronization, or sync, license. If you will play the music without video (as in a radio broadcast or audio streaming, etc.), the copying license is called a mechanical license.

In *Frank Music Corp.* v. *CompuServe,* 93 Civ. 8153 (JFK) (S.D.N.Y. filed 1993), members of the NMPA filed suit against CompuServe, claiming that a CompuServe music forum was illegally permitting forum participants to upload and download musical works without the necessary mechanical licenses. CompuServe settled the case in

1995 not only by paying approximately $600,000 to the music publishers, but also by agreeing to use an electronic licensing procedure under which forum users notified The Harry Fox Agency when they made copies of music and to take a license. For more detail on The Harry Fox Agency's on-line services, see www.nmpa.org/nfa/online.html.

Sound Recording Rights.   As noted earlier, the owners of sound recording rights, usually record companies, have rights in their sound recordings (that is, their CDs, tapes, albums, etc.). These rights are more limited than the rights held by owners of musical works, but they are growing and cannot be ignored. For example, if you plan to make and distribute copies of sound recordings through webcasting, you may well need to obtain permission from the record companies. Section 115 of the Copyright Act does contain a compulsory license that permits you to make and distribute copies of sound recordings under some circumstances in exchange for a relatively small statutory fee. Still, there are a number of Websites that exist for illegal sharing and distribution of sound recordings. In the summer of 1997, the Recording Industry Association of America (RIAA) successfully sued and shut down three such sites, indicating the beginning of heightened efforts to stop this illegal activity.

Digital Performance Right in Sound Recordings.   As if this mess was not complicated enough, Congress recently enacted the Digital Performance Right in Sound Recordings Act of 1995. As a result of this complex new law, which applies only to digital audio retransmissions (that is, not to original audio transmissions or to audiovisual transmissions or retransmissions), some webcasters of audio material will be required to obtain yet another license. This time, a performance license from the owners of the sound recording rights in the relevant music must be acquired. The law also provides a compulsory license for some of the types of users who have been snared in the law's new licensing requirement.

Because this law is still relatively new, and the fees and other structural elements of the compulsory license have not yet been established, it is still unclear exactly how this new law and license will operate. In Figure 8.1, we have constructed a flowchart that you can use to determine whether your webcasting activity will fall within the licensing requirements of this new law.

Shortcuts in Music Licensing.   There are some shortcuts through this maze. One is obtaining rights to one or more cleared music or production music libraries. These libraries contain music that has already been precleared for many production uses. You should review any license agreements for such libraries to make sure that they cover webcasting. These libraries are limited in scope and may not contain the particular music you want to webcast, but they can be simple and convenient tools when you have the luxury of flexibility in your webcasting production plan. In addition, there are several companies that specialize in the often time-consuming task of clearing music rights.

Other Major Webcasting Licensing Issues

Webcasters obviously use many types of third-party material other than music. As with music, it is important that you have the licenses necessary to authorize your use of the material. The licenses should be broad enough to cover the specific activity in which you are engaging and the geographic territory in which you are webcasting.

Many broadcasters have obtained rights to syndicated broadcast programming. In these agreements, the syndicator typically limits the granting of rights to broadcast only, not webcasting or on-line transmission, and also typically limits the granting of rights to the local radio or TV market. Webcasting of these programs would, therefore, almost always require additional licenses from their syndicators. Ironically, you may also need to consider whether you are free to transmit commercial spots or other interstitial material over the Internet. The advertisers or other parties placing this material usually want maximum exposure at minimum price, but may have reasons why they do not want the material transmitted outside a particular territory (for example, broader distribution may trigger additional copyright, talent, or guild rights fees for the advertiser).

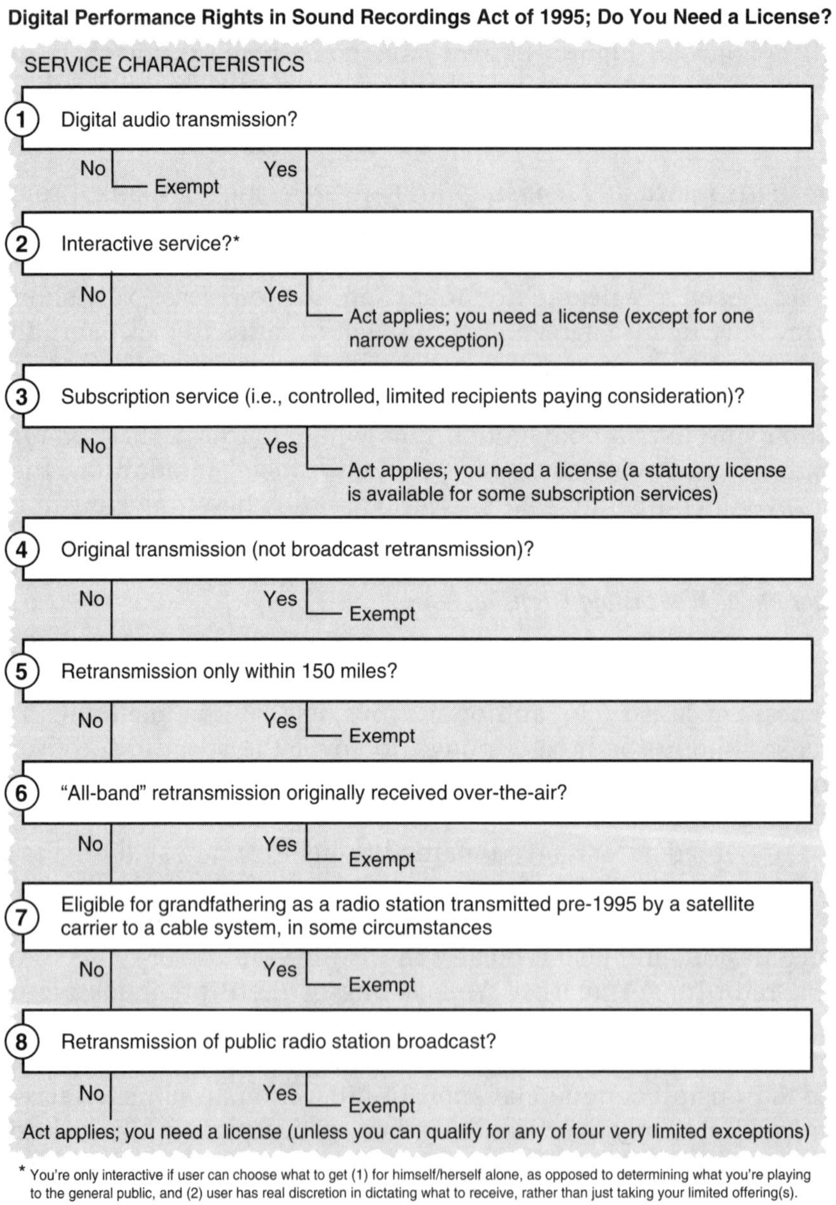

Digital Performance Rights in Sound Recordings Act of 1995; Do You Need a License?

SERVICE CHARACTERISTICS

(1) Digital audio transmission?

No   Yes
   └─ Exempt

(2) Interactive service?*

No   Yes
       └─ Act applies; you need a license (except for one narrow exception)

(3) Subscription service (i.e., controlled, limited recipients paying consideration)?

No   Yes
       └─ Act applies; you need a license (a statutory license is available for some subscription services)

(4) Original transmission (not broadcast retransmission)?

No   Yes
       └─ Exempt

(5) Retransmission only within 150 miles?

No   Yes
       └─ Exempt

(6) "All-band" retransmission originally received over-the-air?

No   Yes
       └─ Exempt

(7) Eligible for grandfathering as a radio station transmitted pre-1995 by a satellite carrier to a cable system, in some circumstances

No   Yes
       └─ Exempt

(8) Retransmission of public radio station broadcast?

No   Yes
       └─ Exempt

Act applies; you need a license (unless you can qualify for any of four very limited exceptions)

* You're only interactive if user can choose what to get (1) for himself/herself alone, as opposed to determining what you're playing to the general public, and (2) user has real discretion in dictating what to receive, rather than just taking your limited offering(s).

Figure 8.1   Webcasting licensing requirements flowchart.

Similarly, newspapers and other print publications often obtain substantial material from wire services, such as AP, and newspaper syndicates. This material includes news reports, many types of data, columns, and comic features. AP has, for several years, worked on an evolving license for on-line use of its material, and all of the major newspaper syndicates also have focused on these issues. Actually, all take the position that their basic license agreements were meant only to authorize local print publication, although the issue of whether the agreements can be interpreted to permit use in an on-line electronic version of a newspaper is not entirely resolved. You should, in any case, carefully review your agreements with the wire services or syndicates before assuming that you are free to use their material in webcasting.

Freelancers and media companies have waged a particularly vigorous battle in the past several years over whether, for example, a newspaper can use a freelancer's contribution to the newspaper in other media, such as on-line versions of the paper. In *Tasini* v. *New York Times,* 93 Civ. 8678 (SS) (S.D.N.Y. 1997), a group of freelance writers sued several print publications and their microfilm and on-line vendors, claiming that the re-use of the writers' articles outside the basic print medium exceeded the scope of the rights that the writers had granted to the print publications. In August, 1997, the court held that Section 201(c) of the Copyright Act authorized the publishers and on-line defendants to distribute the freelancers' articles as part of recognizable electronic versions of the original print publications. The scope of this statutory exception is still not entirely clear, but it does give hiring parties somewhat greater flexibility in dealing with freelancers than before.

Even after the Tasini case, disputes with freelancers, and any question about the ability to use freelance materials in webcasting, will hinge largely on how you have written your agreements with your freelance contributors. (Figure 8.3 contains a checklist of issues you may want to cover in your agreements with freelancers.) As we discussed earlier, the best approach for a party hiring a freelancer is to enter into a works made for hire agreement which gives the hiring party all of the rights in the freelance contribution. Some freelancers fiercely (and understandably) resist such agreements. Whether you insist on works made for hire agreements or use agreements that grant you more limited rights, we recommend that you develop, with your attorney, a set of standard freelance contributor agreements that grant you rights that are broad enough to give you flexibility to use the freelance contributions in a variety of useful ways without having to return each time to the freelancer to seek additional permission (and presumably to pay an additional fee or, worse yet, to have your request denied).

You will also need licenses to webcast films or film clips of more than trivial length. To use films, you should obtain an exhibition license (for transmitting or publicly performing the material) and a reproduction license (for making a copy of the material that resides on your server) from the relevant movie studio. Whenever you obtain any material by license, you should consider several issues in addition to the types of uses permitted by and the geographic scope of the license. You should also address whether the material is licensed exclusively to you, what the length or the term of the license is, how (and how much) you will pay for the material, and you should obtain representations from the licensor that it owns all rights necessary to grant the license, and will indemnify you if there are any problems.

In addition to all of these rights, which are essentially based in copyright, there are other rights clearances to consider. For example, you may need to consider additional talent clearances (or guild or union issues) in webcasting. We discuss these issues later in this chapter.

Uses That Do Not Require a License

As we noted earlier, some uses of material do not require a license. Unless you have agreed not to, you can webcast material that is not protected by copyright or some other law. As the sidebar explains, some material is not eligible for protection.

Public Domain Material. Some material that was once subject to copyright protection may now be in the public domain, and freely available, because its copyright protection has expired. Some very old radio shows, movies, books, songs, and other material that date from the early part of the twentieth century and before may well be in the public domain by now.

You should, nevertheless, be careful about using even material that appears to be in the public domain. It is not always clear whether a particular work—or a particular version of a work—is in the public domain. Public domain vendors of films and other material sometimes give assurances about the public domain status of works that have not been carefully researched, and these vendors may be of little assistance if a party surfaces and threatens to sue for violation of its rights. The Copyright Office or copyright lawyers can search the status of a work for you if you want to remove as much doubt as possible.

Copyright Exceptions and Exemptions. The copyright law contains numerous exceptions and exemptions that permit use of copyrighted work without a license. So far, few of these narrowly crafted exemptions have shown great promise for webcasting. For example, there are exemptions in Section 110 of the Copyright Act that permit the performance of copyrighted material in the course of face-to-face teaching activities, but that do not appear broad enough to benefit webcasters engaged in distance learning or telecommunicated learning activities. In addition, under Section 112 of the Copyright Act, broadcasters enjoy a narrow exemption from the restrictions on making a single copy of copyrighted material, but the exemption is limited to transmissions within the broadcaster's local service area. Therefore, it does not apply to webcasting, although you may have a chance to qualify for the exemption if you are employing only a LAN, a limited WAN, or an intranet, or have some other method of limiting the geographic scope of your webcast transmission.

As a final example, telephone companies, superstation carriers, and other carriers rely on the so-called passive carrier exemption of Section 111(a)(3) of the Copyright Act. This exemption, which applies to carriers that do not control the content of the signals or the recipients of the signals they transmit, clearly does not apply to webcasters, which exercise full editorial control over their signals.

The exemption has also been found, however, to not even apply to Internet service providers (ISPs) in *Religious Technology Center* v. *Netcom,* 907 F. Supp. 1361 (N.D. Cal. 1995), although we believe that there is a reasonably strong argument that the exemption should apply to some or most ISPs that do not attempt to control the content of material sent or received by their customers.

Fair Use.   The primary, and catchall, exception of copyright law is the fair use doctrine, which is codified at Section 107 of the Copyright Act. Briefly, the fair use doctrine permits users, in certain fairly narrow circumstances, to make limited use of the copyrighted material of others without obtaining permission. The doctrine is fuzzy and imprecise; analyses are based on weighing and balancing the facts of each case according to at least four factors enumerated in the copyright law (and sometimes based on other factors as well). Accordingly, the results of these analyses are not always predictable. You should rely on fair use (instead of obtaining clearance) only after consulting a lawyer with some background in copyright law.

The fair use doctrine is more likely to apply for purposes such as news reporting, criticism, comment, teaching, scholarship, and research than for other purposes. Analyses are based on the following four factors:

1. The purpose and character of the use, including whether it is for commercial or for nonprofit educational purposes
2. The nature of the copyrighted work (e.g., fact-based or fictional; published or not)
3. The amount of the portion used in relation to the copyrighted work as a whole
4. The effect of the use on the market for or value of the copyrighted work

Some courts have indicated that they believe that the final factor is the most important one. Because fair use cases are highly fact-specific, legal precedent is of somewhat less help in this area than in others.

Other Content Issues

Webcasters are subject to many content restrictions other than copyright. State laws prohibiting the misappropriation of the rights of privacy and publicity; state laws on defamation, union, and guild issues; and efforts by various governments to censor or regulate Web content may affect your unfettered ability to use the content of your choice in webcasting.

Right of Publicity

State laws generally prohibit the unauthorized taking of an individual's name, likeness, voice, nickname, and other elements of his or her persona and using them for commercial purposes. Most state laws, however, provide fairly broad exceptions that permit the use of persona rights in the context of news reporting or the provision of educational or informational content to the public. The most prominent on-line decision in this area, featuring a picture of Howard Stern's bare buttocks, *Stern* v. *Delphi Internet Services,* 626 N.Y.S.2d 694 (NY Sup. Ct. 1994), confirmed both that individuals have the same publicity rights on-line that they have elsewhere, and that the useful exceptions also apply and are therefore available for webcasters.

Invasion of Privacy and Libel

State laws against invasion of privacy protect against the intrusion into a private person's seclusion, the portraying of a person in a false light, and the public disclosure of private, embarrassing facts. Libel and defamation laws protect against false statements about a person that injure his or her reputation.

Publishing on the Web virtually eliminates limits on the volume of content a publisher can disseminate, makes publication nearly instantaneous, and allows an unprecedented level of interaction between a publication and its audience. Each of these strengths of this new medium also brings heightened levels of legal exposure for libel and invasion of privacy.

Much of the information gathered by the traditional print and broadcast media is ultimately not published. The facts may not be nailed down; the writing may be imprecise, or it may simply not be newsworthy. With nearly infinite space available, a webcaster may be strongly tempted to use as much of this material as possible. The webcaster who submits to the temptation to relax standards in cyberspace simply because space limitations are no longer an issue likely does himself or herself a disservice.

Publishers have long recognized that lawsuits can often be avoided if demands for retraction are handled promptly and sensitively. The immediacy of on-line publishing introduces another layer of complexity into this already delicate process. Though potential libel plaintiffs ordinarily recognize that a print product cannot be altered once it is published, they are likely to demand that offending material be removed instantly from the Web. Editors, however, accustomed to the permanence of print, may be uncomfortable altering the text of an article or other piece once it has been published. But plaintiffs' counsel will doubtless contend that the failure of an on-line publisher to correct an alleged error appearing on the Web as soon as it is brought to the publisher's attention should be punished as an additional injury to the plaintiff.

Bulletin boards and chat areas offer webcasters an unprecedented opportunity to build a community in which users interact with the webcasters they visit and with other visitors who share their interests. But as soon as a webcaster opens a bulletin board, it effectively enters the talk radio business, in which people about whom the webcaster knows little or nothing speak (often with the enthusiasm that comes with anonymity) in a forum for which the webcaster may bear legal responsibility. Opportunities for libel and invasion of privacy abound; you should consider steps to limit your legal exposure, such as including warning language in your site's user or visitor agreement (see the section entitled "Visitor Agreements and Statements"). The Communications Decency Act, most famous for the recent Supreme Court holding that its indecency and obscenity provisions are unconstitutional, also contains a provision (still valid) that provides webcasters and other on-line publishers a safe harbor from certain state laws based on negligence, including negligence in publication or distribution of defamatory statements. See *Zeran* v. *America Online, Inc.,* 958 F. Supp. 1124 (E.D. Va. 1997); *Doe* v. *America Online, Inc.,* No. CL 97-631 AE (Fla. Cir. Ct., Palm Beach County 1997) for examples.

Talent, Union, and Guild Issues

Agreements with talent, such as on-air television news anchors, reporters, hosts and actors, and radio DJs, sometimes limit the distribution of the talent's picture, voice, and so forth to a particular medium, such as radio or television broadcast. In such a situation, you likely need to negotiate with the talent or his or her agent to obtain the additional webcasting right.

More generally, you may obtain rights to use third-party material, such as music, films, or shows that have been created wholly or partially by members of guilds or unions of actors, musicians, and the like. This material may require payment of residuals, which are fees for re-use. Even if you are not a signatory to any guild or union collective bargaining agreements, your use of the material may trigger these payment obligations. We recommend that you put the burden of residual payments on the seller or licensor of this material when you enter into agreements to obtain any third-party material.

Attempts to Censor or Regulate Content

The federal government, several state governments, and the governments of a number of foreign countries have been unable to resist the temptation to regulate or attempt to regulate content on the Internet. Though sometimes stemming from noble motives, these laws often are crafted in sloppy, broad fashion by legislators who do not understand the new medium or the relevant technology. Some of the most prominent attempts to regulate on-line speech in the United States have been struck down as violations of the First Amendment.

The first attempt by the federal government to regulate content, the Communications Decency Act, failed when the Supreme Court held the relevant portions of the CDA unconstitutional in June, 1997 in *Reno* v. *ACLU,* No. 96-511 (U.S. June 26, 1997). Congress enacted the CDA in 1996; among other things, the CDA purported to ban, and criminalize, the transmission of obscene or indecent material to minors and also banned patently offensive depictions of sexual or excretory activities.

The Supreme Court concluded that the language of the CDA was far too vague and created substantial uncertainty as to precisely what had been criminalized. The Court also concluded that, in its zeal to protect children, Congress had also imposed an unacceptable chill on on-line speech between adults.

In its decision, the Supreme Court concluded that Internet speech, unlike speech or expression in radio and television broadcasting, is entitled to the highest possible level of First Amendment protection. The Court signaled that it will be quite skeptical and suspicious of future efforts to regulate Internet speech.

Just as the Court was bestowing on Internet speech a special and highly protected status, it was also setting the stage for potentially anomalous situations for some webcasters. It now appears that broadcasters will have greater freedom as webcasters than as broadcasters. For example, a broadcaster that streams its signal may be violating federal law in broadcasting indecent programming, but the webcast of the same programming would be lawful speech, fully protected by the First Amendment.

States have also attempted to regulate speech on the Internet, generally without success. One court struck down a Georgia statute making it a crime to communicate anonymously over the Internet or to misrepresent a Website as having been created or maintained by another person, and another court invalidated a New York law that restricted the transmission of pornography to minors. However, state laws criminalizing acts such as transmitting child pornography over the Internet or prohibiting harassing or threatening e-mail are likely to be upheld, as they simply mirror the laws that states have successfully applied to more traditional media such as films and the telephone.

In addition, at least one state, Minnesota, has made it clear that it intends to enforce state laws regarding contests and lotteries against people who promote such games on Websites accessible to Minnesota residents. Webcasters using contests, lotteries, or sweepstakes will need to keep abreast of federal, state, and perhaps, foreign regulation.

Not surprisingly, some foreign governments, including Germany, Singapore, and China, also have sought to regulate or limit Internet speech, and their efforts obviously are not hindered by the First Amendment. In Germany, for example, the government has filed criminal charges against German citizens for acts such as distributing Nazi propaganda and maintaining Websites with links to sites promoting terrorism. Other countries have simply blocked their citizens' access to Websites that the government has found objectionable. This has worked more easily in countries, such as China, where the government is the only ISP. In addition, some places (most notably, France and Quebec) have sought to enforce laws requiring that Websites maintained and hosted within their borders be maintained in the favored local language.

Jurisdiction over Webcasting

If the Web is worldwide, you may wonder whether you need to worry about whether your shock jock's streamed audio, or other material that you webcast, may violate laws in distant states or foreign countries. In the United States, courts generally recognize that it is unfair for a court to assert its jurisdiction over a person unless that person has established what are called minimum contacts with the state where the court is located. Ordinarily, courts look to contacts such as purposefully advertising or otherwise seeking the business of consumers in a particular state or signing contracts with citizens of that state. For example, a court is likely to find that a magazine publisher who sends 10,000 copies of a magazine to a particular state has established sufficient contacts with the state to make it fair for the publisher to be hauled into court to face a libel suit there. U.S. courts have struggled with jurisdictional issues in recent decades, as businesses have spread their operations over wider areas. Courts are just beginning to determine these answers in the context of Internet commerce. In deciding whether the Website operator has established the minimum contacts required in a particular state, courts have considered factors such as the number of people from the state who have accessed the site and whether the site has content geared specifically toward people of that state. The mere fact that a Website can be seen in a particular place has not, so far, generally been considered sufficient to establish jurisdiction over the operator of that site.

FCC Regulation of Webcasting

The early indications are that the Federal Communications Commission will try to avoid regulating the Internet. See "Digital Tornado: The Internet and Telecommunications Policy, FCC Office of Plans and Policy Working Paper No. 29," (March 1997) by staffer Kevin Werbach (without necessarily representing the views of the FCC). Certainly the blueprint recently released by the Clinton administration, A Framework for Global Electronic Commerce, available at www.iitf.nist.gov/eleccomm/ecomm.htm, calls for little or no such regulation.

Nevertheless, FCC regulations may affect webcasters indirectly. For example, the FCC rules require any FCC-licensed broadcast station to place in its public inspection file any written comments or suggestions from the public about station operations or programming. The FCC's staff has taken the informal position, which the FCC is now trying to codify, that e-mail comments do have to be included in the public inspection file. We believe that there are strong arguments that messages posted to station Website bulletin boards, chat rooms, or other forums need not be included in the station's public inspection file, but the matter remains in some doubt.

Technological or Industry-Driven Solutions to Content Problems

Because U.S. court decisions so far have strongly suggested that U.S. legislators or regulators will have great difficulty crafting legislation that can survive First Amendment scrutiny, the methods for protecting children from possibly inappropriate Internet content are likely to be technological or industry-driven. One possible solution is software, such as Net Nanny, that restricts children's access to certain Websites. A variety of such programs exist, many of which have the ability to block access to sites containing words that are likely to indicate objectionable content. Other programs allow parents to block access to sites that have been screened by employees of the company that produced the filtering software. Parents using these programs can periodically download lists of new sites with inappropriate material.

Unfortunately, these programs are not foolproof. Software that blocks access to sites containing certain words may inadvertently block Websites that contain discussions regarding science and health that may be appropriate for children but that contain words that also appear on sites containing pornography. Parents who rely on software that blocks access based on the judgment of people reviewing Websites may find they have differing views on what is acceptable for children. Nevertheless, at least two bills currently pending in Congress, H.R. 774 and H.R. 1180, would require ISPs to offer screening software to subscribers.

Some groups have advocated a ratings system for Websites, with either the site or an independent rating authority assigning ratings similar to movie ratings. Software would then enable parents to block children's access to sites carrying certain ratings. The ratings approach to shielding children from sex and violence on television has not received universal acclaim, and it remains to be seen whether ratings would work for the Internet. While these early attempts to engage in self-policing clearly are far from perfect, it may be appropriate for webcasters and others providing Internet content to concentrate on acceptable forms of self-regulation, to avoid the continued threat of government regulation of the medium.

Some Current Web Content Disputes

There are several unresolved disputes or controversies that affect the way that webcasters and other content providers on the Web will do business in the future.

Framing

As most webcasters know, framing is a variation on the more typical Web practice of linking between sites. While linking involves
the clean hand-off of the visitor from the first site to the second,
with framing, the first site does not relinquish control of the visitor.
Rather, the first site permits the visitor to follow a link to a new site,
but it places a frame of its own content around the second site. This
practice is often troubling to the framed site. Because of the frame,
the framed site is displayed through a comparatively small part of
the screen, blocking ads or other content that the framed site
designed to be seen as part of a single screen. The framed site's URL
may not appear, and it may be difficult or impossible to bookmark
the framed site through the frame. The framing site may be selling
advertising in its frame against the content of the framed site, and
advertisers on the framed site may complain about the clutter
caused by simultaneously displayed ads on the framing site. And
with some framing techniques, the visitor's normal navigational
options are limited, and he or she remains framed by the original
framing site as surfing continues.

In *Washington Post Co.* v. *Total News, Inc.,* 97 Civ. 1190 (PKL)
(S.D.N.Y. filed 1997), a number of prominent media companies filed
suit against a framing site called TotalNEWS (www.totalnews.com),
claiming violations of their copyright and trademark rights, misappropriation, and false suggestions of association between Total-
NEWS and the plaintiffs. The case was settled quickly, and the
settlement agreement is posted at www.ljx.com/internet/totalse.htm.
The settlement requires, among other things, that TotalNEWS stop
framing the plaintiffs' sites, that it not use the plaintiffs' logos or
imply a connection with plaintiffs, and it also grants TotalNEWS a
limited linking license that the plaintiffs can revoke if they choose.

There are still a number of sites practicing a variety of framing
techniques on the Web, and the settlement of this case means that
webcasters will have to wait longer for definitive guidance on this
issue. In the meantime, we believe that a framing practice is more
likely to be found legal if the framing site either gets the framed
site's permission or:

1. Does not sell ads directly against the framed site's content
2. Does not delete or obscure the framed site's ads
3. Uses as small a frame as possible
4. Avoids giving the false impression of a connection or association between the two sites

Linking

Hyperlinking obviously is central to the Web's existence and utility, but some Web content providers continue to struggle with the question of how to handle unwanted links to their sites. Sometimes they do not want the link because it is coming from an unsavory site with which they do not want to be associated. In the only reported lawsuit filed so far, the objection was a commercial one.

In *Ticketmaster Corp.* v. *Microsoft Corp.,* No. 97-3055 DDP (C.D. Cal. filed 1997) (for complaint, see www.bna.com/e-law/docs/ ticket.html), Ticketmaster has sued Microsoft to stop one of Microsoft's city-oriented Sidewalk sites from deep-linking far into the Ticketmaster site to the specific page at which visitors can order tickets. As of this writing, there has been little reported development in the case, perhaps in part because Ticketmaster has succeeded in making it technologically difficult for the Sidewalk site to link to its desired internal page target, and perhaps because of recently added disclaimer language on the Sidewalk site.

We believe that sites fighting unwanted links generally will have an uphill battle, but we can envision situations in which they have improved odds, for example, when the link is accomplished in a way that causes public confusion or misunderstanding and particularly when the site providing the link is disreputable. There is also a chance that some forms of deep-linking may ultimately be prohibited, but it is currently too early to predict such a result.

Proxy Caching

AOL and other ISPs cache certain popular Websites in order to speed ISP customer access to the sites; the ISP can provide the customer nearly immediate access to the cached content, rather than having to fetch the content over the open Internet. This shortened access time is clearly good news for both the ISP and the visited site, but a number of visited sites have nevertheless complained about proxy caching.

The two main complaints have been that the visited site does not get credit for the visit for advertising and other traffic purposes, and that the ISPs are not refreshing their versions of the cached sites as quickly as the sites are refreshing themselves, so that visitors may be looking at stale versions of the sites. The cached sites have argued that the act of caching involves the making of an unauthorized copy of the copyrighted material on their site, which is a copyright infringement. There has not yet been litigation on this issue, and we hope there will not be. The solution appears to be cooperation between the ISPs and the cached sites to refresh content in coordination and to share relevant traffic information.

Liability for Copyright Infringement by Others

For the past few years, ISPs and the telephone companies that provide the Internet backbone have pushed hard for legislation that would insulate them from liability for infringing conduct by people who merely use them for Internet access or for conduit services, respectively. Their fears are based on a few cases, such as the *Religious Technology Center* v. *Netcom* case, cited earlier in the section entitled "Copyright Exceptions and Exemptions," that have suggested that they may have liability in some circumstances for the infringing postings of users. The ISP/telephone companies negotiations with interests on the copyright side have not yet succeeded in producing consensus legislation.

This debate has become somewhat more relevant for webcasters because legislation introduced in the summer of 1997 might, if enacted, provide some protection for webcasters that sponsor bulletin boards, chat rooms, or other public forums. Representative Coble (R-N.C.), the chair of the relevant House subcommittee, introduced H.R. 2180, which would insulate providers from liability for infringing material if they did not choose the material or place it on-line themselves, endorse the material, determine the recipients of the material, and did not know the material was infringing or benefit financially from the infringement of the material. The language clearly is designed primarily to help ISPs and telephone companies, but it is deliberately written to apply more broadly. The language could well insulate webcasters from liability for infringing postings of participants on forums provided by webcasters. This bill undoubtedly will go through significant change in the course of a hotly contested legislative battle. At this writing, the bill does not have any immediate prospect of being enacted, but we believe that the debate will continue until some form of legislation is ultimately adopted.

Protection for Databases

As we noted earlier, in the sidebar, U.S. law currently provides only limited protection for databases. The Web provides a significant opportunity to provide access to a variety of constantly updated databases, from timely financial and stock market information to sports statistics, weather updates, classified advertising, and far more. Under the present law, however, the ability of database creators to stop competitors from digitally taking much or all of a database is quite uncertain.

As with the third-party liability efforts described above, there currently are legislative efforts domestically, and there are also treaty efforts internationally, to provide increased protection for databases. These efforts probably will not succeed until some accommodation can be reached between the publishers and others in the information industries (the prodatabase protection side) and the organizations representing librarians, researchers, and scientists who fear that increased database protection will limit their access to information. However, until databases receive greater legal protection, you should proceed with caution before making a commercially valuable database available in the webcasting medium, or in any other accessible digital form. One possible strategy for protecting your databases is described in the next section on visitor agreements.

Visitor Agreements and Statements

A visitor or user agreement is a potentially valuable tool, and we recommend that every webcaster use one. This agreement is a device by which you can set the terms and conditions for the use of your webcast. You will want to customize your agreement or statement to suit your needs. Nevertheless, many visitor agreements cover the following areas:

1. They disclaim responsibility or liability for participant postings on bulletin boards or in chat rooms (generally by indicating that the webcaster reserves the right to delete objectionable postings, but does not assume the obligation to do so).
2. They assert the webcaster's copyright and trademark rights to material in the webcast, warn users not to violate the webcaster's rights or anyone else's, and set limits on what the user can do with the material.
3. They disclaim any warranties or liability for a host of possible problems, ranging from inaccuracies to other possible hazards.
4. They prohibit various objectionable practices, from commercial solicitation to framing to unauthorized use of databases.

You may want to look at the visitor agreements at prominent webcasting sites for other areas you may want to cover. (See Figure 8.2.)

The courts have not yet provided definitive guidance as to whether this kind of visitor agreement actually creates a binding, enforceable agreement between an owner of a Website and a visitor to the site. Nevertheless, a recent decision in the analogous area of computer software shrink-wrap licenses (that is, the fine print on

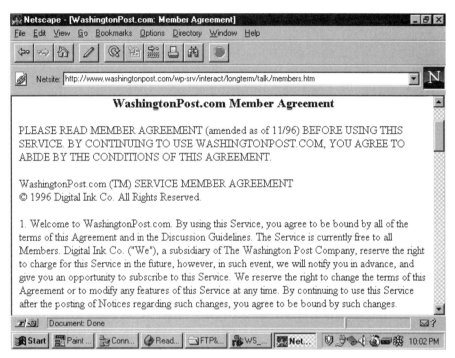

Figure 8.2 Sample visitor agreement (from any Website).

the agreement contained inside the shrink-wrap packaging around the outside of the software box) provides support for the validity of these visitor agreements under some circumstances. The key to creating a valid and enforceable agreement is to indicate—prominently—its existence and to provide a prominent opportunity for visitors to read it. It is not critical that visitors actually read it; the more important element is that you have made sure that visitors know it exists, know that it provides the terms and conditions under which they interact with your webcast, and know that they can easily find it and read it.

Privacy

One of the most intriguing and promising aspects of the Web is its potential for close interaction between content providers and users.

Webcasting promises to make this relationship even more direct and intimate through the use of the push and pull technologies discussed in detail earlier in this book. But even before the development of webcasting, consumer advocates were pressing for new laws and regulations to protect the privacy of Web users, and these advocates will likely be even more alarmed by the heightened level of information that some webcasters obtain from users. Currently, there are efforts to regulate protection of privacy on the Internet, as well as efforts by Web content providers to establish technological or other safeguards, as alternatives to government regulation.

Attempts to Impose Government Regulation

There is not currently any direct regulation of Internet privacy. As of this writing, there are two bills pending in Congress that are of direct interest to webcasters. H.R. 98, introduced by Representative Vento (D-MN), would regulate the use of personally identifiable information provided by users to interactive computer services and would require the service to obtain the user's informed consent before making disclosure of such information. H.R. 1964, introduced by Representative Markey (D-MA), would prohibit the use of personally identifiable information unless the users know that the information is being collected and may be disclosed, and have an ability to opt out of the use or sale of their personal information. For these bills, see http://thomas.loc.gov.

The Federal Trade Commission also is investigating on-line privacy issues, and the momentum for legislation or regulation is likely to come, if at all, from an FTC report to be delivered to Congress by June 1998. The FTC held a workshop on consumer on-line privacy issues in June 1997, focusing on four major topics:

1. Computer databases containing personally identifying information
2. Unsolicited commercial e-mail
3. Consumers' on-line privacy
4. Children's on-line privacy

The FTC is continuing to monitor Web practices. It will make recommendations in its 1998 report to Congress as to whether it believes that industry self-regulation will be sufficient to address the concerns that have been raised, or whether it believes that there is a need for regulation or legislation in the area.

Industry Responses to Privacy Protection

Web services clearly have a stake in avoiding government regulation, and some services have made efforts to address privacy concerns. One of the primary tools has been the development of company or site privacy policies. In a letter sent in July 1997 to the chairs of the House and Senate Commerce Committees (see www.ftc.gov/os/9707/privac97.htm), the FTC commissioners discussed the useful elements of privacy policies and cited the privacy policy adopted by McGraw-Hill as a model. You can find the McGraw-Hill privacy policy at www.mcgraw-hill.com/corporate/news_info/privacy.html.

In addition, a Clinton administration task force recently released a report, available at www.iitf.nist.gov/ipc/privacy.html, that explores options for protecting privacy. Among the principles that the report cites as important are:

◆ Notifying consumers that you are collecting information

◆ Explaining what information you are collecting

◆ Why you are collecting information and how you will use it

◆ What protection you are providing and what remedies consumers have if information is misused

◆ How consumers can opt-out of the information collection

The policy should be clear and easy to find on your site.

While many Web companies have adopted privacy policies, a study in the summer of 1997 found that only 17 of the top 100 Websites have privacy policies, while 49 of these sites collect personally identifiable information. See www2.epic.org/reports/surfer-beware.html. Other Web businesses presumably will adopt privacy policies in the coming months; the Direct Marketing Association has developed a model policy for adoption by companies. See www.the dma .org/home_pages/business_affairs/onlinebd.html. Needless to say, before you adopt a policy, it is important for you to take the time to think about the ways in which you intend to use consumer information and to tailor your policy to meet your business needs.

Labeling

At the FTC's privacy workshop, the Electronic Frontier Foundation and a consortium of companies, Commerce.net, demonstrated a labeling scheme called TRUST-e. TRUST-e assigns *trustmarks* to sites based on the sites' use of personally identifiable information. Sites that do not use any personally identifiable information are labeled "No exchange" sites; sites that collect and use personal data but do not share it with others are labeled "One-to-One"; and sites that provide such data to third parties are labeled "Third party." TRUST-e will automatically notify its user customers of the rating of a site as they arrive at the site, giving the users the relevant information about the site's privacy policies so that the users can decide whether to visit.

Other Technical Solutions

There are various technical solutions that empower consumers to control the amount of information they release to Websites. These products and solutions include the Platform for Privacy Preferences (P3) project developed by the World Wide Web Consortium (W3C), which permits consumers to store their information on their own computers and control what information they release, after reviewing a Website's privacy policy. As of this writing, i33 Technology Corporation is near release of its cupcake tool, which will perform a similar function. Microsoft also has announced its plan to release a Profile Assistant feature in future releases of its Explorer browser, which will provide similar functions to users. There are other approaches as well; the W3C has developed a Platform for Internet Content Selection (PICS) that functions as a filtering technology controlled by the user.

Security

The success of webcasting hinges to some degree on the ability to provide webcasts in a secure way, with only minimal piracy, and within a predictable framework that will facilitate and even encourage electronic commerce. These areas may be the fastest moving targets of all, but we can at least identify the issues that need to be resolved to help facilitate the growth of webcasting.

Encryption and Privacy

The first building block to protecting digital information is the ability to use sophisticated encryption to secure electronic documents. The digital community has been hampered by U.S. laws limiting the export of the most sophisticated encryption algorithms and government requirements with respect to the accessibility of the keys necessary to unlock the encrypted message. The information technology industries continue to fight these battles with the government and particularly with the law enforcement agencies. Encryption is an important tool for providing security for information products on-line, for preserving privacy, and for facilitating sensitive business transactions on the Web.

Moreover, one of the main objectives of security is to fight piracy of Web providers' graphic, audio, or video material. While copyright law and other laws provide at least the theoretical framework for fighting piracy, unauthorized duplication is so easy in the digital environment that webcasters and others are turning to technological solutions as well to protect their material. For example, companies such as Digimarc, NEC Research

Institute, and Aris Technologies provide digital watermarking for audio, video, and multimedia materials. See, for example, www.digimarc.com. This technique involves embedding an invisible sequence of code in material, like a watermark, that travels with the material even if it is digitally lifted and reproduced on another site or in another place. This technology has benefits—it can establish that material has been stolen. It does not, however, have clear deterrent benefits, unless potential pirates know that you are using it. Another company, Liquid Audio, uses encryption technology to block streamed, rebroadcast, or other unauthorized use of music, plus digital watermarking technology.

Other companies are working to develop secure containers, which function essentially as unbreakable electronic envelopes that only legitimate users could open. IBM's Cryptolope software package is designed to protect distribution of virtually any kind of digital content, and to facilitate electronic commerce by incorporating all of the elements of content authentication, transaction audit capabilities, and intellectual property rights management. For more information on the Cryptolope product, see www.cryptolope.ibm.com/products.htm.

Other methods of preserving Web security range from familiar approaches, such as use of password-protected areas and anonymity, to newer practices, such as the use of smart cards. Smart cards have an embedded computer chip that stores personal information and cash credits. A smart card user plugs the card into his or her computer to be read by a Web vendor. The benefit of a smart card is that personal information is stored on a card that is not an integral part of the computer, rather than on the computer's hard drive. This means the information is not accessible to hackers and others with access to the user's personal hard drive. One smart card vendor is Schlumberger Electronic Transactions at www.slb.com/et.

The Role of Security in Electronic Commerce

There are significant efforts at the state and federal levels to try to create a uniform and universal set of standards and model laws to

1. Agreement for Hosting/Server Warehousing/Connectivity

  ◆ *Equipment and services.* Customer provides equipment through purchase or lease; Internet access provider installs equipment within specified time frame, provides Internet connection service, maintains equipment, supplies backup tapes, and provides support staff on specified schedule.

  ◆ *Facility.* Details of host-supplied facility and safety or security features required, such as fire suppression, security protocols, and battery backup.

  ◆ *Term and fees.* Customer to pay equipment installation fees, monthly access fee; access provider will reduce fees in the event of downtime.

  ◆ *Copyright.* Intellectual property rights in all content on the site to be retained by the customer.

  ◆ *Warranties/indemnification/limitation of liability.* Provider not responsible for customer's Website content; provider has all rights to software it utilizes; neither party liable to the other for damages, except that provider is liable to customer for damage to equipment at the facility outside customer's control, and perhaps for downtime damages.

  ◆ *Termination/relocation.* Renewal by mutual agreement, either party may terminate in the event of a material breach or provision of written notice; provider to make available promptly to

Figure 8.3   Some basic webcast agreement checklists.

customer all equipment in the event of termination; if provider terminates, must reimburse for cost of supplying Website access during transition period.

2. Agreement for Site Design or Production

- *Overview.* Provisions and time frame for phases—statement of work, production of Website, testing and acceptance of Website.

- *Content.* Developer to be provided with content for Website.

- *Support.* Provisions for analysis and support services by developer for limited period.

- *Modification to statement of work.* Developer may request written statement of changes; customer recognition of delays in event of modification request.

- *Payment to developer.* Fees and schedule of payments linked to development phases; customer may reject Website as unacceptable (with time to cure permitted) and not pay a predetermined percentage of the cost.

- *Ownership and proprietary rights.* Customer has intellectual property rights to all content, developer assigns rights to all materials developed for customer, source code to be delivered to customer, Website to include copyright notices.

- *Representations/warranties.* Developer warrants that all work is original and does not infringe upon rights of third parties; customer

Figure 8.3   (*Continued*)

warrants that its site content does not infringe upon third party rights.

- *Confidentiality.* Developer pledges confidentiality regarding customer's Website and content.

- *Noncompetition.* Developer will not work for third party to develop a site which would directly compete with the one covered by the agreement.

- *Termination.* In the event of early termination, developer will deliver work completed to date and be paid on a pro rata basis.

3. Agreement for Production of Content: Freelancers

- *Basic terms.* Specification of type of work to be done (generally writing, photography, art, or music), due dates, fees, form of payment, reimbursement, if any, for expenses.

- *Rights.* May be agreement in which limited rights are granted to the hiring party—generally including rights to Web display, reproduce, transmit, license, distribute, and promote using freelancer's name and likeness; or, freelancer's product is a work made for hire and thus the property of the hiring party; alternatively, freelancer assigns all rights to hiring party. If agreement is a license, the territory should be broad (e.g., the world) and the license should be perpetual or for a very long term. Consider whether license is exclusive or nonexclusive.

Figure 8.3 (*Continued*)

- *Editing.* Hiring party may edit or otherwise alter the work in question as it sees fit; hiring party may or may not pay a kill fee if work is rejected.

- *Representations and warranties.* Freelancer represents authorship and that the work will not infringe on the rights of any third party.

- *Independent contractor.* Freelancer is an independent contractor, not an employee.

4. Advertising Agreement

- *Terms of payment.* Specify time and manner of payment, including interest; responsibility of advertiser for expenses and legal fees in the event of failure to make payment.

- *Positioning/audience guarantees/information.* Unless otherwise agreed, Website provider determines where an ad will be positioned on Web page, and provider makes no guarantees regarding usage statistics or levels of impression; provider has all rights to personally identifiable transactional information, click stream data, and other information.

- *Advertising agencies.* To be jointly and severally liable with the advertiser.

- *Renewal.* Provider has sole discretion to renew and may change price for renewal period.

- *Ownership.* Website provider owns any and all creative content it supplies.

- *Assignment and resale.* Advertiser may not attempt to resell or transfer rights.

Figure 8.3   (*Continued*)

◆ *Limitation of liability and indemnification.* Website provider not liable to the advertiser for loss or damages.

◆ *Right to reject.* Web page provider has right to reject or cancel ads on any grounds and at any time, and may also reject URL links embodied in ads.

5. Agreement for Software Licensing/Development

◆ *License of technology.* Granting of rights to Website to use, copy, display, and transmit software for prescribed time period; customer agrees not to reverse engineer or decompile software; customer to pay license fee; software provider to provide prescribed support and maintenance.

◆ *Development of software application.* Specifications for goal of development, step-by-step (milestone) procedure process and conditions of acceptability, fee schedule linked to milestones, penalties for missed milestones, price protection for customer within a fixed percentage.

◆ *Ownership.* Sometimes customer maintains ownership of software under works made for hire doctrine or alternatively by assignment; sometimes vendor/developer only grants a limited license.

◆ *Fees or sharing of site revenue.* Will customer pay vendor predetermined fees or a percentage split of revenue between customer and software developer?

Figure 8.3 (*Continued*)

- *Exclusivity.* Prohibition on vendor regarding licensing or developing same or similar software for third parties or direct competitors.
- *Promotional activities.* Permission for designation of software origin on Web pages; consent required for press releases; encouragement of promotional campaigns; provision for links to software designer's Website.
- *Representations and warranties.* Software designer gives representations on quality of software and its intellectual property rights in it; also gives warranties on absence of malicious code and year 2000 compliance of software.
- *Confidential information.* Restrictions on disclosure of information about customer activities by software provider, allowable exceptions.
- *Vendor failures.* Provide for escrow of and access to code, penalties, and other remedies if vendor fails to provide required service, support or maintenance.

Figure 8.3   (*Continued*)

encourage electronic commerce. The Clinton administration is supportive of these efforts; its general position is outlined in its report, "A Framework for Global Electronic Commerce," which we cited earlier in the section on the FCC regulation of webcasting. Among the most important issues are achieving uniform and secure practices for electronic and digital signatures, how to establish reliable certification or authentication authorities that can verify identities and authorizations within secure electronic commerce, and how to apply laws on credit card transactions to the Web.

The standards for electronic commerce, and the methods for effective provision of security, continue to be in a state of rapid evolution. It is critical that uniform laws develop to make electronic commerce predictable and trustworthy, and that encryption and other methods of security develop to provide the public confidence necessary to permit substantial business to be transacted on the Web.

Agreement Checklists

Webcasters must enter into a wide range of agreements in order to do business. While it is not possible to cover every agreement you may face, or provide agreements in great detail, we have provided at least some minimal checklists for five types of typical webcaster agreements in Figure 8.3.

WEBCASTING RESOURCES

Dial-Up Multicasting Resources

Multicasting service is becoming available to select dial-up Internet users. Until now, almost all webcasting on the Internet has been delivered using unicast transmission. Unicasting sends out one copy of each webcast data packet for each viewer through the entire Internet connection between webcaster and viewers. This means that a 20-Kbps stream webcast with 50,000 simultaneous viewers will require 1 Gbps of server bandwidth. A single ISP would have trouble handling this much traffic, and indeed such a webcast might clog up the network access points (or NAPs) of the Internet.

Multicasting requires transmission of only one copy of each webcast data packet through any Internet connection. The webcast server sends out a single data packet, and only at points in the Internet where the data needs to go in different directions to reach different viewers (such as routers or switches) is the data packet cloned, and a copy of the packet is sent in each of those different directions. Multicasting is the most efficient way to do live event webcasts to large numbers of viewers. Webcast events with millions of simultaneous viewers are possible using multicasting. Multicast is the key to turning webcasting into true mass media.

Thanks for the Dial-Up Multicasting Information to Thomas Edwards, The Sync, Inc. (thomas@thesync.com), whose website contains an updated list of the lastest additions to the Dial-Up Multicasting marketplace: www.thesync.

Until recently, multicasting was only implemented as unicast "tunnels" between specially equipped Unix machines on high-speed networks, known as the MBONE (short for "multicast backbone"). In the last two years, multicast-capable routers have been deployed by some ISPs, and only in the last year has the hardware that dial-up users call into (known as "access servers," "WAN switches," or "terminal servers") been available with multicast capability. A handful of ISPs have now announced the availability of multicast to their dial-up users.

For example, UUNet has announced UUCast, a service that webcasters can use to send multicast webcasts to UUNet dial-up users. The significant limitation of this service is that you can only reach UUNet users, and not other multicast capable ISPs. AudioNet, however, is currently in trials to deliver multicast webcasts to partners Erols Internet, The Microsoft Network, IDT, GTE, InReach Internet, and UUNet. This kind of "commercial MBONE" service, which allows multicasters to reach multiple multicast enabled ISPs, will be required at first because ISPs do not currently exchange multicast traffic.

For more information on developments in this area, go to Webcast Week's dial-up multicast information page at http://webcast-week.com/multicast.html.

Multicast Webcast Services

UUNet (UUCast Service)
www.uu.net
3060 Williams Drive
Fairfax, VA 22031
1-703-206-5600
1-800-488-6383

AudioNet
www.audionet.com
2914 Taylor Street
Dallas, Texas 75226
1-214-748-6660

Multicast-capable Access Servers

Ascend Communications (MAX Series)
www.ascend.com
Ascend Communications, Inc.
One Ascend Plaza
1701 Harbor Bay Parkway
Alameda, CA 94502
1-800-621-9578

Miscellaneous Multicasting Products, Services

Mobile Internet Broadcast Devices
www.audible.com
www.audiohwy.com

Digital Watermarking Companies
BBN
Aris Technologies (MusicCode)
Dice (Argent)

Music Delivery—Sound Technology
Cerberus Central Limited
Eurodat
www.liquidaudio.com
www.dolby.com
A2bmusic.com (ATT's New Music Net Distribution System)

IP Multicast Product and Service List

Review www.ipmulticast.com for a complete listing of products
and services. These different companies, from software, hardware,
and consulting, provide support, services, and products that work
with multicast networks. This list is not inclusive and is comprised
of members of the IP Multicast Initiative. You will note that these

companies include streaming media, push, technology, infrastructure, and Internet Service Providers who are working together to implement multicasting delivery of audio and video on the Internet and other digital networks. Go to ipmulticast.com and review the products and services and the links to these executives' Websites. After review, here are the specific contacts for your corporation related to your multicasting needs.

3Com
Bob Roman
Director, Business Development
408-764-5237
Bob_Roman@3mail.3com.com

Adaptive Media
Deven Kalra
CEO
408-481-1700
kalra@adaptivemedia.com

Ascend Communications, Inc.
Steve Thomas
Director ISP Marketing
510-747-2324
sthomas@ascend.com
www.ascend.com

AT&T
Steve Nurenberg
District Manager
908-949-1020
s.nurenberg@att.com
www.att.com

AudioNet
Mark Cuban
President

214-748-1125
mcuban@audionet.com
www.audionet.com

BackWeb Technologies
Mikki Nasch
VP Business Development
408-437-0200
http://backweb.com

Bay Networks, Inc.
Adam Dunstan
Senior Product Manager
508-916-8498
adunstan@BayNetworks.com

BPG
Dan Fortune
VP Business Development
www.bpgnet.com

Cable Television Laboratories
Jerry Bennington
Sr VP Internet Technology
303-661-3790
j.bennington@cablelabs.com

Cabletron Systems/Zeitnet
Dave Roberts
Product Marketing Manager

408-565-9307
dave.roberts@zeitnet.com

Cascade Communications Corp.
Fred Sammartino
Director, IP Marketing
508-952-1201
fred@casc.com

Cisco Systems, Inc.
Lisa Birch
Product Manager, Multicast
    Technologies
408-527-2462
libirch@cisco.com

Condat, Germany
Dominik Zimmermann
49-30-39-094437
dz@condat.de
www.condat.de/uk/index
    .htm

DataBeam Corp.
Susmitha Bellam
415-368-1800
sbellam@databeam.com
www.databeam.com

Digital Equipment Corp.
Nancy Cappuccio
Internet Marketing Manager
508-486-6434
Cappuccio@mail.dec.com
www.dec.com

Ericsson
Tapio Anttila
Manager, Business
    Development

468-719-4494
tapio.anttila@lme.ericsson.se

Exodus Communications, Inc.
B.V. Jagadeesh
VP Engineering
408-486-5018
bvj@exodus.net
www.exodus.net

Fantastic Corporation, The
Wen Liao
Director of Marketing
212-363-4226
wcliao@fantistic-usa.com

FORE Systems, Inc.
Andy Reid
ForeThought Product Manager
412-635-3657
areid@fore.com
www.fore.com

FTP Software
J.D. Stanley III
Product Manager, Kernel
    Products
508-684-6348
jdstanley@ftp.com
www.ftp.com

Genuity, Inc.
www.genuity.com

GigaLabs, Inc.
Alice Homolka
Marketing Manager
408-481-3030 x233
ahomolka@gigalabs.com
www.gigalabs.com

Gilat Satellite Networks
Yoram Zylberberg
Director, Internet Products
972-392-52195
yoram@gilat.com
www.gilat.com

GlobalCast Communications, Inc.
Albert Chen
Director of Marketing
510-266-0404
achen@gcast.com
www.gcast.com

GTE Internetworking
Rich Blatt
Service Line Manager
617-873-4281
rblatt@bbn.com

Hewlett-Packard Company
Paul Congden
Senior Architect Lab and
   Marketing
916-785-5753
paul_congdon@hp.com

Hughes Network Systems
Dennis Conti
VP of North American Sales &
   Marketing
301-428-5581
conti@lando.hns.com
www.hns.com

IBM
John Tavs
TCP/IP Technology Manager
919-254-7610
tavs@raleigh.ibm.com
www.raleigh.ibm.com/icf/
   icfnww.html

ICAST Corporation
Vinay Kumar
CEO and President
408-874-0700
vinay@mbone.com

Icon CMT
Bret S. Brase
Director, Advanced
   Development
800-572-4266 x1364
bbrase@icon.com

Intel Corporation
Pierre Laurent
Marketing Manager, PC RSVP
503-264-9168
pierrel@ibeam.intel.com

Intelligent Devices Inc.
Mitch Robinson
President & COO
301-874-5800
mrobinson@idinets.com
www.idinets.erols.com

INTELSAT
Susan Gordon
Manager, Media & Industry
   Relations
202-944-6890
susan.gordon@intelsat.int
www.intelsat.int

Internet Initiative Japan
Naoto Fujii
Assistant Manager, Engineer
816-459-4788
fujii@iij.ad.jp
www.iij.ad.jp/

Loral/CyberStar
Mark Rafter
Director of Engineering
650-852-7398
rafter.mark@ssd.loral.com
www.cyberstarcom.com/

Lucent Technologies, Inc.
David Stahl
Business Development—Bell
  Labs
908-949-1767
dstahl@lucent.com
www.bell-labs.com

MCI
Howard Hempenius
Senior Manager, Internet MCI
703-715-7161
0002047189@mcimail.com

Media4, Inc.
John Martinez
Application Developer
404-870-0001
jvm@m4.com
www.m4.com

MediaOne
Kip Compton
617-854-3245
kcompton@mediaone.com

Microsoft Corporation
John Paddleford
Program Manager, Microsoft
  NetShow
425-703-9397
jpaddle@microsoft.com

Microspace Communications
Greg Hurt
Account Executive
919-850-4561
ghurt@microspace.com
www.microspace.com

**Multimedia Research Group,
  Inc.**
Gary G. Schultz
President, Principal Analyst
408-524-9767
ggs@mrgco.com
www.mrgco.com

NASA Ames Research Center
David Meyers
415-604-0735
dmeyers@vod.arc.nasa.gov
www.nasa.gov

Netcast Communications
Robin Wang
Marketing Manager
212-248-2989
robin@netcast.com
www.netcast.com

Netscape Communications
Christopher Walton
Product Manager, Media Server
415-937-3271
cwalton@netscape.com

Newbridge Networks, Inc.
Marc Pfeiffer
Director of Product Marketing
703-736-5916
mpfeiffe@us.newbridge.com
www.newbridge.com

Novell, Inc.
Steve Stokes
Software Development Manager
408-473-8475
stokes@novell.com

ONE TOUCH Systems, Inc.
Steve Lewis
408-436-4610
lewis@onetouch.com
www.onetouch.com

Open Horizon
Andrew Philips
Development Manager
415-869-2223
andy_philips@openhorizon.com
www.openhorizon.com

Orion Network Systems
David Puente
VP Business Development
301-258-3232
6936035@mcimail.com
www.OrionNetworks.net

Packet Engines, Inc.
Kevin Sheehan
Product Manager
509-922-9190
kevins@packetengines.com
www.packetengines.com

PeerLogic, Inc.
John Roberts
VP Development
415-626-4545
jroberts@peerlogic.com
www.peerlogic.com

Precept Software, Inc.
Judy Estrin
President and CEO
415-845-5200
jestrin@precept.com
www.precept.com

Progressive Networks
Mike Metzger
General Manager
206-674-2227
mikem@prognet.com
www.prognet.com

Rapid City Communications
Ross Schibler
Director of Software
415-937-1370
ross@rapid-city.com

Silicon Graphics, Inc.
Bill Melohn
Director, Network Engineering
415-933-2628
melohn@sgi.com
www.sgi.com

Sitara Networks, Inc.
Malik Khan
Founder & CEO
617-487-5910
mkhan@ktwonet.com
www.ktwonet.com

StarBurst Communications
Stephen A. Collins
Vice President Marketing
508-287-5560
scollins@starburstcom.com
www.starburstcom.com

StarGuide Digital Networks
Larry Hinderks
CTO
702-686-5050
dr_musicam_audio@msn.com
www.starguidedigital.com

Starlight Networks, Inc.
Sanjit Shah
Product Line Manager
415-528-7310
sanjits@starlight.com
www.starlight.com

Sun Microsystems, Inc.
Bob Bressler
Chief Scientist, Networking
415-336-7135
bob.bressler@sun.com

Target Vision, Inc.
Michael Hasenauer
Director, R&D
716-248-0550
mhasenauer@targetvision.com
www.targetvision.com

Telemedia Systems Ltd.
Andy Jackson
Director of Business Strategy
ajackson@telemedia.co.uk
www.telemedia.co.uk

TIBCO, Inc.
Mark Bowles
Vice President, TIB Products
415-846-5073
bowles@tibco.com

Torrent Networking, Inc.
Gordon Saussy
VP of Marketing
301-918-3984
gsaussy@torrentnet.com
www.torrentnet.com

USC Information Sciences Institute
Joe Bannister
Associate Director
310-822-1511
joseph@isi.edu

UUNet Technologies, Inc.
Kelly King
Product Manager for IP
703-208-3890
kellyk@uu.net
www.us.uu.net/

VDOnet
Ori Cohen
Director of Technical Marketing
617-621-1517
orico@vdo.net
www.vdo.net

ViaSat, Inc.
John Puetz
Director, Business Development
760-438-8099
jpuetz@viasat.com
www.viasat.cerfnet.com

Vivo Software, Inc.
Dr. Staffan Ericsson
Chairman
617-899-8900
staffan@vivo.com

VXtreme, Inc.
Kendra Anderson
408-617-2328
kendra@vxtreme.com

White Pine Software, Inc.
David O. Bundy
Vice President, Engineering
603-886-9050
dbundy@wpine.com

Xerox PARC
Bill Fenner
Member of Research Staff
415-812-4816
fenner@parc.xerox.com

@Home Network
Mark Green
Senior Scientist
415-569-5242
markg@home.net
www.home.net

Push Media Companies

AirMedia
11 East 26th Street, 16th Floor
New York, NY 10010-1402
212-843-0000
www.airmedia.com, airmaster@airmedia.com

Thanks to Peter Chislett, president of Pushconcepts.com, whose site www.push-concepts.com includes a list of all the current articles found on the Internet about push and an updated listing of new push companies and the focus of their products. Some push vendors and consultants are specializing in certain areas such as medicine and education and this Website should be referred to for current additions to this marketplace. Peter can be reached at peter@pushconcepts.com.

Astound Incorporated
3160 West Bayshore Road
Palo Alto, CA 94303
415-845-6200
www.astound.com, sales@astound.com

Back Web
2077 Gateway Place, Suite 500
San Jose, CA 95110
408-933-1700
www.backweb.com sales@backweb.com

BroadVision, Inc
333 Distel Circle
Los Altos, CA 94022
415-943-3600
www.broadvision.com, jkromhout@broadvision.com

Desktop News
350 Fifth Avenue, 77th Floor
New York, NY 10118
212-290-5000
www.desktopnews.com, feedback@desktopnews.com

Diffusion
321 Castro St.
Mountain View, CA 94041
650-237-8500
www.diffusion.com, websales@diffusion.com

FirstFloor Software
444 Castro Street, Suite 200
Mountain View, CA 94041
650-968-1101
www.firstfloor.com, lobby@firstfloor.com

inCommon, Inc
1875 South Grant Street, suite 110
San Mateo, CA 94402
415-345-5432
www.incommon.com, feedback@incommon.com

Intermind Corporation
217 Pine Street
Seattle, WA 98101-1500
206-812-6000
www.intermind.com, peterh@intermind.com

Marimba, Inc.
445 Sherman Ave.
Palo Alto, CA 94306
650-328-5282
www.marimba.com, info@marimba.com

Microsoft, Inc.
One Microsoft Way
Redmond, WA 98052-6399
206-882-8080
www.microsoft.com/ie/ie40/features info@microsoft.com

NETdelivery Corporation
4900 Pearl East Circle, Suite 109
Boulder, Colorado 80301
303-448-1110
www.netdelivery.com, info@netdelivery.com

Netscape
501 E. Middlefield Rd.
Mountain View, CA 94043
415-937-2555
http://home.netscape.com/comprod/products/communicator/
    netcaster.html, info@netscape.com

PointCast Inc.
501 Macara Avenue
Sunnyvale, CA 94086
408-990-7000
www.pointcast.com, info@pointcast.com

Tierra Communications Inc.
300 March Rd., Suite 303

Kanata, Ontario, Canada, K2K 2E2
613.591.8000
www.tierra.com, info@tierra.com

Vitria Technology, Inc.
500 Ellis Street
Mountain View, CA 94043
415-237-6900
www.vitria.com, getreal@vitria.com

WavePhore, Inc.
3311 N 44th Street, #100
Phoenix, AZ 85018
602-952-5500
www.wavephore.com, info@wavephore.com (Wavephore is a
  broadcast type push using the Vertical Blanking Interval of a TV
  Signal)

Wayfarer Communications, Inc.
2041 Landings Drive
Mountain View, CA 94043
800-300-8559
www.wayfarer.com, info@wayfarer.com

XcelleNet, Inc.
5 Concourse Parkway, Suite 850
Atlanta, GA 30328
800-322-3366
www.xcellenet.com, info@xcellenet.com

Additional On-line Push Resources

AfterDark Online	http://www.afterdark.com
AlphaConnect StockVue	http://www.alphaconnect.com
DataChannel	http://www.datachannel.com
NetDelivery	http://www.netdelivery.com

Push Enhancement, http://www.netperceptions.com, slarsen@netperceptions.com, 800-466-0711

Push/Pull Intelligence, http://www.agentware.com, info@agentware.com, 415-326-6300

www.channelsoftware.com, channel@intekom.co.za, Rivonia, South Africa

www.digitaldeliverance.com, crosbie@well.com

www.pushconcepts.com, peter@pushconcepts.com, New York, NY

www.pushgroup.net, mike@pushgroup.net, New York, NY

Streaming Content

Select sites demonstrating innovative use of Webcasting and Resources, as well as aggregated content sites, guides, and enhancements.

Alternative Entertainment Network TV	http://www.aentv.com
Audible	http://www.audible.com
Audio Highway	http://www.audiohwy.com
Audionet	http://www.audionet.com
Blue Platypus	http://www.blueplatypus.com
BPG	http://www.bpgnet.com/
Cheetah (Captioning)	http://www.cheetahcast.com/ framesx.html
C-Span On-Line	http://www.cspan
Daily Briefing	http://www.dailybriefing.com

Deadradio.com	http://www.deadradio.com
Entertainment News Daily	http://www .entertainmentnewsdaily.com
Grit Broadcasting	http://www.grit.net/
ie40.audionet.com	http://www.ie40.audionet.com
INTV NET	http://www.intv.net
ITV.NET	http://www.itv.net
JamTV Corp,	http://www.rollingstone.com, http://www.jamtv.com
Live Concerts	http://www.liveconcerts.com
Mediacast	http://www.mediacast.com/ Company/
Mediadome	http://www.mediadome.com
Microsoft Netshow	http://www.microsoft.com/ netshow
MIT List of Radio Webcasters	http://wmbr.mit.edu/stations/list
MSNBC Desktop	http://www.businessvideo .msnbc.com
Music Net	http://www.musicnet.com
N2K Inc	http://www.musicboulevard.com
NetRadio	http://www.netradio.net
Plugged In	http://www.pluggedin.com
Policescanner.com	http://www.policescanner.com

Radio Channel	http://www.radiochannel.com
Radio Stations in RA	http://www.geocities.com/ ResearchTriangle/1803/
Radio Tower Radio Live Lists	http://www.radiotower.com/ console/
Real Time Reporters (Captioning)	http://www.rtreporters.com/
Real	http://www.real.com
Sportsradio.com	http://www.sportsradio.com
Sportsworld.com	http://www.sportsworld.com
Super Sonic Boom	http://www.supersonicboom .com
The Sync	http://www.thesync.com
Timecast	http://www.timecast.com/
vcall.com	http://www.vcall.com
Webactive	http://www.webactive.com
WebTV	http://www.webtv.com
Westerns.com	http://www.westerns.com
Wordcasters (Captioning)	http://www.wordcasters.com
Xing	http://www.xingtech.com/content/ sw2_content.html#Webcast
Yahoo (webcasting listings)	http://events.yahoo.com/events .html
Yahoo/Timecast Alliance	http://yahoo.timecast.com/ livenow.html

Streaming Hardware, Software

Compression	http://www.iterated.com
Zephyr	http://www.zephyr.com
Rightsholder Issues	http://www.majorleaguebaseball.com/special/nrfaq.sml

Streaming Media Companies

Macromedia, Inc. (Shockwave)
600 Townsend, San Francisco, CA 94103-4945
Telephone: (415) 252-2000
Fax: (415) 626-0554
http://www.macromedia.com

Microsoft Corporation NetShow
One Microsoft Way, Redmond, WA 98052
Telephone: (425) 882-8080
Fax: (425) 936-7329
http://www.microsoft.com/netshow

Real Networks Progressive Networks (RealAudio, RealPlayer)
1111 Third Avenue, Suite 2900, Seattle, Washington 98101
Telephone: (206) 674-2700
Fax: (206) 674-2699
http://www.real.com/
http://www.real.com/products/ra3.0/index.html (Audio)
http://www.real.com/products/realvideo/index.html (Video)

Vivo (VivoActive)
411 Waverley Oaks Road, Waltham, MA 02154-8414
Telephone: (617) 899-8900
Fax: (617) 899-1400
e-mail: info@vivoc.com
http://www.vivo.com

VDOnet Corporation (VDOLive)
4009 Miranda Avenue, Suite 250, Palo Alto, CA 94304
Telephone: (415) 846-7700
Fax: (415) 846-7900
http://www.vdo.net

VXtreme, Inc. (Web Theater)
675 Almanor Avenue,
Sunnyvale, CA 94086
Telephone: (408) 617-2330
Fax: (408) 245-9770
e-mail: info@vxtreme.com
http://vxtreme.com

Telos Systems (AudioActive)
2101 Superior Avenue, Cleveland, OH 44114
Telephone: (216) 241-7225
Fax: (216) 241-4103
http://www.telos-systems.com/

Xing Technology Corporation (StreamWorks)
810 Fiero Lane, San Luis Obispo, CA 93401
Telephone: (805) 783-0400
Fax: (805) 783-4930
http://www.xingtech.com

Streaming Media/Webcams, Components

Cinecom	http://www.cinecom.com/
CineWeb	http://www.digigami.com/cineweb/
GTS—Graham Technologies	http://www.graham.com/company
InterVU	http://www.intervu.net
LiquidAudio	http://www.liquidaudio.com
Netscape Media Server	http://home.netscape.com/eng/media/

TrueSpeech	http://www.dspg.com/
Vosaic	http://www.vosaic.com
WebCams	http://www.mattheij.nl/webcam.html
Digital webcam	http://www.quickcam.com

Streaming Media/Push API, and Enhancements

RCS Software (Scheduling Programs/Automation Software)
914-723-8567
http://www.rcsworks.com

STD, Solana Technology Development Corporation (Electronic DNA)
619-677-6522
http://www.solanatech.com

Liquid Audio, Digital Commerce for Music
415-562-0880
http://www.liquidaudio.com

Agent Technology
http://www.cs.umbc.edu/agentslist/

Video Conferencing and Internet Telephony Sites

Duplexx	http://www.duplexx.com/
Inext	http://www.inext.com
Intel	http://www.intel.com
Iris	http://irisphone.com
Summersoft	http://www.summersoft.com
Transphone	http://www.transphone.co.uk
VocalTec	http://www.vocaltech.com
Voxware	http://voxware.com
White Pine	http://www.wpine.com

Webcasting and Broadcasting Information Sites

Broadcast Net	http://www.broadcast.net
BRS Radio Directory	http://www.brsradio.com
Gebbie—Broadcast Lists	http://www.gebbieinc.com
Intervox Webcasting Reference	http://www.intervox.com
Iradio	http://www.iradio.com
NewsProNet	http://www.NewsProNet.com
Old Radio	http://www.oldradio.com
Push Concepts	http://www.pushconcepts.com
The Antenna	http://www.theantenna.com
TV Net Streaming List	http://www.iep.com/rti.html
Ultimate TV	http://www.ultimatetv.com
Video Webcasting Info	http://www.racc.org/~samc/cable7.html
WWWAC-Webcasting Sig	http://www.wcsig.org

Webcasting Industry Associations

International Radio Symposium, Radio Montreux, 41 21 963 32 20, message@symposia.ch

International Telecommunications Union, 44 22 730 6039, itumail@itu.ch, http://www.itu.int

International Webcasting Association (Europe), http://www.iwa-europe.org

International Webcasting Association, http:/www.webcasters.org, info@webcasters.org

IP Multicasting Initative, http://www.ipmulticast.com, martyb@stardust.com

National Association of Broadcasters, http://www.nab.org

North American National Broadcasters Assoc., 416-205-8533, nanba@tvo.org, Bill Roberts, Sec. General

WWWAC Webcasting Special Internet Group, http://www .wcsig.org

Webcasting Reference Sites

Business, Dun and Bradstreet Companies Online, http://www .companiesonline.com

Business Name Search, such as http://www.bigbook.com.

Business Telephone Directory, http://www.switchboard.com

Business Telephone Numbers, http://www.bigbook.com

Business, U.S. Incorporation Records, http://plains.uwyo .edu/~prospect/secstate.htmlx

Content Design for Search Engines, http://www.searchengine watch.com/

Content Design for Search Engines, http://www.searchhelp .com/sitereg/tips.html

Event Notification Yahoo! Submission form, http://add.yahoo .com/fast/add?+Events

Event Notification Yahoo!, http://events.yahoo.com/, http:// www.yahoo.com/new/

Government, http://www.nii.org, voa.gov

Government PACER (Public Access to Court Electronic Records), http://www.uscourts.gov/PubAccess.html

Government, State and Local Government Websites, http:// www.piperinfo.com/state/states.html

HDTV Advanced TV, http://www.attc.org/dtv.html. This site has a number of links to High Definition Trials and Programs and Standards Organizations related to Advanced TV, Digital TV and High Definition TV.

Legal, U.S. Copyright Office, http://lcweb.loc.gov/copyright/cpywel.html#new

Legal, Intellectual Property, http://www.arvic.com/Guide_IP.htm

Legal, Government Patent Name Search, http://www.micro-patent.com/trademarkwebindex.html

Legal, Government Patent Search, http://patents.uspto.gov/

Legal, Government U.S. and Canadian Intellectual Property, Trademarks Reference

Lyrics, http://www.harmony-central.com/Guitar/tab.html

Lyrics, http://www.lib.washington.edu/libinfo/libunits/soc-hum/music/resource.html

Lyrics, http://www.lyrics.ch/search.html

Lyrics, International Lyric Server, http://www.lyrics.ch/

Marketing Promotion, Book, http://www.amazon.com/exec/obidos/ISBN=0471172499/wilsoninternetseA/

Marketing Promotions, Getting Your Website Seen, http://Stars.com/Location/Promotion/

Reference, Computer-Assisted Reporting and Research Page, http://www.ryerson.ca/~dtudor/carcarr.htm

Reference, MEGASOURCES for journalists, http://www.ryerson.ca/journal/megasources.html

Reference, Reporting, http://plains.uwyo.edu/~prospect/sec-state.htmlx

Reference, University Websites, http://www.clas.ufl.edu/CLAS/american-universities.html

Search Engine By Popularity, http://www.mmgco.com/t1006in1.html

Search Engine Discussion, http://goldray.com/register.htm

Search Engine information, http://www.searchhelp.com/

Search Engine Registration Site, http://www.submit-it.com/

Search Engine Registration Site, http://www.mmgco.com/top100.html

It is highly advised that you seek legal advice for your trademark, service mark, and other copyright issues. The following Websites are intended to give you a basic understanding of the concepts to discuss the details with your attorney or the company you choose to select, process, and enforce your trademark and patent issues.

Copyrights, Trademarks, and Publication, http://www.name-city.com/corporate/search.htm

Legal Trademark Links and International References, http://www.arvic.com/Links.htm

Patent, Copyright and Trademark Attorney Answers, http://www.moc.govt.nz/patent/intertm2.html

Registration of Trade Mark Information, http://www.usd.edu/~jwortham/copyright.html

Copyrights, Trademarks, Trade Secrets, http://www.ccpit.org/attn2.html

Trademark applications, http://www.twistedhelices.com/music/making/tips/copyrights_publication.html

Trademarks and Business Names, http://www.ggmark.com/welcome.html

Trademarks Information, http://www.patentpending.com/

U.S. Copyright Office Information, http://lcweb.loc.gov/copyright/cpywel.html#new

Webcasting Resource Sites

Broadcast Reference Desk, http://www.intervox.com/desk.htm oriented to broadcasters

IP Multicasting Dial-Up, www.thesync.com, listing of news and companies serving multicast dial-up

Talkmagazine.com, www.talkmagazine.com, publication includes internet broadcasting and webcasting

Webcastweek.com, a site that has audio interviews with the leaders in webcasting

Webcasting Mailing List by Intervox Communications, http://www.intervox.com and backed up by www.broadcast.net. This list is also mirrored on the ipmulticast.com Website.

- Webcasting (discussion group of executives in webcasting, CEO's, Presidents, Broadcasters)
- Webcasting-Events (Postings of daily events, channels in webcasting)
- Webcasting-Digest
- Webcasting-Events Digest
- Internet-Broadcaster (Radio and TV Broadcasters involved in New Media and the Net)
- Ivox-Webcasting Report—Quarterly E-Mail State of the Webcasting market reports compiled by the strategic alliance of www.ultimatetv.com, Intervox.com, brsradio.com, VooDoo Agency in France, www.mediamanager.com.sg in Asia

MARKETING AND PROMOTION*

Following Your Website Launch

Now that you have completed your Website design and got it up and running on your server, you have to get the word out on the Internet that you have something unique to offer, and you must also make your site easy to find.

The old Madison Avenue cliche "let's run it up the flagpole and see who salutes" may have worked in the days when mass media dominated the marketplace, but it just doesn't work in cyberspace. There may be 200 million people using the Internet but you still have to reach them with the message that you are now open for business—then convince them to stop and shop.

---

* Thanks to Noel Moore, Greenbush Electronic College, noelm1@mulberry.com, for this extensive appendix on tips and techniques for promotion. In addition, the extensive support from Dean Sakai, dsakai@sprynet.com, writer and contributor for the Promotions and Marketing chapters and Developing Content chapters, coauthor of the National Association of Broadcasters book, *Internet Age Broadcaster*, published January 1998, info: bseals@nab.org, http://www.nab.org.

This involves Website promotional campaigns using search tools, links and associations, on-line advertising, publicity, direct marketing, response tracking, and other techniques. These tasks need as much thought and planning as the content, technical, and software components of your webcast service.

Content Counts

A successful business site is more than just designing a few graphics or transferring a printed brochure onto your Web page. It is what you offer that counts, and if you are offering something of real value the message will get through to the reader.

Many sites offer contests, free giveaways, and other inducements, but these are for large, well-heeled operations. Your best bet—if you are organizing a webcasting cooperative—is information about what you are doing, how you are doing it, and the advantages of cooperating with you.

The first step is to send your URL and get it listed on Web search engines, which are the first place most people go on the Internet when looking for information.

Key Words and Search Engines

While a lot of people just surf the Net looking for anything of interest, most are looking for specific information, so when they discover through the use of key words on search engines the kind of services or products you are offering and visit your site, they want details. Success depends on how quickly and efficiently they can get that information.

If you use the right key words in your submission to the various search engines they will come, but you must also offer some incentive in the form of a free gift of information or some other inducement to get them to respond to your message. The best way to do this is to offer something of real value for free.

Provide Useful Content and Free Advice

When you provide useful and meaningful information that people need and that others don't have, then it will draw lots of people to your site. People will bookmark your page and add you to their links.

While you may not make money on free advice, a lot of people who visit your free advice page will go on to explore the rest of your site. Good free advice establishes you as an expert and creates goodwill with your users and makes your site the place people come to when they want to get ideas.

Information Is the Most Effective Freebie

You have to lure customers into your Web Store to get them to interact with your site—you don't want window shoppers, you need to evoke a response. There are many ways to do this. The best way is to provide free information that will be of value to them. People really appreciate getting information relevant to their interests.

Don't be afraid to give it away. Information is only of use at the moment a person needs to use it. The rest of the time it is mere data, and like lettuce on the shelves of a supermarket produce section, data has a limited shelf life.

Like electricity, information is valuable only when in use and there is no point in storing anything except proprietary information about your products and services on your site. Get it out and in circulation and reward people who visit your site by giving it to them free. It's of no use on your hard disc.

You must capture the attention of prospective customers and the best way to do this is to offer them a bargain in the hope that it will motivate them to buy your products and services.

Some of the best and most successful sites on the Internet use this free information technique, and one is Sitelinks—http://www.sitelynx.co.uk—to whom I am indebted for much of the following information in this chapter.

A good example of other Websites that not only present advice about free marketing on the World Wide Web but also offer inducements to browsers to get them to respond is MarketPlace Information (www.mktplace.com), which offers two free booklets full of marketing tips for entrepreneurs and small-business owners on the World Wide Web: *Introduction to Desktop Marketing* and *5 Steps to a Successful Direct Marketing Campaign.*

1. *Introduction to Desktop Marketing* shows entrepreneurs how to sell and market with a PC. The booklet explains how software can control the marketing and sales process, including developing and introducing new products, identifying and targeting potential customers, generating lists, and performing customer service following a sale. The booklet also includes case studies of small businesses that have successfully used desktop marketing, and helps readers decide whether the method can work for them.

2. *5 Steps to a Successful Direct Marketing Campaign* explains the "15-second rule" and why it is so important to direct marketers. The booklet also tells entrepreneurs how they can set up a direct-mail promotion, fashion and format a direct-mail offer, and build a list of people likely to be receptive to the offer. Instructions on printing and mailing also are included.

"Since its debut last November, our Web site has provided thousands of computer users with time- and labor-saving resources for business-to-business market research," says John Wang, MarketPlace Information's general manager of Internet business. "The new Bookstore adds one more benefit. It's the place where entrepreneurs can find solid advice on marketing strategy and great ideas for cost-effective marketing tactics."

This is an excellent example of a free giveaway of information used for market promotion.

Direct Email Campaigns

You can also use Direct Email campaigns, but whatever you do, do not subscribe to one of those Web-based Junk Email direct marketing services that promise you 27 million readers, because the majority resent being spammed in this manner and will immediately put up software blocks to keep you out—permanently.

You may get through once or twice but members of Listservs and other specialized forums on the Net resent being spammed in this manner and have installed software procedures to keep junk mail off their lists.

Check with Your ISP

Before using software that automates mass e-mail clear it first with your ISP, because many will cut you off when they note the increased traffic. AOL, CompuServe, MSN, and Prodigy are, of course, the best places to start getting the word out, but make sure you join a subscriber list if you want your message to get through to sympathetic readers.

A Place on the Web Map

The first step you take is to let readers and surfers know you exist, and in this chapter we present various strategies to make sure your efforts are not wasted and will attract more traffic, customers, and revenue without losing time and money on trial and error.

It's a big job so approach it carefully and methodically and you will be successful.

Search Engine Registration—Four Key Steps

Search tools are the key method for your target audience to find what is of interest to them. Therefore a cornerstone of any promotion campaign is comprehensive registration in relevant search tools.

1. *Research.*   There are the primary global search tools that every Website needs to be in. Yahoo, Altavista, Excite, Infoseek, Lycos, Hotbot, and Webcrawler; for almost every subject there are specific search sites to help. These you need to research and identify according to your specific requirements.

2. *Enhance.*   The next step is to use various methods, appropriate to the particular search tools targeted, to enhance the HTML to allow for better indexing. This increases the page's position in specific key phrase searches.

3. *Submit.*   While automated software is available, you will achieve better results according to Sitelynx if you personally handle the contacting part. ("We have used the automated services in the past and have had various problems.")

4. *Register.*   You will have to check to ensure that all search tools targeted have accepted the registration; if not, then you should resubmit the entry.

Advertising

This includes banners for Websites, text ads for discussion lists, and applications of "Push" media techniques.

Publicity

The best kind of free advertising is publicity in the mass media and trade press. To get it, you will have to write a press release describing your services and get it out to journalists and editors of both on-line and printed media.

Direct Marketing

The key points to remember in direct mail marketing, according to Sitelynx, are to develop a wide range of direct marketing initiatives in a site-promotion campaign; but never use spamming, which is unsolicited or unrelated contact via e-mail. If the contact has been requested there is no fear of retaliation from anti-spammers.

You first identify and locate Newsgroups and Discussion lists; then contact them with a carefully worded letter or release telling them exactly what you hope to gain from direct participation with a network of subject experts.

Visitor Tracking

It is very important to keep track of people who visit your site and to do this there are a number of visitor tracking solutions from simple CGI scripts to full log file analysis or independent auditing.

Essential Search Engines

After your Website has been up and running for some time you need to analyze your main home page and provide additional information to enhance your search/results positions. Next you submit and register that page with the primary search engines on the Web, some of which are:

    www.Yahoo.com
    www.Excite.com
    www.Infoseek.com
    www.Altavista.com
    www.Lycos.com
    www.Hotbot.com
    www.Webcrawler.com

There are more than 50 search tools apart from the primary ones mentioned previously, including many others more specific to your target markets, but you will learn about these from interaction with others on your growing Community Network.

Even if you reached them initially via someone else's Listserv or Discussion group you will soon establish interpersonal relationships with individuals on these other groups and will soon start to develop a separate community of your own—but always remember to notify the Sysop of what you are doing and get his or her cooperation.

Reciprocal Linking

Research and arrange reciprocal links with Websites that are complementary to yours. This involves contacting the Web masters and/or site editor to exchange links between the two sites. This means you will have to include a "hot links" section on your home page where reciprocal links can be placed.

This process will also open up possibilities of alliances between industry partners, as well as helping you to identify niche and mass-market sites and on-line services.

How to Find Related Sites

Use the Web to locate other related sites already attracting your target markets or that might relate to your project and arrange reciprocal links with them. The best place to start this process is at The Bay State Internet Mall on the Common Wealth Network at http://www.baystatemall.com/addlink.html.

With more than 600 links listed, this is a site where you can find information on just about everything you need to run and operate a money-making home business like webcasting.

Internet Link Exchange, the Web's largest advertising network with over 100,000 member sites, at http://www.linkexchange.com/, is another site that offers free linkages to use its paid services.

Banner advertising. If you are willing to accept other banners placed on your site, then you should sign up with the top reciprocal banner networks at no additional cost.

Magnet came on-line in April 1995 and since then has provided a continuous learning experience of what works on the Web and what doesn't. As an inducement to people to use their services, they provide a "How-To-Do-It" section on their site to help you increase traffic to your site without your having to use the trial-and-error approach. Their sales pitch is: "Anything you read here we can do for you—so feel free to contact us." They provide over 50 strategies that will increase traffic to your site.

Strategies to Increase Your Website Traffic

Here are some general ideas as thought-starters and tips from Noel Moore. You should refer to the Promotion and Marketing chapter to prioritize your approach and choose the most beneficial marketing program for your webcast. These are general Website traffic builders that are also of benefit to a webcaster.

1. Target your market.
2. Conduct market research to determine who's most likely to buy—study Web demographics.
3. Scope out your competition.
4. Use search engines and keywords to find competitors.
5. Use business data sources to find out who else is in your field.
6. Provide free high-quality useful content.
7. Give some good free information.
8. Update your content often.
9. Provide your content in interactive and entertaining ways.
10. Provide a monthly newsletter.
11. Offer to send info by fax or mail.
12. Design your site for maximum viewing impact.
13. Match your "look" to your product and your target audience.
14. Provide high-quality graphics.

15. Update your site often.

16. Make it easy to navigate your site.

17. Use a standard header and navigation bar on each page.

18. Make your home page draw people into your site.

19. Make sure your home page loads quickly.

20. View your pages with several different Web browsers and design accordingly.

21. View your pages on a laptop and design your site that many people see it this way.

22. View your pages with images off and design accordingly.

23. Make sure your URL is on every page that gets printed by a surfer.

24. Use HTML extensions to assure quick loading times.

25. Keep each graphic under 65K so it will load quickly.

26. Avoid large imagemaps.

27. Use the "ALT" tag with all of your images to define width and height.

28. Announce your site.

29. Get listed in all relevant Web directories and search engines.

30. Determine where to find listings of the directories and search engines.

31. Find out how to get listed in all of those directories and search engines.

32. Determine what else it takes after you've submitted your info to all those sites.

33. Find out how to place higher in search results.

34. Get recognized in what's new listings.

35. Get recognized in what's cool listings.

36. Write a press release and distribute it every way, everywhere.

37. Local and regional newspapers.

38. On-line national newspapers newspapers.

39. On-line magazines.

40. On-line newsletters.

41. On-line mailing lists.

42. On-line radio stations.

43. TV stations—newsgroups.

44. Should I use direct mail, e-mail, or both?

45. Announce your site on AOL.

46. Other sources of information.

47. Send bulk e-mails to interested recipients.

48. Encourage people to make your home page their start-up page.

49. Utilize newsgroups to establish your expertise and credibility.

50. Monitor newsgroups and provide expert answers.

51. Submit FAQs to newsgroups monthly.

52. Include your URL in your newsgroup signature.

53. Get as much free publicity as possible.

54. Announce site changes everywhere, every way.

55. Be an expert speaker at local and national events.

56. Get listed on all relevant link lists.

57. Get recognized in "best of the web" link lists.

58. Ask owners of relevant link lists to include your URL.

59. Request on your site that people add you to their bookmarks/hotlists.

60. Run contests.

61. Keep your contest as simple as possible.

62. Interactive contests are fun; just don't make them too complicated.

63. Invite people to join your mailing list and/or ask if they want an e-mail reminder about next month's contest.

64. Provide a "Thank You" page.

65. Put lots of information about your site on your contest page.

66. Offer more than one prize.

67. List the winners.

68. Get people to "join"—offer a membership to your site.

69. Offer special deals just for members.

70. Make it easier for members to enter your contests.

71. Automatically include members on your mailing list for catalogs and newsletters.

72. Sponsor other Web sites.

73. Sponsor a site like Yahoo or Netscape if you have the money.

74. Traditional approaches: direct mail and advertisements.

75. Conduct a direct-mail campaign to your target market.

76. Place e-mail address, URL, and site name on business cards, stationery, and all sales/marketing literature.

77. Demonstrate the credibility of you and your business.

78. Provide a section on your site called, "about us"; include quotes from satisfied customers; make reference to awards you've earned.

79. Provide excellent customer service.

80. Treat the customer with kid gloves.

81. Send "Thank You" gifts to top customers.

82. Conduct a customer-satisfaction survey.

83. Include FAQs on your site.

84. Be prepared to respond quickly to leads.

Target your market. Who is most likely to buy your product or service? Directing your efforts to those people will attract them to your site.

Conduct market research to determine who's most likely to buy. Knowing your target market will maximize the effect of the time and money you spend on PR and advertising for your Website.

Demographics. There's another approach you can take to get on the Web, which is to study the statistics of who's using the Web, who's buying on the Web, and choose to sell the products and services that they are most likely to buy. There's some good research at Commerce Net.

Scope out your competition. Use search engines and keywords to find competitors. What are the keywords for your site? Search on all of them in the major search engines such as WebCrawler, Excite, and Lycos. A great site that lists all of the best search engines is C/NET at www.cnet.com. Then visit as many of your competitors' sites as possible. What do you have that your competitors don't? Those are the things you should emphasize in newsgroups, press releases, and Web announcements (more on these areas later).

Excite at www.excite.com has an incredible Live! offering where you can set up your own customized news/magazine article search. In an e-mail they sent us, they made a helpful suggestion for using the "Live!" capabilities: "Create topics to track your business competition. If you want to track a particular sector of an industry, try typing in relevant company names, the type of industry and the product the companies sell. For example, if you wanted to create a topic on search engines, enter words like: excite, lycos, yahoo, search, engine, engines, internet."

Use business data sources to find out who else is in your field. Do you know the Standard Industrial Classification (SIC) code for your business? Every business has one, so yours does, too. Most business listings you can buy on CD have an SIC code listed for each business. You can buy them pretty easily and do searches to find your competitors. Some places where you can get information on other businesses that might be competitors or allies are: Dun & Bradstreet; MarketPlace; American Business Information (ABI), and PhoneDisc.

Where to find standard industrial classification codes. If you don't know your SIC code(s), select the most appropriate business categories from the list provided by Ellips at http://www.ellips.nl/sicsel.html or The Blue Cross Blue Shield Blue Care Network of Michigan at http://www.bcbsm.com/induscode.shtml, both of which provide a free partial list of SIC codes.

Ellips, a Dutch company that specializes in designing electronic control systems, is another site where you will be able to find codes relating to your business: e-mail: info@ellips.nl.

Update your pages often. Provide reasons for people to come back to your page. Be sure to add new features to your site to maintain interest. Perhaps you add a new product or service, you hold a contest (see Contest section following), or maybe you have a "sale."

What you must include in your Website:

♦ At the bottom of every page put a comment like this: "Last Updated: September 1, 1998" to emphasize that your site has fresh content.

♦ Have a "What's New" Section. People have become accustomed to the "What's New" sections of Websites. As a matter of fact, that's one of the first places they'll check when they come to your page.

Ideas on how to provide interactive and entertaining content for your Website in addition to your webcast material or as a focus of your webcast material:

1. Reviews/articles
2. Calendar of events
3. Commentary
4. Searchable directories and/or databases
5. On-line Seminars/Discussion Groups/Forums
6. Library with on-line periodicals; FAQs or Q&A; advice (ask the expert)

7. How-to sections—step-by-step instructions
8. Hot link of the day
9. Chat areas
10. Vote in a weekly virtual poll
11. Have a trivia section
12. Audio clips
13. Video clips
14. Listings
15. Downloadable articles or software

Provide a monthly e-mail newsletter. You'd be surprised how many people will choose to subscribe to your newsletter if you give them a chance. Mention the newsletter on your home page and throughout your site and provide a short form with a check box and a submit button. It will fit anywhere.

Offer to send info by fax or mail. Often people want to hold something in their hands and think about it before they buy. Also, by providing information by fax or mail, the potential customer is more likely to have faith that you are a legitimate business and not just a scam.

Design your site to attract your target market. Who is your target market? (See chapter in book on Marketing and Promotion.) What type of design appeals to the type of person in your target market? For example, if you're targeting executives to get them to use your stock brokerage service, it would be a mistake to use the black, starry-night background cyberspace look even though you're on the Web. You'd more likely go with an upscale, polished look and feel of a white background with precise graphics.

Provide high-quality graphics.

◆ Excellent graphics are essential for a high-traffic page on the Web, especially if you're trying to make money. If you have a low-graphic page, be sure it is information rich. When you're competing with other sites for business, it's a different story. You'll need to either learn to make your own graphics or contract out this part.

◆ Animation of graphics and interactivity is appealing to many people.

◆ Keep in mind, though, that a large percentage of Web users are still using nongraphical browsers and there are people who choose to turn graphics off. Make sure you use the ALT tag with every graphic to describe it to the person who doesn't download the image.

Make it easy to navigate your site

◆ Provide a site map if you have more than 25 pages.

◆ Keep the site map low-graphics (a plain-text menu is often preferable) so it will load quickly for the user.

◆ Provide a navigator bar at the top and/or bottom of each page.

Use a standard header and navigation bar on each page. You want to be sure that people don't get lost when they're surfing your site. It's a good idea to use a standard header with a navigation bar on every page and link it to your home page. It's also a good idea to include the navigation bar on the footer. You'll enable your users to be able to quickly move to other areas on your site. You also increase your likelihood that the surfer will see more of your site when you make it easy to navigate.

Make your home page draw people into your site. When you're surfing the Web, how many sites do you actually explore? Maybe 10 percent of the sites you visit? You want people to "come on in" so your home page must have quick-loading high-quality graphics and compelling content.

Don't keep them waiting! This is most important! On your home page don't use a graphic that has a long load time. Also, be sure to use ALT tags with every graphic.

Make sure your pages load quickly.   How long will you wait for a Web page to load? If you're like most, you'll become impatient after about 30 seconds. And we doubt you'll wait much longer than a minute before you abandon the site.

Quality assurance procedures:

1. Empty your cache. (When someone first loads your page, none of your graphics will be in cache, so to get the real load time, you need to be sure your graphics are not in your cache.)

2. Log onto the Web.

3. Load the Web page you want to test.

4. Time the load from the second you hit "enter" until the word "Done" appears on your browser. (More than 30 seconds?)

5. If it's not graphics slowing you down, then consider breaking your page into multiple pages to give readers the choice of which one they want to load.

View your pages with several different Web browsers

◆ Download from the Web all of the browsers you can get, such as Netscape, Microsoft Explorer, NetCom's browser. Keep in mind, too, that on-line services like AOL have their own browsers.

◆ Subscribe to major on-line services like AOL just so you can test your pages and see how their users will view them.

◆ Be careful not to create your pages using HTML extensions that aren't understood by the most heavily used browsers unless you're prepared to provide pages with alternate formats.

◆ Pay attention to versions, too.

View your pages on a laptop and remember . . . when designing your site that many people see it this way.   We use a laptop when we're traveling and it's very difficult to view some Websites this way. Keep in mind the types of people who are likely to be using laptops—salespeople and corporate executives who travel a lot. If you are targeting either of these groups for your products, then avoid the use of frames and keep your design readable.

View your pages with images off and design accordingly. Since many people view your site with images off, it's a good idea for you to see how it looks to them. This will highlight the need for ALT tags.

Make sure your URL is on every page that someone might print out. Your URL and site name needs to be at the top and bottom of every page. Why? Many people will print out your Web pages for future review and/or reference. If your URL and site name aren't on the page, they won't be on the printout. If there's no identification on the printout, how will the user ever return to your site?

Sure, Netscape has the capability to put the site URL at the top of a printed page, but users have to set their preferences to do this, and how many people ever get around to it? Don't take a chance that someone will print your page because they're interested in your business, but when they read it a few days later, they don't remember where they found it.

Also, be sure you use the ALT tag and put your URL and site name within your HTML code. As an example: ALT = "Web Magnet at URL: http://www.webmagnet.com." (See our section on Using ALT tags.)

Use HTML extensions for quick loading time. If it seems that it's taking forever to load your page, the viewer probably will surf on to something else. You want to be sure to use every possible strategy that will shorten the load time for your site.

Keep each graphic under 50K so it will load quickly. Most Web surfers don't have the time or patience to wait for large images to load. Even with a 28.8 modem, it's often a long wait for a large image. Imagemaps are popular, but they take more time to load than individual images. Remember, when you use a large graphic on your entry page lots of people will abandon the site before it ever finishes loading.

Here's some good advice we read at Moller Digital University. Never use GIF files over 80 × 80 in size unless you have a special GIF animation or the GIF file has four or fewer colors. It will increase the load time of your Web page for no reason. You should use JPEG files for large images with many colors (photos). There's a lot of other useful information at this site.

Avoid large imagemaps. Large imagemaps (these are large graphic images that have the ability to clickthrough on certain pictures) take so much time to load it's guaranteed that some people won't stick around to wait for them to load. A good alternative is to use multiple GIFs to make up the picture. The Web Magnet opening page is a good example of a group of GIFs that would be in an imagemap on many other sites. These individual GIFs load much more quickly than the imagemap would.

Use the ALT tag with all of your images to define width and height. The ALT tag is an HTML coding term that allows those without a graphic browser to view the description of an image or picture on your page. This is advised to also assist in helping the blind navigate through your Website. You want to do everything in your power to make your viewers have the best experience when they visit your site. If you're not using the ALT tag with your images then you're slowing things down for a lot of your viewers.

You've probably been on a page where the images took forever to load and you couldn't even scroll down to read the text portion of the page while you were waiting. That's what happens when you don't use ALT tags. It's a very frustrating experience for the surfer who wants your information, but has to wait . . . wait . . . wait . . . wait. . . .

Using the ALT tag with all of your images tells most browsers to reserve a defined amount of space on a page for your image when it's preparing your page layout for viewing. That means the text will go ahead and load and your viewers can get immediate gratification.

Alex Knowles has written an excellent explanation of why using the ALT tag is a good idea. You can read it and also download a program he has written called WWWis V1.8 that will go through HTML and automatically add the right HEIGHT and WIDTH tags for you! Wow!

Search engine registration and design tips:

◆ How to design your Web pages for best search-engine registration:

http://www.searchenginewatch.com/

http://www.searchhelp.com/sitereg/tips.html

◆ How to get your Website seen:

http://Stars.com/Location/Promotion/

A book: http://www.amazon.com/exec/obidos/ISBN=0471172499/wilsoninternetseA/

◆ List of the top search engines:

http://www.mmgco.com/t1006in1.html

◆ Recommended do-it-yourself registration sites:

http://www.submit-it.com/

http://www.mmgco.com/top100.html

◆ Other good sites:

How to use search engines: http://www.searchhelp .com/

Good wide-ranging discussion: http://goldray.com/register.htm

Is it good enough just to submit my site to these free services?

◆ Submit It! and other services like it are great for people who don't have the time to submit their listing themselves to the directories and who don't have the money to pay anyone else to do it.

◆ If you have the time to submit your own listings to directories, or if you have the money to pay a firm to individually submit your listing to directories, then that's usually a better approach than using free submission services. Why?

◆ You need to utilize the 10-word, 25-word, 60-word, 80-word, and 100-word descriptions that some directories allow you to submit. Some of these autosubmit services put only your 25-word description in every directory.

◆ Also, you need to submit your listing in multiple categories of a directory whenever possible. Some automatic services only allow you to submit in one category.

Once I've submitted my information to the sites, is that all it takes? Unfortunately, no. Once you send in your information, you'll need to confirm that your information, indeed, did show up in the directories. The bad news is that one month after you've submitted your site to all those directories and search engines, only about 60 percent will have displayed your listing.

It takes months and many resubmittals to get listed in them all. You'll need to make a checklist of the sites you submitted to and put a check beside the site when you find your listing there. We recommend that you keep checking for up to three weeks.

For those sites that never put up your listing you'll need to resubmit. Then keep checking back for another three weeks. Then submit again. It could get to be a real headache! Keep in mind that some places choose who will appear on their sites, so they may never list you (they usually tell you that on their entry form).

Web magnets tips to help your page place higher by a search engine query:

◆ Make use of META tags within each Web page. Remember, though, that not all search engines utilize META tags, so don't stop here.

◆ Make use of keywords within META tags. (Don't use a string more than five times. Search engines such as Lycos will omit a Web page that is obviously loaded with keywords.)

◆ Place strings of keywords in text the same color as your background so the words will be invisible. (Once again, don't use a string more than five times.)

◆ Make separate directories for each keyword so it will be in your URL.

◆ Use that keyword in all titles to Web pages belonging to that directory.

◆ Make special Web pages that have full sentences, using the keyword a different way in each of the sentences. This is for the Excite search engine that catalogs full sentences.

Webcasting-Events. http://www.intervox.com provides an e-mail list of webcasting events around the globe to post your new events and channels.

This is an Email Announce Website Announcement Updates list. If you wish to change your subscription status, point your Web browser to the following URL: http://www.EmailAnnounce.com/entesubs.html. And then just check the appropriate box to subscribe or unsubscribe from the list.

Get recognized in what's cool listings:

◆ The Spider's Pick of the Day

◆ Yahoo—Entertainment:COOL links

◆ The Dynamite Site of the Nite

◆ Also, see the best list of cool listings: Spider's Lists of Hot Lists

On-line mailing lists.   Michael Mathieson's book *Marketing on the Internet* provides the following information (p. 117): "To find mailing lists of interest to you, send an E-mail message to mail-server@nisc.sri.com and in the body of the message type—send netinfo/interest.groups. You will receive back a list of mailing lists that will help you find lists of interest. You can get another list of lists by sending an E-mail message to listserv@vm1.nodak.edu. In the body of this message, put—get new list routers."

Newsgroups.   Post only to the ones that are appropriate—don't damage your image by angering people by posting in irrelevant newsgroups. Also, use Netiquette. Internet Marketing Group can help you find the right newsgroups and help you to use proper Netiquette.

Here are a few newsgroups where you can place announcements:

◆ comp.infosystems.www.announce
◆ How to Announce in comp.infosystems.www.announce
◆ How comp.infosystems.www.announce Works (FAQ)

Also, it's a good idea to submit information such as free advice and link lists monthly to newsgroups.

Should I use U.S. Mail, e-mail, and newswires to send press releases?   If you can afford both U.S. Mail and e-mail, then Magnet recommends both. For those of you who have limited funds, e-mail is a great way to get your press release out to important on-line sources and news editors. (Author's note: For global penetration and to be picked up by newswire, it is advised you submit your news releases to prnewswire. http://www.prnewswire. Although there is a fee and you can select your distribution whether to magazine editors, high-technology and your industry, or the geographical location, we highly recommend the use of prnewswire or a company that provides services that are recognized and used by leading media companies.)

Where to get the e-mail and U.S. and Canadian mail addresses for the media? Gebbie Press provides listings of radio, TV, magazines and can send you this via e-mail from their Website at www.gebbiepress.com. You can also review Media listings at www.parrotmedia.com.

There's a group called The US All Media E-Mail Directory that, for a very reasonable rate, provides a list of 7000 electronic-mail (e-mail) addresses for key editors, columnists, correspondents, and executives in magazines, newspapers, radio, TV, and news syndicates across the United States and Canada.

The directory is organized by the type of media and by subject for targeting public relations efforts. In addition to the e-mail address of the media organization, the directory provides the name of the contact, his or her title (e.g., news editor), address, phone number, and fax number.

In the hard-copy perfect-bound edition, there is a subject index and a media locator to identify the page number for a given source, at the end of the directory. The diskette or electronic e-mail version has industry descriptors for each media category, and contains all the data in ASCII comma-delimited so that you can bring it into a spreadsheet, sort and search it, and bring a targeted list into your e-mail program.

Announce your site on AOL. Announce and advertise your product/service with your URL on AOL and other on-line services. It's amazing how many people read them. And AOL users have good Web access now, so they'll make it a point to check out some of the sites they read about. You need to be a member to place a free classified ad, but it may be worth the $9.95 a month.

Utilize newsgroups to establish your expertise and credibility. Monitor newsgroups and provide expert answers. You have information that people need and that others don't have. Monitor newsgroups for questions relating to the subject matter of your Website, and then answer those questions concisely and politely. A good answer will draw people to your site because they'll say, "Hey, this person knows his/her stuff. I'll visit the Website they've listed to see what else I can learn." These same people will bookmark your page and add you to their links once they've visited your site. Giving good advice as a newsgroup participant establishes you as an expert and creates goodwill.

Ask owners of relevant link lists to include your URL.   Many Websites have link lists specializing in a particular category. Contact those sites and ask them to include your URL as a link. As an example, let's say you're a real estate firm. There are several excellent real estate link lists on the Web. Check out Web Magnet's LinkAppeal Awards for a list of those sites.

Request on your site that people add you to their bookmarks and hotlists.   Often just a simple reminder like this is enough to make people add you to their hotlists and linklists. Check out Spider's Web for an example of this sort of request.

Make sure your e-mail, URL, and site name are on the following:

◆ Business cards
◆ Stationery and envelopes
◆ Brochures, all business materials, annual reports
◆ Press releases
◆ Speciality items
◆ Banners
◆ Building signs

(*Note:* In reverse, one item of importance is to include the phone number and address of your business on your home page. This is one of the most frequent complaints from consumers when they want more information to complete their inquiry or purchase a company's products.)

Provide a section on your site called, "About Us".   In your "About Us" section, provide a brief history of your firm, including its address and phone number. Also provide brief biographies and qualifications of key personnel.

Include quotes from satisfied customers.   When you receive positive comments from customers ask if it's OK to post a quote on your site. Perhaps you could even link to their site to show off your work if you had a hand in it.

Include frequently asked questions (FAQs) on your site. Include on your site a list of frequently asked questions (FAQs). Current and potential customers will read them and will often come back to read them several times before they contact you for your products or services.

Respond quickly to leads.   Develop a way to quickly respond to leads. If your site hits the mark you will get many requests for more information, catalogs, and so forth. Be prepared! Have a system worked out ahead of time to send mailings and have someone available to answer all e-mails and phone calls. This helps build good customer relationships and customer loyalty. Perhaps you'll get so many requests for information you may even need automated e-mail responses of a mailbot.

Research and Analyst Publications and Industry News

Cowles Simba Information 800 307-2529, ext 344, simbainfo@simbanet.com, http://www.simbanet.com, Stamford, CT

Min's New Media Report, 301 424-3338, clientservices.pbi@phillips.com

News Pro Net, http://www.newspronet.com TV News

The Antenna, http://www.theantenna.com, TV Industry News

Ultimate TV, http://www.ultimatetv.com, TV Entertainment Industry News & Webcasting, TV Webcast Sites

Kagan World Media Analysis, 408 624-1536

Intervox Communications, http://www.intervox.com

APPENDIX C

RECOMMENDED READING

Angel, Jonathan. *Realmedia Complete; Streaming Audio and Video Over the Web [Complete].* New York: McGraw-Hill, 1998.

Brinkley, Joel. *Defining Vision: The Battle for the Future of Television.* San Diego: Harcourt Brace, 1998.

Campbell, Roy, and See-Mong Tan. *Streaming: Video, Audio & Data Transport.* M & T Books, 1998.

Dean, Damon. *Web Broadcasting Development for Dummies.* Foster City, CA: IDG Books Worldwide, 1997.

Fisher, David E., and Marshall Jon Fisher. *Tube: The Invention of Television.* Cambridge, MA: Counterpoint, 1996.

Fox, David. *I Want My WebTV™.* San Francisco: Waite Group Press, 1997.

Keyes, Jessica. *Webcasting: How to Broadcast to Your Customers over the Net.* New York: McGraw-Hill, 1997.

Magne, Lawrence, ed. *Passport to Web Radio: Music, Sports, News and Entertainment from the Hometowns of the World.* International Broadcasting Service, 1997.

Miles, Peggy, and Dean Sakai. *Internet Age Broadcaster.* Washington, DC: National Association of Broadcasters, 1998.

Mitchell, Joan L., ed., William B. Pennebaker, ed., and Chad E. Fogg. *Mpeg Video: Compression Standard* [Digital Multimedia Standards Series]. London: Chapman & Hall, 1996.

Purcell, Lee, and Jordan Hemphill. *Internet Audio Sourcebook.* New York: John Wiley & Sons, 1997.

Real Time Web Broadcasting: With CD-ROM Que Corporation. Que Format, 1996.

Van Tassel, Joan. *Advanced Television Systems: Brave New TV.* Chicago: Focal Publishers, 1996.

GLOSSARY

For a fuller Internet glossary, see the site www.santel.lu/SANTEL/ DOCS/internet_glossary.html, and also www.onelook.com. I recommend www.phillipsmagnavox.com since it lists many broadcasting and Internet convergence terms; and for more PC-oriented terms, Philip Margolis, www.pcwebopaedia.com, includes graphics and diagrams with select definitions. www.egeek.com also has glossary resources available on its Website.

Ad banner. Advertising banner or typically an advertisement that appears on a Web page. The Internet Advertising Bureau (www.iab.net/) has set standard sizes for different shapes and preferred download times for the advertisements. Ad banners incorporate animation, sound, and video. This is also called a banner ad and a typical size is $7'' \times \frac{3}{4}''$, with pixels at 468×60.

Ad view. The number of times that a banner ad was downloaded within a specified period of time. The actual number of times the ad was seen by viewers may be higher due to caching, which is an automatic process by your computer to download a graphic once but provide multiple views. An ad view is the same as an "exposure."

A special thanks to the senior vice president of the National Association of Broadcasters, Rick Ducey (rducey@nab.org, www.nab.org), who was key in assisting on many of the terms and allowed us to use 90 of the terms found in the book *Internet Age Broadcaster*. Thanks to Rick Ducey and his staff for their work throughout the world on digital and convergence, along with the NAB director of technology assessment, Marcia DeSonne.

ADSL.   Asymmetric Digital Subscriber Line. This is a fast digital connection that may be a rival to ISDN. The speed of connections is 2 Mbps downstream (to the user) and slower speeds upstream (to the Internet or network).

Analog.   A means of encoding information by varying phase, amplitude, or frequency of a carrier wave.

ASF.   Advanced streaming format is an industry standard introduced by Microsoft to define the storage format for streaming media. It is intended to replace a variety of separate file formats such as WAVE and AVI and allow streaming of the multimedia content.

ATM.   Asynchronous Transfer Mode. A method to allocate bandwidth using a fixed-size packet (called a cell). ATM is also known as "fast packet."

ATV.   Advanced Television. Refers to the standard selected for digital television in the United States. ATV incorporates both Standard Definition Television (SDTV), which is equivalent or better than conventional NTSC signals, and High Definition Television (HDTV), which is equivalent to 35-mm film quality. One television channel can accommodate a single HDTV signal or multiple SDTV signals as well as some ancillary data services.

AVI.   Audio Video Interleave. The Microsoft file format used for displaying Video. AVI provides ability to develop video and animation files on the World Wide Web. The files (which end with an .avi extension) require a special player that may already be included with your Web browser or may require downloading.

Bandwidth.   This is a measure of bits per second or transmission capacity of data sent over a particular wire, cable, satellite, fiber-optic, cable, interface, or bus. More bandwidth is needed to send faster and more complex data and assure accurate and real-time delivery. Thus, audio and video, datacasting, and webcasting require more bandwidth due to the complexity and swiftness of changes than does ordinary text or phone communications. So, the larger the bandwidth, the greater the quality and capacity of voice, video, or data. Bandwidth also refers to the range of frequencies that can be passed over a given channel.

Banner ad. The actual graphic that displays the on-line advertisement. The sizes and shapes vary. Usually they are about $7'' \times \frac{3}{4}''$, which in pixels is 468×60.

Broadcasting. Delivery of information, data, audio, or video in a one-to-all transmission method, where the source sends one copy of the message to all users, whether they wish to receive it or not.

Browser. This is a software program that allows users to view World Wide Web pages. New versions of browsers allow one to listen to audio and watch video from the World Wide Web. This is called webcasting or internet broadcasting. The most popular browsers are Netscape Navigator and Microsoft Internet Explorer.

BWTP. BackWeb, a push company's UDP-based protocol, www .backweb.com.

Cable modem. A device typically provided by a cable company to access the Internet over coaxial cable. This could provide a fast speed connection to your TV at around 1.5 Mbps. www.cablelabs.com provides information and research on cable modems.

CAD. Confirmed Advertisements Delivered. Advertising traffic as confirmed by a management tracking or auditing system. (CAD also stands for Computer Aided Design.)

CDF. Channel Definition Format is a specification promoted by Microsoft to allow the pushing of data to users. If software is written with the CDF specficiation, any channel that uses CDF will be able to post the information to the push channel or a Web server. Many push companies have agreed to support CDF, although some browser companies have in the past shown a reluctance. The specification has been sent to the World Wide Web Consortium (W3C) for approval as a standard.

CD quality.   The informal benchmark for consumer audio of all types. Equal to or exceeding the frequency range of 20 Hz–20 kHz audio, with –90 dB noise floor, and sample rate of 44.1 kHz or 48 kHz.

CD-ROM.   Compact Disk–Read Only Memory. A digital laser storage device holding data that can be video, text, graphics, music, or data of any type. This type of disk can be written to only once and then becomes "read only." Storage capacity is typically 600MB.

CGI.   Common Gateway Interface. A method to let information pass from the client to the server, and allow programs that run through this gateway.

Channel.   A term used to specify a location of audio/video on your TV or cable or satellite system to dial or select a program or broadcast signal. The term is also being used on the Internet in much the same way to designate a location or program or information sent or received by a commercial. Some companies may refer to their Websites or programs within their Websites as their Internet channels.

Clickthrough.   The number of times an ad banner has been clicked on by viewers within a specific period of time. The mouse or your keyboard can activate a link. When you activate a link (by pressing or clicking on it) you go to another page on a Website. This counts as one clickthrough. In advertising, one click of the mouse that takes one person to another page is counted as one clickthrough.

Clickthrough rate.   Clickthroughs described as a percentage of "ad views," or the number of clicks by a viewer on a banner as a percentage of the number of times that ad was downloaded by end users. The ad gets downloaded as part of a page requested by the user, a clickthrough occurs only when the viewer activates the link by clicking on the portion of the HTML page containing the ad banner link. Therefore, if a specific HTML page is downloaded by 100 viewers and 10 click on the ad banner, the clickthrough rate is 10 percent.

Client. A computer that requests and exchanges information from a server or host computer where it resides. In the case of the Internet, an individual user's computer is typically the "client" and requests information via the World Wide Web (or other networked connection) to reach a computer at the other end called a "server."

CPM. Cost per one thousand ad views.

Database. A collection of information, data, audio, and/or video organized so a computer can select this information for you in a swift manner. It could contain your Rolodex, your files, your record library, and other information in an easy-to-retrieve manner. Databases use the terms fields, records, and files. A field is a piece of information such as a first name or a zip code; a record is one complete set of fields such as a name, address, zip code, and phone numbers; and a file is a collection of records such as an entire Rolodex. Datamining, datawarehousing, database marketing, and intelligent databases are other terms used in association with database uses.

Datacasting. The ability for a broadcaster or any other communications company to send data over the airwaves.

Datagram. See **Packet.**

Digital. Information sent by modulating a carrier wave to carefully control binary states of phase, frequency, or amplitude.

Download. If you want to view, listen, or save a file, you may need to transfer the file from another computer "server" to your computer "client." This process of requesting information and the transfer to you is called "downloading." Information is downloaded from the server or host to the client. Uploading is when information moves from the client to the server machine.

DS-1. Digital Signal Level 1. Same as T-1, 1.544 Megabits per second (Mbps).

DS-3.   Digital Signal Level 3. Synonym for T-3, 44.736 Mbps data per second.

DSS.   Direct Satellite Service. The ability to receive data, audio, or video from a satellite. Another term used in conjunction with this is DBS, Direct Broadcast Satellite, which uses medium- to high-powered satellites to transmit programming or data directly to small satellite receiver dishes at user's home or to mobile receivers.

DVD.   Digital Versatile Disk or sometimes known as Digital Video Disk or Digital Variable/Versatile/Video Disk. The disks can read data from DVD-Video and DVD-ROM disks. These disks are like a CD-ROM with up to 17GB storage. The disks are marketed to replace VCRs and laserdisc players.

DVD-R.   DVD-Recordable. The technology records data once and allows storage of up to 3.95GB of information on a disk.

DVD-ROM.   You may record over the DVD disk multiple times like a VCR.

E-commerce.   Electronic commerce. Transactions that occur on an electronic or digital network. It is the process of buying and selling, or ordering of products, typically on the World Wide Web.

E-mail.   Electronic mail. Electronic messages that are sent to a specific person across the Internet (or across a local area network or wide area network). Popular e-mail programs include Eudora, Netscape. Most Internet access subscriptions include a preinstalled e-mail software program. You also receive or request a unique Internet mail address that has a very specific format. The first portion of the address is your unique identification. For example: pmiles@intervox.com. "pmiles" stands for Peggy Miles. The information after the @ sign stands for the computer where her mail is sent, stored, and forwarded. The computer is assigned a number (an IP address), but for ease of remembering on the Internet, domain names (like "intervox .com") have been assigned to correspond to the numbers.

Names are easier to remember than numbers. By convention, Internet e-mail addresses, user names, and domain names are in lowercase letters.

EPG. Electronic Program Guide is a method of display of different live and on-demand audio and video and data elements. The ITU is setting standards for interoperability between different program guides that may resemble *TV Guide*–type listings or more audio and video–based icon-driven guides. It can be related to a directory or a search engine that may or may not include real-time information and updates.

Extranets. This is usually an intranet that can be accessed by certain people outside the company or outside employees using a password on a Web page.

Frame/Framing. On a Web browser, you can break up the screen into different windows or compartments. Each compartment can show different graphics, text, or different Web pages. It is a way to divide information on a graphical user interface (GUI). Different frames can perform different operations or go to different Websites.

Frame relay. This connects devices on a wide area network. Data transfer rates can connect to T-1 (1.544 Mbps) and T-3 (45 Mbps) speeds and typically start at 56-Kpbs connections. In Europe the rates range from 64 Kpbs to 2 Mbps.

FTP. File Transfer Protocol. This is a method of moving files across the Internet using the TCP/IP protocol. You can transfer files from a Web browser or download a piece of software for the purpose.

Hard drive. This is a disk-storage device found in a computer, or is a separate piece of equipment that holds data. It can be recorded over again. A typical capacity is 1 GB or larger.

HDTV. High Definition Television. A higher-quality resolution using a digital format for the transmission and reception of television signals. Future television sets, some in use in Japan already, have higher picture resolution, wider aspect ratio (wider picture), and digital quality sound. HDTV screens will have a 16 × 9 aspect ratio that is the same shape as a movie screen.

Hit.   A hit is generated by every request made to a Web site, whether the file is found or not. Every graphic and link on an ad page can count as a hit. It has no predictable relation to users, visitors, or pages and is therefore not a reliable advertising measurement. For example: When a user requests a Web page using your URL (such as http://www.nab.org), the computer (located at the National Association of Broadcasters) is contacted. It locates the page on its hard drive (storage disk) and sends it over the network (e.g., phone lines) to that user's computer (client). When it gets to the Web page, it downloads graphics, text, and so on, to build the page. Each graphic and sometimes other items on a page are considered a "hit." Most servers count hits as every item or graphic that is on the page. One Web page may have 10 graphics registering on the server as hits. If you are tracking traffic on your site, hits are not a valid measurement of users. Hits are a valid measurement of the amount of graphics and other items that the server has to pull down to build a full Web page. Page views are a better traffic measurement to give to advertisers.

Hosting/Host.   An Internet Service Provider (ISP) typically provides space for rent on its computers (servers) to hold the contents of your Web pages and to allow a connection to the Internet. The process of holding and maintaining your Web pages, software, and hardware is called hosting. The data is stored on a host computer, or a computer you are renting space from for the delivery of your Web pages. Hosting can also mean other services besides World Wide Web access, and can include FTP, Telnet, IRC, e-mail services, database service, audio and video streaming services, and other new technologies that connect to the Internet. Different hosts or Internet Service Providers have better connections, software, or computers. Prices for hosting depend on how reliable you want the network; what services are needed; and the popularity of your site.

HTML.   Hyper Text Mark-Up Language. This is the standard language used to build World Wide Web pages. It is like a word processing language, where you put in indicators called tags to denote boldness of text, text size, margins, graphics, photos, multimedia objects, and other attributes.

http.   Hyper Text Transport Protocol. Web Pages are built with a language called HTML (Hyper Text Mark-Up Language). These pages must be requested and transmitted in a standard format that can be understood by different machines on the Internet. This protocol or standard is called the Hypertext Transport Protocol. It is the standard necessary to request and serve specific Web pages.

Hyperlink.   A designation in HTML, the language on the Internet, that allows you to select an item on a Web page and be transported to a new location, Website, or another Web page. When selecting a hyperlink, typically represented on a page as an underlined word, you are transported to a Web page that (by convention) has more information about the item that you just read. Graphics and other icons, or pictures on a Web page are also hyperlinked, taking you to a page that relates to the picture or icon. Arrows are a frequently used hyperlink graphic to designated going forward, backing up, or jumping to another site or Web page. Also video and graphic files have hyperlinks in them called "hot spots" (i.e., rather than underlined text, hot spots are mapped areas of an image that are activated as hyperlinks) that transport you to other video, audio, or text about the selected object.

IETF.   Internet Engineering Task Force, standards organization for the Internet, comprised of an international community of experts and interested parties involved in the growth and smooth operation and architecture of the Internet.

Interlaced.   Refers to how a PC monitor can produce the picture. Because the speed to refresh is faster, the resolution can be greater.

Interlacing.   Refers to preparing a graphic file typically for a GIF.

Internet.   Network of interconnected networks and computers all sharing TCP/IP protocols. The Internet evolved from technologies first developed about 30 years ago by the defense community (ARPANET and its progeny).

Intranet.   A private network of computers hooked together using TCP/IP as the standard communications protocol. This is a private "Internet" for companies, or individuals with access limited to approved users, employees, or participating companies.

IP.   Internet Protocol, part of a standard protocol that computers use to communicate with each other over the Internet. An IP address is a "dotted quad" used to uniquely address Internet resources. This unique number consists of four parts separated by dots (e.g., 199.113.245.2).

IPMI.   Internet Protocol Multicasting Initiative. An association of businesses or technology companies involved in the support of IP multicasting that provide research and promotion. White papers and other reference information are available at www.ipmulticast.com.

IP multicast.   See **Multicast.**

IRC.   Internet Relay Chat. Multiuser, real-time chat service. People can type in comments that everyone can see. Some IRCs are voice-based.

ISDN.   Integrated Services Digital Network. A 128-kilobyte-per-second communications line. This is a digital communications line that carries data at relatively high speeds. It can connect to the Internet. There are different versions of ISDN: PRI, primary rate interface; and BRI, basic rate interface. BRI is a 56-Kbps service, which uses half of the ISDN line's bandwidth; PRI is the 128-Kbps version, which uses both the 56 Kbps channels on the line. The remaining 16 Kbps are split at 8 Kbps for the back channel of each line. (If the term 2B+D is used, it is meant to combine the two B and the one D channel that feed a digital connection and totals to 128K. Each home ISDN connection has two 2 "B" channels; each B channel can carry up to 64K of information. It also has one "D," or signaling channel.)

ISO.   International Organization for Standardization. The name comes from the Greek word *iso* (equal) This international organization founded in 1946 has members from 75 countries and is located at www.iso.ch.

ISP.   Internet Service Provider. A company that has a connection to the Internet (usually the regional backbone) and sells Internet connections on a dial-up or dedicated basis to customers. Popular ISPs include America Online, Netcom, and BBN-Planet.

ITU.   International Telecommunications Union at www.itu.int. Sometimes refered to as the UN of the Telecom World, this intergovernmental organization develops and governs telecommunications standards. The ITU was founded in 1865 and became a United Nations agency in 1947, and is responsible for adopting international treaties, regulations, and standards governing telecommunications.

IWA.   International Webcasting Association. An association of content, technology, and interested companies promoting the advancement of webcasting around the world. Chapters have formed in the UK, New York City, Washington, DC, Singapore, France, and the West Coast, with more planned. www .webcasters.org is the originating group in the United States and www.iwa-europe.org is based in the UK. Information can be received at info@webcasters.org. Members include broadcast networks, as well as Real Networks, Microsoft, and many others.

Java.   A self-contained programming language that can be used on different operating systems, most commonly used in conjunction with World Wide Web browsers. It is a platform-independent programming language designed by Sun Microsystems.

LAN.   Local Area Network. This is a network of computers connected together to communicate and exchange files and other data in real time. Popular LAN techologies include Ethernet, Windows NT, and Novell Netware.

List server.   A special type of server computer that handles e-mail membership lists. List servers are used to communicate with a number of people at one time by e-mail. There are various services you can subscribe to that reside on a list server and are accessible by the Internet. A popular list Website providing lists to which you can subscribe can be found at www .lizst.com. Webcasting lists can be found at www.intervox .com/webcast.htm. In this case, the list server is a computer in Houston, Texas, operated by Broadcast.net that sends out hundreds of thousands of messages to subscribers. The list content is generated by Intervox Communications. Lists and list names can be owned by individuals who moderate the lists. Common list server software includes ListServ and Majordomo.

Mbone.   Multicast backbone on the Internet. The Mbone uses IP multicasting to send audio, video, or data multicasts.

Memory.   (versus "Storage") The ability of your computer to process information and how fast it can process a lot of information at the same time. Sometimes called RAM, or Random Access Memory; the more RAM, the quicker your computer can process, draw, and display audio, video, and process programs.

Modem.   Modulation-demodulation. A piece of equipment that allows you to transfer data typically by the telephone. New modems can be connected to any data source, cable, phone, or satellite, and can be inside or outside a computer, or attached to a TV set or wireless communications device. Modem speeds range from common telephone connections at 28.8 to 56 Kbps.

MPEG.   Motion Picture Experts Group, a group that sets the standards (under the auspices of the ISO, the International Standards Organization) for digital video (sequences of images in time) and audio compression. This is the standard to compress and decompress audio and/or video files using compression algorithms. The different standards typically start out with the term MPEG before them, such as MPEG 1, 2, 3, and so on.

Multicast.   Multicasting takes one of your available Internet data streams and allows many users to connect to it. For example, the National Association of Broadcasters Website often has audio and video files on its Web servers. Unicasting is when a file, say a keynote speech, is served to one user at a time. Multicasting allows the same file to be served simultaneously to multiple users. This allows a much larger audience to be served far more efficiently as you no longer need to dedicate one stream to each user. This technology requires special software and hardware to be installed at different connections on the Internet. (This infrastructure is being built as you read this book.) The Internet Protocol Multicast Initiative at www .ipmulticast.com has formed an alliance of the leading computer and technology companies to bring multicasting equipment into the market faster, and works with the International Webcasting Association at www.webcasters.org.

Multichannel. In digital broadcasting from a TV station, a TV station could send on its digital spectrum one HDTV program or several (four or five with current technology) programs of SDTV quality that would be superior to today's NTSC. When operating in "multichannel mode" a television station could be transmitting several SDTV signals as well as ancillary data services, including HTML pages and associated objects.

Navigating. When you open a program or browser, and click or move around a page with your keyboard, mouse, or with a touch screen, you are navigating on a computer. Navigation allows you to go from program to program, or from Web page to Web page.

Net. A short way to say the Internet, which is a collection of computers that can communicate with each other using the same TCP/IP language.

Object. Data structures (sometimes called containers) that conform to specific templates, classes, and rules. For example, an HTML page may contain a video "object," which is accessed via a hotlink to initiate a streaming video file transfer. Generally, objects refer to different types of elements that developers may incorporate into documents, databases, programs, or other software.

OC-3.   Synonym for the 155 Mbps ATM protocol. This is a fast transmission link to send data.

On-demand.   The request of information at your convenience. On the Internet or on a video tape recorder, you can access the information at anytime. This process is called on-demand. It is the instant retrieval and viewing, listening, or reading of audio, video, or data.

On-the-fly pages.   HTML pages built dynamically (or "on the fly") from a database with user provided parameters (e.g., a weather page for a given local city). On-the-fly Web pages are built based on a user request with preprogrammed criteria and instantly selects the right information and builds a customized Web page or graphic at the time of request with the latest or appropriate information. These personalized pages are based on information found in a database that stores your preferences and are built on-demand or on-the-fly each time you request them.

OSD.   Open Software Description is a specification written to provide a standard data format for describing software and different relationships of software. It is based partly on Marimba's technology.

Oversampling.   When you record data, such as music, you can select to oversample, a process that provides more information about the signal, which when played back provides a smoother, more natural CD-quality sound.

Overscan.   In some areas of your TV screen, areas are scanned that are not visible. Some overscan areas are now being used to send data, specifically the Microsoft Actimates Technology sending signals to remote devices.

Packet.   A piece of data or message sent over a network.

Page.   An HTML document that may contain text, images, and other on-line elements. It may be static or dynamically generated, and may be a stand-alone HTML document or one that is contained within a frame.

PC.   Personal computer. A computer that has one primary person who uses it, versus a computer that is shared by multiple users.

PDA.   Personal Digital Assistant. A handheld hardware device that combines services that may feature a handheld telephone, pager, fax, e-mail, and organization software. More features can be found on certain PDA systems.

PERL.   Program Extraction and Reporting Language. This is a programming language often used by CGI programmers for Internet programs to create interactive applications for sending and receiving data.

Post (as in "posting a page").   Posting a page is sending data to your Web server, typically a new HTML page, audio, or video, that updates a Web page or a Website. You put a new file up on the computer that is assigned a file name. When you do this, the page is live or "posted" to the Website.

Progressive scan.   Electronics provide a better image on a monitor and will be used in the USA HDTV system.

Proxy server.   This server checks all client or users requests to see if it can fulfill a file, data, audio, or video application request. It may fulfill the request itself or forward to another server. It typically sits between the client and your main server.

Pull.   A term used for information that you seek out. You search out Web pages or information and pull them down to your browser or e-mail.

Push.   A term for technologies delivering information to your computer usually on a regular basis. It is information that comes to you typically after signing up for it. The simplest form of push is e-mail. The more complicated forms of push involve a personalized, one-to-one interaction with you, based on customized information. You either tell the computer the information you desire upon signing up, or it learns from your behavior patterns on the Internet your interests, and sends you information based on these clues. An example is a set of stock quotes or electronic newsletters you select for periodic downloading. The information is automatically sent or pushed to you, rather than you having to specifically request every time it gets updated.

Qualified hits.   Hits to a Web server that deliver the requested items to a user. Qualified hits exclude error messages (e.g., "URL Not Found" or "Permission Denied"), redirects, and requests by computer programs.

RAM.   Random Access Memory is typically a computer holding space or a computer space that allows you to process information quicker. More RAM allows you to display more complicated and quickly changing graphics or video. This is a space in your computer where the programs that are currently running reside and process information.

Real time.   The delivery of content, data, audio, or video at almost the same moment it originates, very similar to a "live" interaction or delivery of information. The origination of data, audio, or video is sent and transmitted and received at the same time it is created.

Repurpose.   Using the same text, audio, or graphics content over again, either identically or enhanced with other information. In this way, content created for one purpose (e.g., a radio newscast) can be used again in a different form (e.g., an Internet unicast) to provide more services efficiently and economically. It can also be reedited or reconfigured to deliver a different viewpoint or perspective. Different content can be used in different places, in printed material, on the Internet, on different Websites, or sent via e-mail. The distribution as well as the content may be altered, but the original material holds some consistency or could be recognized to protect the content under copyright law.

RSVP.   Reservation Protocol enhances the current Internet architecture to support requests for a specific quality of service to maintain data or streaming transmissions, www.isi.edu/div7/rsvprsvp.html.

RTCP.   Related to RTP, this protocol checks the status of webcasts from time to time as a monitoring and management protocol in which sender and receiver reports are transmitted from time to time, so that applications using RTP can get RTCP reports on how well the packets are delivered.

RTP. Real-Time Transport Protocol provides end-to-end network transport functions suitable for applications transmitting real-time data such as audio, video, or simulation data, over multicast or unicast network services.

Scripts/Scripting. Scripting has dual meanings. In traditional entertainment production, it is the semantic or language storyboard of action on the set. On the Web, it denotes setting the stage and flow of text, programming, graphics, or video in a manner specifying how the user can view, listen to, or use the data. Scripting can also be used as a term for programming for Internet applications.

Search engine. Search engines hold a database of information and use different computer programming language to locate information. These engines query computers connected to the Internet and compile massive catalogs or databases, which are searchable. Many search engines use keywords to locate information on a Web page or other locations on the Internet. Common search engines, which are a library or directory in digital format, can search for audio, video, and text, or look for similarities in language or visual markers. There are common text search engines such as Yahoo (www.yahoo.com), Infoseek (www.infoseek.com), and Webcrawler (www.webcrawler.com).

Server. A computer that contains information you wish to access to use. It is typically used with the term client/server. Your computer (the client) accesses another computer (server) to get information or to have another computer perform a program for you either on that computer or on your computer.

Set-top boxes. Devices that can sit on your television set and act as a connection to the Internet, game systems, or cable systems.

SGML. Standard Generalized Mark-up Language. The ISO standardized this language in 1986 for organizing elements in a document. The more common type of mark-up language used for the Internet today is HTML. However, SGML is being used for certain applications on the Net.

Site.   A location on the Internet specified by a domain name and unique IP address. A domain is a name for your home on the Internet. The domain or site on the Internet for the National Association of Broadcasters is www.nab.org. Domain names are structured in a standard way. In the case of NAB's "nab.org" the first part, "nab," stands for National Association of Broadcasters. The second part, "org," denotes a nonprofit organization.

Site traffic.   The number of page views or unique visitors that are counted and added up over a period of time equals your site traffic.

SMIL.   Synchronized Multimedia Integration Language. The World Wide Web Consortium (W3C) has a new proposed markup language, Synchronized Multimedia Integration Language. SMIL is designed to allow the easy mixing of simple media objects in different formats. These formats could include audio, images, text, and streaming audio/video. The coding would be with simple tags, a method to designate elements on a Web page. If this is approved, the streams and images would be scheduled together to make it easier for the average person to design and add webcasting elements to Web pages. SMIL is a proposed language and not a media format.

Software.   The program or programs that run on your computer (the client) or on another computer remote from you (the server). A computer is useless without software to tell it what to do.

Storage.   (versus "Memory") When you save information such as data, files, word processing documents, audio, video, or software, it needs space on a computer. This space is the storage media inside or attached to a computer. Your data can reside inside your computer on a hard drive. Your data can also reside on other devices (such as a Zip drive, CD-ROM, DVD, diskette) or on other computers in a remote location.

Streaming or Streaming media. The ability to send a continuous data signal that remains in the same order, or is connected to software that makes sure the order of the data is constant to allow for the delivery of audio or video broadcasts over the Internet. A stream of data connects the originating server to the client software. One stream is dedicated to one user, listener, or viewer. One stream per user is called a unicast. A "stream" is one continuous digital signal that sends audio or video. "Streaming" is the process of sending the digital signal of audio or video.

T-1. This is a fast connection that allows you to move data at a quick rate. It is two pairs of copper wire that carry data at a rate of 1.544 Mbps. T-1 lines are used to carry 24 DS-0 signals. They can be used to carry 24 phone lines or an Internet connection capable of 1.544 Mbps data transfer.

T-3. You can send 44.736 Mbps data per second through a T-3 line. Twenty-eight T-1 lines together make up a T-3, which can carry 672 separate voice channels or up to 44.736 Mbps data throughput. Large Internet providers have T-3 connections called "backbones" to the Internet.

TCP/IP. Transmission Control Protocol/Internet Protocol. This is a method for computers to interconnect with each other and transfer data back and forth. This protocol (a standard for the Internet) originated at the Department of Defense Internet in 1983. This protocol or communications method allows computers of different types to understand each other when connected.

Time-shift. Time-shifting used in the context of the Internet designates a program, usually audio or video or an event, that you can view at a later time or at your convenience. It is like on-demand, where you can time-shift a program to your convenience. New Internet programs allow you to make your own program guide, which allows you to time-shift programs at your convenience. You may wish to view a program at 9 AM and follow that program up with another program at 10 AM, and devise your own program schedule. In traditional TV or radio, the station was in control; with the Internet and with webcasting, the user, visitor, viewer, or listener can schedule programs in any order, at any time. This results in time-shifting programs for their convenience.

UDP.   User Datagram Protocol, a protocol that runs on top of IP networks. This protocol provides a way to send/receive datagrams over an IP network.

Unicast.   A means of serving a multimedia file in real time to a single user. (*See* **Multicast** and **Streaming.**) A stream of data connects the originating server to the client software. One stream is dedicated to one user, listener, or viewer. One stream per user is called a unicast.

Unique user.   The number of different individuals who visit a Website or page within a specific period of time.

Unix.   An operating system for multitasking and multiusers created at Bell Labs in the 1970s. Many Websites run on Unix systems.

Upload.   The transfer of a file, data, video, or audio from your computer to another remotely located computer. Downloading is pulling information down from another computer.

URL.   Uniform Resource Locator. This is the Internet name of the machine containing the data and the path to a file. It is the address of your Website or home page. Sometimes referred to as a Universal Resource Locator.

User.   The person who is interacting with you via a computer. It may be a visitor to your Website, someone who uses your software, enters a database form on your site, plays a game, sends you an e-mail, signs up for more information, or interacts with you by a computer. It can also specify a person who uses a computer program, software, or a game.

VCR.   Videocassette recorder. A machine that uses magnetic analog tape to tape and play back programs.

Vertical blanking interval. After a television image has been displayed, it takes a certain amount of time, the "vertical blanking interval" or VBI, for the electron gun to be moved into position for the next image. This occupies 21 lines' worth of the 525 lines transmitted per second in NTSC television. No picture information is sent at this time, but other data may be sent. This is the black stripe at the top/bottom of a television picture. To decode the data, users need a set-top box or specially enabled television receiver to decode this data. Closed captioning is sent on the VBI (line 21), but other information such as Web pages, stock market information, weather, or sports scores can be sent over remaining lines. The new Intercast system (see www.intercast.org), as well as other systems make use of the VBI to broadcast data in HTML format to personal computers and to television sets. HBI is a term used in reference to the Horizontal Blanking Interval. Microsoft Actimates is using a similar signal (*see* **Overscan**) to send signals to receivers found in plush stuff toys resembling the popular cartoon character Barney. This program is being sent through the Public Broadcasting Network.

Virtual. Something that is not real but has the appearance, texture, or feel of being real. A virtual experience is an experience that resembles a real environment. It may be a fake representation of any of your five senses.

Virtual community. A community of individuals who work together or communicate together by the use of networks or the Internet. Communities can form from those who visit your Website, your listeners or viewers, or those who subscribe to your e-mail lists. Typically, it is an interactive experience between users, who tend to form like interests, bond, and may start to communicate with others, and may participate in an interactive process.

Visit. A single unit of measurement that encompasses all activity by a user to a specific Website during a specified amount of time. If a user makes no requests from that site during a prede-termined period of time (30 minutes is standard), the next hit would constitute the beginning of a new visit. A visit can con-tain several ad views. It is a way of trying to understand how many different people may be using your Website, not just how many resources are being served to clients. One person may request 100 objects, generating lots of site traffic; another person may request only one HTML page.

Visitor.   This is a person or a computer who contacts your com-puter (server). It is more typically a user who accesses your Web page. That person is a visitor to your Website.

WAN.   Wide Area Network. A network of computers that usually extends outside a building and may reach across a metropoli-tan area, region of the country, or even the world. It is typically a private network of connections and proprietary to the com-pany who owns the network.

WAV.   A way to store sound developed by Microsoft and IBM. These files end with the extension, .wav. WAV files are large: A minute of audio can require more than 1MB of storage.

Web.   World Wide Web. This is a collection of data and associated resources that is assembled on pages accessible through a browser on the communications network called the Internet. These pages (Web pages) use the same language, HTML (Hyper Text Mark-Up Language), to display on a computer: text, graphics, animations, audio, and/or video. These Web pages may be connected to a Website or domain that is found by an address. This address is called the URL (Universal Resource Locator).

Webcast.   Internet content served using a streaming protocol. Web-casting is the publishing, subscription, broadcast, and tune-in methodology for the distribution of information from one to many recipients. Webcasting usually embodies audio/video streaming, push, or electronic software distribution.

Interactivity may also be possible by the addition of tele-phony, conferencing, textual, and graphical communication capabilities. Webcasting is used to distribute digital—often multimedia—content to audiences or communities over the Internet. Popular content types include news, business information, and entertainment. Content formats include digital text, graphics, audio, and video.

Combined with individual, community, or audience profile databases, this is the most powerful medium yet invented for delivering information and entertainment.

Webmaster. The person who typically is responsible for Website functions, such as programming, server upgrades, html, and administration of the technical Internet functions.

INDEX

A

Accounting department, webcasting responsibilities, 272
Adaptive processing, 22
Advanced Streaming Format (ASF), 107
Advertiser, per-inquiry/per-transaction, 86
Advertising, 84–87, 364
    banners. *See* Banner ads
    interstitial, 85
    traditional media, 246–247
Agent technology, 22
Agreement checklists, 327–333
ALT tag, 376–378
AOL, announcing site on, 382
Archiving, automatic on-demand, 195–196
ASAP Webshow, 219
Assignment agreements, 296
Astound, 220
Audio:
    capture, 120, 210–211
    determining bandwidth requirements, 138–139
    editing, 211–212, 217–219
    encoding, 121
    replication, 121
    storing, 121
    transmitting, 121
AudioNet, 131–132, 184–186
AudioPoint System, 220

Audio specialists, 277–278
AudioVCR, 196
Audio webcasts, implementing, 119–121
Automated listings, 259
Automated pull, 132–133

B

BackWeb, 26–27, 206–209
BackWeb Channel Server, 158–159
Bandwidth, 32–33
    determining requirements, 138–139
    issues and requirements, 113–115
    T1, number of viewers supported, 138
Banner ads, 84–85, 256–260
    audio- and video-enhanced, 85–86
    costs, 257
Barter links, 258–259
Bookmarks, 383
Brand deconstruction, prevention, 63–68
Broadcasting:
    definition, 97
    information sites, 354
        live-event, 149–150
    medium, 58–59
        traditional vs. live webcasting, 32–33

Broadcast Websites, 131
Browsers:
   default Websites, 66
   webcasting channels, 63
Browsing, 59–60
   medium, 58
   off-line, 152
Budgeting, webcasting department, 284–287
Buffering, 29–30
Bulletin boards, 310–311
Business applications, 15–20
   high-end, 45–46
Business-to-business, 47, 76–77
Business-to-consumer, 76–77

C
Capture, 119–120
   audio, 211
   data, 123
   video, 213
Case study:
   AudioNet, 184–186
   BackWeb, 206–209
   Boeing Company, 12–13
   CNET, 203–205
   GRIT Internet Broadcasting, 190–192
   Heineken Brewery, 68
   House of Blues Inc., 81–83
   Intranet EIS, 175
   MediaCast, 214–217
   MSNBC Business Video, 17–19
   New Century Network, 79–80
   New Orleans Web, 142–148
   N2K, 200–202
   Sundance Film Festival, 9–10
   The Sync, 160–167
   TheDJ, 187–189
   Time Warner Interactive TV, 49–54
   Yves St. Laurent, 240–242

CDF, 152–154
Censorship, 311–313
Channel Definition Format, 152–154
Chat areas, 310–311
Children, restricting access, 314–315
Clients, targeting, intranet, 229–233
CNET, 203–205
   Radio, 193–194
Codec, 112
Comedy Club, webcasting, 43–44
Commerce, electronic, security role, 326, 332–333
Commercials, webcasting, 86
Communications Decency Act, 310, 312
Compression. *See* Codec
Conferencing medium, 59
Connection speed, 198–199
Connectivity:
   costs, 165–167
   to Internet, 124–125
   providing, live-event webcasting, 148–149
Content:
   censorship, 311–313
   development, 181–221
      audio and video editing tools, 217–219
      buying sources, 186–189
      creating new, 190–192
      design considerations, 197–209
      end-user created, 189–190
      multimedia presentation conversion tools, 219–220
      producing, 209–220
      repurposing existing content, 183–186
      scheduling, 192–197
   selecting content, 183–192

ideas for, 372–373
importance, 360–361
protecting, 292–298
strategy development, 181–183
updating/refreshing, 289–290
webcasting, 109
Content developers, 279–280
Contests, 313
Conversion tools, 219–220
Cool Edit 96, 218–219
Copyright:
exceptions and exemptions,
307–308
infringement by others, liability,
318–319
law, 293–295
licenses, 299
registration, 295–296
rights, policing on-line, 298
Copyright Act:
fair use, 308
passive carrier exemption,
307–308
Cost justifying, 89–90
Costs:
banner ads, 257
connectivity, 165–167
distribution, 168–169
e-mail marketing system, 39
establishing a Website, 160–167
hosting, 170–171
live webcasting, 44
on-demand webcasting, 44
outsourcing, 286–287
personnel, 164, 173
training/retraining, 286
production, 169–170
push system, 171–176
recurring expenses, 164
traditional advertising media, 246
webcasting department management, 287

Customers:
defining, 264
gathering user input, 265
Customer support department,
webcasting responsibilities,
270

D
Data:
capturing and translating, 123
storing, 123
transmitting, 123–124
Database:
legal protection, 319–320
marketing, 89
Delivery medium, 59
Demographic survey, 235
Department manager, 275–276
Digital Performance Right in
Sound Recordings Act of
1995, 302–304
Direct Internet, 125
Direct marketing, 364–365
Distribution costs, 168–169
Dynamic Publisher, 197

E
Editing:
audio, 211–212
tools, 217–219
video, 213–214
Editorial links, 259
e-mail, 59
graphical richness, 78
marketing, 38–39, 363
set-up cost, 39
Employees, targeting, intranet,
229–233
Encoding:
audio/video, 121
live video, 137
Encryption, privacy and, 325–326

Exploders, 108
Exposure sponsorship, 84
Extensible Markup Language, 106
Extranet, 76

F
Fair use, 308
Fan-out server products, 108
FCC regulation, 314
Feasibility, determination, 69–76
   business-to-business vs.
      business-to-consumer con-
      siderations, 76–77
Federal Express, 73
Federal Trade Commission, work-
      shop on privacy issues, 322
Framing, 316–317
Freelancers:
   copyright issues, 305–306
   hiring, 297–298
Free Range Media, AudioVCR, 196
Free webcasting, 89
Frequency domain coding, 113
Frequently asked questions, 384

G
Graphics, quality, 373–374
GRIT Internet Broadcasting,
      190–192, 231–233

H
HDTV, 126
Header, 374
High-end webcasting:
   applications, 45–46
   requirements, 131
Hosting costs, 170–171
Hotlists, 383
H.323 specification, 104
HTML, extensions, quick loading
      time, 376
HTTP, 115

Hybrid revenue models, 89
Hyperlinking, 317

I
IETF, standards, 96–101
Indirect Internet devices, 125
Industry associations, 354–355
Information, as freebie, 361–362
Intelligent database marketing, 22
Interactive TV, 50–54
Interlaced Internet devices, 125
International Standards Organiza-
      tion, 101–103
International Telecommunications
      Union, 103–105
International Webcasting Associa-
      tion, 99
Internet:
   accountability, 10
   privacy, 322–324
   targeting audience, 233–235
   telephony sites, 353
   webcasting benefits, 8–11
Internet Engineering Task Force,
      standards, 96–101
Interstitial advertising, 85
Intranet, 76
   evaluating audience, 182
   targeting employees and clients,
      229–233
   webcasting, benefits, 11–13
Invasion of privacy:
   legal and regulatory issues,
      309–311
   potential for, 10–11
IP, 125
IP multicasting, 96–99
   definition, 97
   product and service list,
      337–344
IP Multicast Initiative, 99
ISO, 101–103

ISP:
    considerations for webcasting,
        146–147
    proxy caching, 317–318
    streaming charges, 39
ITU, 103–105

J
Java, Castanet applications, 159

K
Key words, 360
Kohesion, 217

L
Labeling, 324
Leads, responding to, 384
Legal and regulatory issues,
       291–333
    censorship, 311–313
    content protection, 292–298
    contests and lotteries, 313
    copyright exceptions and
        exemptions, 307–308
    database protection, 319–320
    fair use, 308
    FCC regulation, 314
    framing, 316–317
    invasion of privacy and libel,
       309–311
    jurisdiction over webcasting,
       313–314
    labeling, 324
    liability for copyright infringe-
       ment, 318–319
    policing copyrights on-line, 298
    privacy of users, 321–322
    protection, industry responses,
       323–324
    proxy caching, 317–318
    public domain material,
       306–307

    rights of publicity, 309
    security. *See* Security
    talent, union, and guild issues,
       311
    unwanted linking, 317
    uses not requiring a license,
       306–308
    using content owned by others,
       298–308
    visitor agreements and state-
       ments, 320–325
Lemming effect, 69
Libel, 309–311
Licensing, 299–308
    music, 300–303
        other issues, 303, 305–306
    uses that do not require, 306–308
    video, 306
Linear predictive coders, 114
Linking:
    live-event webcasting, 147–148
    reciprocal, 366
    unwanted, 317
Link lists, 383
Live-event webcast:
    broadcasting, 149–150
    connectivity, 148–149
    content design, 199–202
    costs, 44
    current volume, 46
    general considerations, 144–145
    group approach, problems with,
       172–173
    ISP/technical considerations,
       146–147
    linking/promoting considera-
       tions, 146–147
    plug-ins, 145–146
    postproduction, 148
    receiving, 36–37
    recording for archives, 149
    transmission, 110

Live-event webcast *(Continued)*:
 vs. traditional broadcasting,
   32–33
 webcasting vendors, evaluating,
   139–150
Live-event webcasters:
 defining responsibilities, 140
 hiring, 141
 production, 141–142
Live video:
 case study, 142–148
 encoding, 137
 sending, 136–137
Lotteries, 313
Low-end webcasting, 38–40

M
Mailing lists, on-line, 381
Management, issues and goals,
   263–265
 responsibility, 266–272
   accounting department, 272
   customer support department,
     270
   marketing department,
     267–268
   MIS department, 270–271
   public relations department,
     266–267
   sales department, 268–269
   site, 288–290
   stand-alone webcasting
     department, 272–275
Marimba, 26–27
 Castanet, 159–160
Market, webcasting, 46–55
 trends, 48–55
Marketing, 223
 advantages, 19
 direct, 364–365
 direct e-mail, 363
 following Website launch,
   359–363

on-line, 252–253
personnel, 276–277
research and analyst publications and industry news,
   384
Marketing department, webcasting
   responsibilities, 267–268
Marketing plan, generating,
   224–242
 budgeting promotion, 237–238
 defining objectives, 227–229
 measuring success, 260–262
 positioning webcast, 238–242
 recognizing hurdles and opportunities, 224–227
 target audience identification,
   229–237
Market research surveys, 70
Mbone, 114
McAfee virus protection software,
   15–16, 73–74
Mechanical license, 301–302
Media:
 e-mail address resources, 382
 shift of control to consumers,
   90–92
Media, choice, 77–89
 advertising, 84–87
 database marketing, 89
 e-mail, 78
 factors, 78
 free, 89
 hybrids, 89
 microtransactions, 87–88
 subscription, 87
Media webcasts, implementing,
   122–123
Microsoft:
 CDF, 152–154
 IE 4.0, crawling capability,
   153–154
Microstudio, 168
Microtransactions, 87–88

Mid-range webcasting, 40–44
Mindshare, battle for, 63
MIS department, webcasting
      responsibilities, 270–271
MPEG, 101–103
MSNBC, Desktop Website, 15–19
Multicasting, 34
   See IP multicasting
   resources, 335–358
      access servers, 337
      broadcasting information sites,
        354
      hardware and software, 351
      industry associations,
        354–355
      IP product and service list,
        337–344
      media companies, 351–352
      miscellaneous products and
        services, 337
      push media companies,
        344–347
      streaming content, 348–350
      video conferencing, 353
Multicast protocols, Reliable IP,
      101
Music, licensing, 300–303

N
Navigation bar, 374
Near video on demand, 111
Netcaster, 152
netPodium, 3
Netscape, Netcaster, 152
NetShow, 135
New Orleans Web, 45–46,
      142–148
News Exchange, 52–53
Newsgroups, 381
   using, 382–383
Newspapers, online, 79–80
N2K, case study, 200–202
NVOD, 111

O
On-demand webcasting, 4, 34–37
   compared to VCRs, 34–35
   costs, 44
   personnel needed, 179–180
   receiving, 36–37
Open Sesame, 22–23
Outsourcing, 282
   costs, 286–287

P
Pagers, Internet capabilities, 126
PCM, 113
PDAs, Internet capabilities, 126
Peak, 218
Per-inquiry advertiser, 86
Periodic webcasting, 110
Personal digital assistant, Internet
      capabilities, 126
Personnel:
   hiring new, 282–283
   maintaining Website, 177–180
   training existing, 281
Per-transaction advertiser, 86
Plug-ins, 145–146
PointCast, 25–26
PointPlus, 219
Postproduction, live-event web-
      casting, 148
Prescreening, 265
Press release:
   sample, 250–251
   sending, 381–382
Privacy:
   encryption and, 325–326
   government regulation,
      322–324
   invasion of
      legal and regulatory issues,
        309–311
      potential for, 10–11
   other technical solutions,
      324–325

Privacy *(Continued)*:
  protection
    industry responses, 323–324
    on Internet, 322
  of users, 321–322
Production costs, 169–170
Program guides, 255–256
Promotion, 243–260
  budgeting, 237–238
  considerations for live-event
    webcasting, 147–148
  finding related sites, 366–367
  following Website launch,
    359–363
  increasing Website traffic,
    367–384
  message delivery, 245–260
    advertising media, 246–247
    banner advertising, 256–260
    on-line marketing and public
      relations, 252–253
    promotional offers, 247–248
    public relations, 249–251
    search engines and program
      guides, 254–256
  message development,
    243–245
Promotional offers, 247–248
Protocols, 94–95
  definition, 96
  Real-Time Streaming, 106–107
  RSVP, 99–100
  RTCP, 100
  RTP, 100
Proxy caching, 317–318
Public domain material, 306–307
Publicity, 364
  on-line rights, 309
Public performance licenses,
  300–301
Public relations, 249–251
  on-line, 253–254

Public relations department, web-
    casting responsibilities,
    266–267
Pull. *See* Push technology
Pull model, 93–94
Pulse code modulation, 114
Push:
  content design, 205–209
  determining if company will
    benefit with, 225–226
  Internet versus intranet, 209
  media companies, 344–347
  on-line resources, 347–348
  target audience identification,
    236–237
Push alert:
  creating, 208–209
  scheduling, 196–197
Push channels, dynamically
    updating, 197
Push notification facility, 134
Push system:
  architectures, 133
  costs, 171–176
  guidelines, 155–157
  vendors
    BackWeb Channel Server,
      158–159
    Marimba Castanet, 159–160
    selection, 157–160
    Tibco, 160
Push technology, 4–5, 20–28, 94
  benefits, 8–9
  content control, 133
  features, 24–27
  future directions, 27–28
  size limits, 207
  software, 117
  systems requirements,
    132–135
  transmission methods, 21–22
  usage by companies, 48

Push Website, implementing,
      150–157
    CDF, 152–154
    Netcaster, 152

Q
Quality assurance, 375
Quality of Service, 99

R
RealAudio, 45
Real Networks, RealServer,
      195–196
Real Player, 135
Real-Time Control Protocol, 100
Real-Time Streaming Protocol,
      106–107
Real-Time Transport Protocol, 100
RealVideo, 45
    hardware requirements, 137
    technology, 12
Receiving webcasts, 124–128,
      135–136
    connectivity, 124–125
    devices, 126
    future, 127–128
Reflectors, 108
Regulatory issues. *See* Legal and
      regulatory issues
Reliable IP, multicast protocols,
      101
Replication, audio/video, 121
ReSerVation Protocol, 99–100
Residual payments, 311
Revenues, generating, 84–89
    advertising, 84–87
    database marketing, 89
    hybrids, 89
    microtransactions, 87–88
    subscription, 87
RSVP, 99–100
RTCP, 100

RTP, 100
RTSP, 106–107

S
Sales department, webcasting
      responsibilities, 268–269
Salespersons, 276–277
Sample Wrench, 218
Schedule guides, 194
Search engine, 254–255, 360
    design tips, 378–379
    essential, 365–366
    registration, 363–364, 378–379
Security, 325–333
    encryption and privacy,
      325–326
    role in electronic commerce,
      326, 332–333
SGML, 106
Site management, issues, 288–290
SmartSound for Multimedia, 219
Software, 116–117
    future, 127–128
    needed in building webcasting
      department, 283–284
    websites for, 136
Sound Forge 4.0, 217–218
Sound recording rights, 302
SpeedRazor Mach3.5, 219
Splitters, 108
Sponsorships, 85
Spring 1997 Internet Demographic
      Study, 235
Standard Generalized Markup Lan-
      guage, 106
Standard industrial classification
      codes, 371–372
Standards, 77, 94–95
    H.323 specification, 104
    IETF, 96–101
    ITU, 103–105
    MPEG, 101–103

Standards *(Continued)*:
  T.120, 104–105
  W3C, 105–106
Storing:
  audio/video, 121
  data, 123
Streaming, 28–34, 111
  buffering, 29–30
  content resources, 348–350
  hardware, 351
  high-end, 45
  live, 30–34, 183
  media companies, 351–352
  on-demand, content design,
      203–205
  push API and enhancement
      resources, 353
  software, 117, 351
  standards, future, 127
  target audience, 235–236 tech-
      nology, 2–3
  video, 39–40
  webcams and components,
      352–353
Subscription, 87
Synchronization license, 301–302
Synchronized Multimedia project,
    105
Synchronized Multimedia Integra-
    tion Language (SMIL), 107
Syndicated broadcast program-
    ming, 303, 305

T
Talent, agreements, 311
Target audience identification,
    229–237
  Internet, 233–235
  intranet, 299–233
  push, 236–237
  streaming, 235–236
TCP, vs. HTTP vs. multicast, 115

TCP/IP protocols, 96
Technicians, webcasting,
    278–279
Telephones, Internet capabilities,
    127
Text webcasts, implementing,
    122–123
TheDJ, 187–189, 195
Tibco, 160
Time domain coding, 114
Time Warner Interactive TV,
    49–54
TotalNEWS, 316
Training:
  costs, 286
  existing personnel, 281
Translating, data, 123
Transmission:
  audio/video, 121
  codec, 112
  data, 123
  types, 110–112
  see also Streaming
TRUST-e, 324
Trustmarks, 324
T.120 standard, 104–105
TV:
  interactive, 50–54
  Internet capabilities, 126–127

U
UDP, vs. HTTP vs. multicast, 115
Unicasting, definition, 97
USB interface, 137
User notification facility, 134

V
V-Active for RealVideo, 218
Vendors:
  live-event/on-demand
      benchmarks, 140
  evaluating, 139–150

push system:
  BackWeb Channel Server,
      158–159
  Marimba Castanet, 159–160
  selection, 157–160
  Tibco, 160
Video:
  capture, 120, 213
  determining bandwidth require-
      ments, 138–139
  digital, editing and compressing,
      120
  editing, 213–214, 217–219
  encoding, 121
  getting onto the Internet, 119
  licensing, 306
  quality of capture, 210
  replication, 121
  storing, 121
  transmitting, 121
Video conferencing sites, 353
Video consultant, 40
Video on-demand, 110
  sending, 137–139
Video specialists, 277–278
Video webcasts, implementing,
      119–121
View later transmission, 110
Visitor tracking, 365
Vocal tract models, 114
Vocoders, 114
VOD. See Video on-demand

W
Watermarking, digital, 326
W3C, standards, 105–106
Webcast, positioning, 238–242
Webcasting:
  benefits, 7–13, 57–58
      Internet, 7–11
      intranet, 11–13
  commercials, 86

  cost justifying, 89–90
  definition, 1
  factors affecting, 32–33
  FCC regulation, 314
  industry associations, 354–355
  information sites, 354
  interactive TV, 54–55
  market, 46–55
      trends, 48–55
  measuring success, 260–262
  reference sites, 355–357
  resource sites, 357–358
  transmission, 109
  types, 2
Website capability expansion,
      61–62
Webcasting department:
  budgeting, 284–287
  management costs, 287
  personnel/staffing issues,
      275–284
    audio/video specialists,
        277–278
    content developers, 279–280
    department manager, 275–276
    hiring new personnel,
        282–283
    outsourcing, 282
    sales/marketing, 276–277
    staffing alternatives, 280–283
    tools, 283–284
    training existing personnel,
        281
Webcasting events, e-mail list, 380
Webcasting page, design, 198–199
Webcasting technicians, 278–279
Webcasts, types, 20
Web magnets, tips, 380
Website:
  "About Us" section, 383–384
  broadcast, 131
  definition, 129

Website *(Continued)*:
  development, 129–180
    choosing vendors and compo-
      nents, 136–160
    evaluating video webcast ven-
      dors, 139–150
    push site implementation,
      150–157
    selecting push system ven-
      dors, 157–160
    sending live video, 136–137
    sending video on-demand,
      137–139
    production costs, 169–170
    push system costs, 171–176

  ease of navigation, 374
  finding related, 366–367
  increasing traffic, 367–384
  maintaining, 176–180
  quick loading time, 373–377
  turning into active media, 62
  URL and site name on pages, 376
  viewing with different browsers,
    375
What's cool listings, 380–381
World Wide Web Consortium,
    standards, 105–106

X
XML, 106